Over the past twenty years debates about pornography have raged both within feminism and in the wider world. Throughout the 1970s feminists increasingly addressed the problem of men's violence against women, and many women insisted that men's sexual coercion was the bedrock of male domination, thus reducing the politics of men's power over women to questions about sexuality. By the 1980s these questions became more and more focused on the issue of pornography – now a metaphor for the menace of male power. However, collapsing feminist politics into sexuality and sexuality into pornography has not only caused some of the deepest splits between feminists, but made it harder to think clearly about either sexuality or pornography – indeed, about feminist politics more generally.

This collection of essays, by well-known feminists on both sides of the Atlantic, aims to open up the widest possible debate about sexuality and feminist politics. It sees its goal as moving beyond current divisions between, on the one hand, those who see pornography as the key to women's oppression, and, on the other, those who defend the private sphere as exempt from political scrutiny.

Lynne Segal teaches psychology at Middlesex Polytechnic and is a member of the *Feminist Review* collective. Her previous works include *Is the Future Female?: Troubled Thoughts on Contemporary Feminism* (Virago 1987) and *Slow Motion: Changing Masculinities, Changing Men* (Virago 1990).

Mary McIntosh teaches sociology at the University of Essex and is a member of the editorial collective *Feminist Review*. She has previously written on the family, social policy and sexuality.

Both women are members of Feminists Against Censorship and live in London.

D0927221

Sex Exposed

Sexuality and the Pornography Debate

**Edited by Lynne Segal
and Mary McIntosh**

Published by VIRAGO PRESS Ltd 1992
20–23 Mandela Street, Camden Town, London NW1 0HQ

A CIP catalogue record for this title
is available from the British Library

Typeset by Goodfellow & Egan Phototypesetting Ltd, Cambridge
Printed in Great Britain by Cox & Wyman Ltd, Reading, Berkshire

Contents

Part 4
To each their own: Differing pornographies

Lynne Segal

Introduction

Ex-porn actress – now Post-Porn Modernist – Annie Sprinkle currently performs onstage in California to promote an active, pleasurable, spiritual enjoyment of sexuality in the service of peace, love and freedom: 'Let there be pleasure and ecstasy on earth, and let it begin with me.' Hearing her call, Senator Jesse Helms, fresh from battles to remove state funding for displaying the works of gay artists Robert Mapplethorpe and Andreas Serrano, immediately instigates a congressional investigation into whether any federal funding supports Sprinkle's 'pornographic' performances. As 'freedom' is bringing commercial pornography into Eastern Europe for the very first time, questions of sex, censorship and pornography continue to rock North American cultural life. In Britain, too, fierce debates over sexuality increasingly focus on pornography, and politicians consider what support they should offer to bills censoring pin-ups and pornographic images.

Pro-sex or anti-sex, Western cultures remain sex-obsessed. This is why the issue of pornography just won't go away. Its presence has dogged and divided Western feminism like no other. The debate over pornography reflects different views about the nature of sexuality, the forms of its representation and its place in our lives. Definitions of 'pornography' have changed dramatically since the word was first used in the mid nineteenth century to separate off the dangers of 'the sexual' from offensive religious and political material. At that time *any* type of sexually explicit writing or image, whether

1

scientific, medical, poetic or popular, was equally liable to censorship. Throughout the twentieth century, however, recurring obscenity trials resulted in the progressive uncoupling of the 'pornographic' from anything which could be claimed to have 'scientific' or 'literary' value. Yet despite this narrowing of legal definitions, the meaning of 'pornography' remains today as contentious as ever; if not more so.[1]

Moral crusaders have always worried about the corrupting effect of explicit sexuality. Sex should be confined to its only legitimate place, in marriage, and linked at least in some way to its only legitimate purpose, procreation. Liberals, in contrast, have worried about public surveillance and censorship of displays of explicit sexuality which may cause little or no harm to others, especially when consumed privately and willingly. The feminist case against pornography is different. Feminists object not to the sexual explicitness in pornography but to the sexism: to its characteristic reduction of women to passive, perpetually desiring bodies – or bits of bodies – eternally available for servicing men. But there is more than one argument about pornography within feminism, from which conflicting conclusions have been drawn. For example, is all pornography necessarily sexist? How do we judge what is and what is not sexist?

The purpose of this collection is to survey these arguments, and in particular to ask why recent feminist debates about sexuality keep reducing to the question of pornography. It has never been easy for women to speak or write about our sexual experience in a culture which is still male-dominated, heterosexist and sex-obsessed. The contributors to this book, however, all share the view that women's discussions about sexuality must remain as open as possible, agreeing on the dangers of simplifying or foreclosing the communications which need to take place. They also share the fear that these dangers exist in current calls for greater censorship of sexual representation, including those which come from anti-pornography feminists. Censorship may cut short women's own search for ways of understanding and expressing the complexities of their sexual lives, and the possiblities for increasing their sense of sexual agency and empowerment – before it has barely begun.

To the bewilderment of some of its founding sisterhood (ridiculed in the early seventies for their concern with their own orgasms in seeking to liberate 'the suppressed power of female sexuality' from male-centred discourses and practices), pornography seemed to become *the* feminist issue of the 1980s. Its eventual domination of the sexuality debates in the second decade of contemporary Western feminism stemmed from the increasing determination of that movement to understand and eliminate rape and violence against women. Two oddly contradictory arguments began to take the lead in feminist debate from the mid to late 1970s. The first, exemplified by Susan Brownmiller in her influential book *Against Our Will*, was to deny that rape was sexually motivated, and analyse it purely in terms of violence, as the timeless and global method by which men had sought and managed to keep women subordinate throughout time and place.[2] The second, existing in implicit but cosy contradiction, was to analyse all of male sexuality in terms of a continuum of violence: to proclaim, as had Susan Griffin in 1971, that the basic elements of rape are involved in all heterosexual relationships.[3]

Two further moves were necessary to push the pornography issue into its present ruling place in the sexuality debates. The first was to insist that sexuality was *the* primary, the overriding, source of men's oppression of women, rather than the existing sexual division of labour, organization of the state or diverse ideological structures.[4] The second was to cite pornography as the cause of men's sexual practices, now identified *within* a continuum of male violence: 'Pornography is the theory, and rape the practice.'[5] As with rape, the same contradictory assertions were made denying the importance of sexuality altogether in men's consumption of pornography, while simultaneously holding pornography responsible for constructing male sexual behaviour. Men in this type of feminist analysis no longer had a sexuality. What they had was something else: a need for power, expressed through violence but *disguised* as sex.

Sexuality had been significant in British feminist analysis and politics from the beginning of women's liberation. At first feminists celebrated female pleasure, and what they saw as the *similarity* between women and men's sexuality. 'Acknowledgement of lust, acceptance of so-called promiscuity must be recognised as potentially inevitable stages in women's escape from sexual conformity', Beatrix Campbell wrote in 1973.[6] But five years later, many would declare that there is a fundamental *difference* between women's sexuality and men's, with women's sexuality once again the inverse of men's: gentle, diffuse and, above all, egalitarian.[7]

With denunciation rather than celebration the new mood of the moment, a type of political lesbianism became the sexual ideal for one influential strand of feminism: 'Women who make love to women are more likely to express their sexuality in a more equal way.'[8] Most feminists simply stopped writing about sex altogether, refocusing on the problem of men's violence. Not to focus thus, in Britain, was to court aggressive attack from the 'revolutionary feminist' faction, increasingly active from 1978. Coincidentally, in the United States, Women Against Pornography groups proliferated rapidly after that same year. Not coincidentally, as Ann Snitow was later to write, this was the time when the mood of the women's movement changed – especially in the USA, where the feminist anti-pornography campaigns first flourished (and US feminism has always had a profound influence on feminism in Britain).[9]

Having just witnessed the defeat of women's rights to state-funded abortion, won only four years earlier, the Equal Rights Amendment (ERA) was coming under serious attack from the growing strength of the New Right, soon to sweep Reagan to power and begin to derail the ERA. With poorer women facing greater hardship, welfare services being removed, and the conservative backlash against radical politics in ascendancy everywhere, 'pornography' served as the symbol of women's defeat. From then on, feminists were less confidently on the offensive, less able to celebrate women's potential strength, and many were now retreating into a more defensive politics, isolating sexuality and men's violence from other issues of women's inequality.

The basic feminist anti-pornography argument is that pornography is central to the way in which men subordinate women. Pornography, it is argued, both depicts and causes violence against women: 'Domination and torture is what it's about.'[10] Pornography which does not depict violence nevertheless objectifies women reducing them to sex objects for servicing men. The production of pornography also involves the brutalization and exploitation of women as sex workers. Pornography 'programmes' women into accepting female identities as subordinate 'dehumanized sex objects'.[11] More recently Andrea Dworkin and Catharine MacKinnon, the leading feminists seeking legislation against pornography in the USA, have argued that pornography violates women's civil rights because it *is* discrimination against women. It convinces men that women are inferior and do not deserve equal rights; it is 'the essence of a sexist social order, its quintessential social act'.[12]

Anti-pornography feminism is compelling because it makes intuitive sense. Much of pornography is at the very least complicit in some of the most offensive aspects of our sexist, male-centred culture: it appears to position men as active and powerful, women as commodified – objects, not subjects. Its target audience – at least until recently – is men, not women. Unlike liberals, concerned only with freedom of speech untroubled by questions of whose speech is heard, feminists have always seen cultural production as a site of political struggle. In recent decades they have consistently condemned the sexist use of women's bodies in the marketing of commodities. More provocatively still, pornography caters to men's sexual fantasies of female availability and eagerness for sex in the context of societies which have proved unable, and until recently unwilling, to offer women protection from widespread sexual harassment, abuse and violence; indeed, unwilling not so long ago, and for many men still today, even to acknowledge the existence of these issues.

Nevertheless, problems and contradictions come thick and fast the instant we look more closely at any one of the premises of anti-pornography feminism. On the contents of pornography, for example, so influential has the feminist anti-pornography message been that it is easy not to realize that in most pornography – unlike some other genres of representation like Slasher and Horror movies – violent imagery is extremely rare. One recent New York survey found between 3.3 and 4.7 per cent of violent imagery in a random sample of pornographic films. Another found around 7 per cent of s/m or bondage imagery with women submissive in pornographic magazines (9 per cent with men submissive).[13] Moreover, contrary to the often-asserted claim that violence in pornography – due to its assumed 'addictive' nature – has been increasing, recent research has consistently indicated a *decline* in violent imagery since 1977, suggesting that the feminist critique is getting through.[14]

There is now a mountain of debate, drawing upon psychological and sociological research as well as experiential reports (most of it collected in the USA), about the effects of pornography on behaviour. Empirical research on soft-core pornography has almost without exception failed to reveal *changes* of any significance in the behaviour of its consumers, whether affecting sexual practices, attitudes about, or behaviour towards, women. Indeed, its most characteristic effect, were we to feel confident generalizing from laboratory research on aggression to behaviour generally, has been to *lower* aggression levels.[15]

For this reason, attention has focused on pornographic material which does depict violence against women (in the form of rape scenes where the victim ends up 'enjoying' it, for example). It may come as a further surprise to many to learn that heterosexual men in general list violence as the least titillating aspect of pornography and, along with most other people, have become less, rather than more, tolerant towards violent pornography.[16] (The surprise is indicative of the influence of apocalyptic feminist rhetoric like that of MacKinnon and Dworkin linking pornography and the Holocaust: 'Dachau brought into the bedroom and celebrated'.[17]) In psychological experiments the majority of men react with distress to pornographic violence.[18]

The fast-accumulating research on the effects of violent pornography is most notable only for its inconsistency. Although many sex offenders, for example, do use pornography, in general (as studies like those of Goldstein and Kant found) they have had access to it at a *later* age than non-sex offenders, and are overwhelmingly more likely to have been punished for looking at it as teenagers.[19] In the great majority of sociological studies, variations in rates of sex crime do not correlate with the availability of pornography: Japan, for example, has an extremely low sex crime rate despite the existence of extensive and extremely violent pornography.[20]

Against Dworkin and MacKinnon's belief that pornography violates women's civil rights because it increases discrimination against them, one recent study of the relationship between circulation rates of soft-core pornography and levels of gender equality in fifty states in the USA discovered a positive correlation between equal opportunities for women in employment, education and politics, and higher circulation rates of pornography.[21] Conversely the researcher Larry Baron found that states with a preponderance of Southern Baptists – followers of the anti-pornography campaigner Jerry Falwell – had the highest levels of inequality between women and men. (This is all the more ironic when one remembers that it was Beulah Coughenour, a Southern Baptist, anti-abortion and 'Stop ERA' activist, with whom Dworkin and MacKinnon worked in Indianapolis to enact their model Minneapolis anti-pornography ordinance.) Baron's conclusion was not that pornography led to more positive attitudes towards women's equality, but that other factors, like greater social tolerance generally, probably explained his findings.

Baron's study is consistent with the far higher levels of overall economic, political and other indices of gender equality in Sweden and Denmark compared to the USA, coupled with far more liberal attitudes towards pornography.[22] This survey also found that gender inequality correlated with the presence and extent of legitimate violence in a state (as measured by the numbers of people trained to work in the military; the use of corporal punishment in schools; government use of violence; and mass-media preferences for violence, as in circulation rates of *Guns and Ammo*).

In contrast to many of these surveys, however, some psychological experiments – including the now often cited work of Donnerstein, Linz and Penrod – have, albeit inconsistently, found that men watching violent pornography are more likely to score higher on laboratory measures of aggression and to display, at least temporarily, more calloused attitudes towards women. These researchers, however, express caution over how far it is possible to generalize from their highly artificial laboratory set-ups to reactions to pornography more generally.[23] Whatever we conclude from this, three points in their research are salient: first, it was those subjects who had said that they were likely to commit rape if they could get away with it *before* watching the violent pornography who showed more calloused attitudes *after* watching it; secondly, it seemed to be the violence, rather than the sexual explicitness, which correlated with the increase in calloused attitudes and the higher measures of aggressiveness towards women (established after using non-pornographic films involving violence against women).[24] Finally, debriefing subjects after watching violent pornography, with information that all rape is harmful, led to lower rather than higher expressions of calloused attitudes towards women in all subjects. This effect was evident for at least six months, which would seem to point to the significance of anti-sexist educational initiatives in undermining the sexism of pornography.

Donnerstein and his fellow researchers have complained – rather inconsistently, given Donnerstein's own former enthusiasm for public testimony – of the misappropriation of their empirical data by feminist anti-pornographers to strengthen censorship laws.[25] But Donnerstein's own inconsistencies, and those within the wider research data, are dwarfed by the far more troubling contradictions within the feminist anti-pornography position itself, especially in terms of what should be done about pornography. For instance, the consumers of pornography are here seen as 'almost exclusively men', yet pornography is seen as 'programming' *women* into adopting identities as 'dehumanized sex objects'.[26] It seems that women learn to imitate pornographic representations, even though they do not read or view them (except, presumably, from a distance, unintentionally). Dworkin and MacKinnon's assertions of what pornography has done to women really do seem, in themselves, astonishingly offensive and discouraging to women. Dworkin declares that because of pornography a woman literally becomes 'some sort of thing', while MacKinnon maintains that women's lives are 'seamlessly *consistent* with pornography': 'For example, men say all women are whores. We say men have the power to make this our fundamental condition . . . Feminists say women are not individuals.'[27]

The anti-pornography position on sex workers is similarly offensive and unhelpful to many women. We are exhorted to save our sisters, the 'coerced pornography models', as represented by Linda 'Lovelace'. But of course most sex workers are not looking for feminist salvation. On the contrary, they complain bitterly about the stigmatization of women who work in the sex industry by anti-pornography feminists.[28] Speaking for themselves, both individually and collectively, some sex workers have described why they choose the work they do and the type of control they feel it gives them over their lives, as well as their feelings of victimization caused not so much by how they are treated at work as by their fears of arrest, low pay, poor working conditions, inadequate health care and social stigmatization. These are all dangers they see as *exacerbated* by state censorship and criminalization of their work. Sex workers provide an important corrective to feminist debates around pornography by suggesting that it is the privileges of largely white and middle-class anti-pornography feminists, who are not as exploited or oppressed as many other women, which enable them self-centredly to present the issue of women's sexual objectification by men as *the* source of oppression of all women.[29]

In 'Confessions of a Feminist Porno Star' Nina Hartley describes why she works in pornographic films in the USA:

> Simple, I'm an exhibitionist with a cause: to make sexually graphic (hard-core) erotica, and today's porno is the only game in town. But it's a game where there is a possibility of the players, over time, getting some of the rules changed . . . I find performing in sexually explicit films satisfying on a number of levels . . . In choosing my roles and characterizations carefully, I strive to show, always, women who thoroughly enjoy sex and are forceful, self-satisfying and guilt-free without also being neurotic, unhappy or somehow unfulfilled . . . I can look back on my performances and see that I have not contributed to any negative depictions of women; and the feedback I get from men and women of all ages supports my contention.[30]

However complex our attitudes to sex workers may be, it is clear that feminists face problems in choosing which women's voices to privilege. However troubled our reaction to pornography may be, it is also clear that feminists face problems choosing to downplay the social *context* of pornographic consumption. When pornography does work to empower men, it works not simply because of the nature of its images but rather because it is being used as a form of male bonding, as in the boys' night out to the strip joint – something quite different from their solitary, embarrassed visits to peepshow or porn arcade.

The problems we face as feminists tackling pornography today, however, are not just those of deciding to which women's voices we should pay most attention, and why. Nor do they reduce to questions of which types of explicitly sexual representation, or which contexts of pornographic consumption, produce the most coercively sexist behaviour from men, why, and what to do about them. They also – at least for some feminists – connect to the fear that the setting of sexual agendas in Britain, as in the USA, is increasingly led by the conservative right, with its traditionally repressive attitudes towards sexuality generally, and towards women and sexual minorities in particular. It is a fear led by the knowledge that, in recent years, moral conservatives interested in attacking gays and lesbians, as well as in controlling women's sexuality, have become more successful precisely through focusing on pornography and, especially in the USA, using the rhetoric and tactics of the feminist anti-pornography project.

Such fears grow stronger in Britain at this time as some of our more progressive politicians on the left, like Clare Short and Dawn Primarolo, have now embarked upon a similar project. In such a political climate, it is more urgent than ever to rethink the highly charged issues surrounding sexuality, which so frequently take the form of debates over pornography.

Part 1

From Minneapolis to Westminster

Feminism and censorship

Elizabeth Wilson

Feminist fundamentalism
The shifting politics of sex and censorship

Debates within feminism

From its beginnings in the early 1970s, the contemporary women's liberation movement has been divided between those feminists who see men as 'the main enemy' and those who have linked female subordination to a number of different structures in society, including the state and capitalist production. The first group have been labelled 'radical', 'revolutionary' or 'cultural' feminists; the second usually – in Britain at any rate – 'socialist' feminists. These labels are not always helpful, and sometimes perpetuate or reinforce stereotypes. For example, these days socialist feminists are often said to have been interested only in employment and welfare issues; yet they always argued that men as a group *were* responsible for the oppression of women, although neither men nor women were to be seen as a monolithic group, nor did the oppression of women emanate from a single source. Their oppression was the outcome of the complex interaction of a number of causes, reinforced by employment practices and state power, not just by men. Radical feminists have been seen as being interested only in issues relating to violence and sexuality, yet they *were* often extremely critical of capitalism and of the state, as well as of men.

None the less, in the context of the politics of sexuality, the differences between radical and socialist feminists were very real. Radical feminists were more likely to be critical of heterosexuality itself as an instrument of male domination.

They also placed greater emphasis on male violence towards women (and latterly towards children, especially in the form of sexual abuse). Socialist feminists were more interested in 'coalition politics' and saw some men as potential allies, capable of being won over to an anti-sexist stance. This rift may seem like ancient history, and something of an irrelevancy in the 1990s, yet it has been recast in recent years and retains its importance in the pornography debate.[1]

The decline of activist feminism has coincided with the 'culturalization' of society – the growth of media technologies and the growing importance of the cultural sphere. This expanding sphere of culture and technology is both economically and ideologically important and has obvious consequences for employment, education and leisure, both nationally and internationally. One feature of this 'culturalization' is the expansion of printed and visual material, and the production of pornography has expanded as part of this more general increase.

Despite their differences, feminists of every kind fought active campaigns in the 1970s – for better or specific provision for women, for changes in the law – and mounted a radical assault on the all-pervasive sexism of British society. Declining feminist activism has meant in practice a shift from struggles to change the world to struggles to change representations. Where once women's groups battled to open a refuge for battered women or a rape crisis centre, they now mount campaigns against *Hustler* and *Penthouse*. To say this is not to deny that there are still groups of women running refuges on a shoestring or running repeated campaigns to halt the recurrent attempts to restrict abortion rights; nevertheless, by far the most visible feminist activity from the late 1980s until now has been that surrounding pornography.

There is a shift here too. Women's liberation always made a critique of representations of women. The 'bra-burning' demonstration may have been a myth, but women demonstrated and campaigned against striptease, against the irrelevant use of women's bodies in advertising, and against the cultural stereotypes which insisted that women must always be young, slender, blonde and white if they were to be considered beautiful. They objected to the division of women into Madonnas and whores, sex objects and mothers, sluts and virgins.

Feminist campaigns were radical in refusing to accept the line drawn by conventional society between the 'decent' and the 'indecent', between 'family viewing' and the 'obscene', between 'clean' and 'smutty' images. This meant that they challenged the norms whereby written or visual material is usually judged. For the purposes of censorship and obscenity, the dividing line is between what is merely suggestive and what is sexually explicit. Thus, in practice, *Penthouse* images of nude or semi-nude women in 'come-on' poses may be freely purchased, but any image containing an erect male prick would be judged sexually explicit and therefore consigned to a sex shop. This (utterly ridiculous if you think about it) convention was rejected by feminists, for whom an image that shows sexual activity is not in and of itself offensive or 'obscene'. What is to be criticized is any image of women that reinforces stereotypes or panders to male prejudice. A film such as *Nine and a Half Weeks*, for example, might be offensive to feminists, not because it has sexual passages but because it suggests that women enjoy bondage and sadomasochistic sex. Even then, the feminist response would not have been – in the 1970s, at least – that such a film should be banned; the idea was rather to generate debate and criticism of sexist images, and to produce alternative 'positive images' of women's sexual enjoyment, and of their bodies. Such demands were linked to demands that women should be depicted in a wider range of social and work-related roles: there should be images of women firefighters and engineers, images of older women and black women. Everything about the way in which our society depicts women was up for grabs, and sexually explicit images were only one part of this.

Although it was objectionable if women were depicted *only* as sexual objects, it was important for women to be able to explore their varying responses to sexually explicit material. We could acknowledge, for example, that some women *might* have fantasies of being raped, without concluding that this therefore meant that women really want to be raped in real life. Rape or other masochistic fantasies might or might not be common, and they might be problematic, but it was important to confront and explore such responses if anything about sexual behaviour was to change.

Today, there has been a shift from the attempt to understand how we respond sexually as women and how we internalize oppressive notions of femininity and female sexual response, to a simpler position which lays the blame squarely on pornography for creating a climate of sexual violence and terrorizing women. Today, too, the context of the debate on Britain has changed. The efforts of Andrea Dworkin and Catharine MacKinnon in the United States to introduce legislation that would enable women to bring an action against pornographers or pornography on the basis that it/they had harmed them – although their strategy failed there – has had some influence in Britain. However, because the constitutional and legislative position is different here, it seems unlikely that similar legislation will or could be placed on the statute books. In true British style, however, the issue has attracted the attention of individual Members of Parliament and is being taken up into the party political system. Thus while there is unlikely to be any legislation that women might use to bring a civil action, it is less unlikely that a private member's or even a government bill to restrict pornography nationally might pass into law. One such bill is the one framed by Dawn Primarolo MP, which aims to relegate *Penthouse, Mayfair* and other similar magazines to sex shops (meanwhile, anti-porn groups in Ms Primarolo's constituency of Bristol are trying to get the sex shops closed down, so there may be a degree of disingenuousness here).

The British Labour Party

Just as the legislative context differs between the USA and the UK, so the support such efforts have attracted is different. In the USA Andrea Dworkin and Catharine MacKinnon gained support from right-wingers, the 'moral majority', but here in Britain – and this is a significant difference – the issue has become the property of the left wing of the Labour Party and particularly, although not exclusively, of its group of women MPs, headed by Jo Richardson, who has a superb record of defending and extending women's rights. Right-wing MPs such as Jill Knight (the scourge of homosexuals, an anti-abortionist and a member of the pro-hanging lobby) and the evangelical (fundamentalist) group of MPs also support moves to restrict further the sale of pornography as part of their traditionalist, 'pro-family' stance.

For feminists who support the anti-porn position the winning of the Labour left to their cause is good news – and no doubt the Labour Party women are trying to 'do the right thing'. Like the 'feminist' campaigns against pornography in Britain – the Campaign against Pornography and the Campaign against Pornography and Censorship – however, their critique of pornography is based on confused thinking and faulty premises, and leads to politically and ideologically reactionary conclusions. Before exploring some of the thought behind the anti-pornography position and suggesting reasons why feminists should adopt a different approach, it may be worthwhile suggesting why the Labour Party has adopted the anti-porn stance as its own.

In a way, it is the inverse of the 1960s. Then, the Labour Party came to power in adverse economic circumstances and was unable to fulfil its promise to modernize British industry and revitalize the economy. In winning the elections of 1964 and 1966, the Labour Party had to gain support beyond its core constituency, which was then still the organized working class. (This it always has to do, just as the Conservative Party always relies on working-class Tory votes.) In the 1960s, the Labour Party accordingly rode the bandwagon of the rising demand for the liberalization of a number of laws relating to personal conduct, in particular to sexual behaviour, but also to other humanitarian causes. This wave of reform had been building since the latter part of the 1950s, with the publication of the Wolfenden Report on homosexuality and prostitution in 1957 and the introduction of the defence of literary merit into trials charging publications with obscenity in 1959.[2] Thus, in the 1960s – the era of so-called permissive legislation – suicide ceased to be a crime, the death penalty was abolished, and the laws relating to abortion were relaxed (in 1967, although abortion has never been decriminalized in this country) together with those relating to divorce (in 1969). In 1967, too, the Sexual Offences Act partially decriminalized male homosexuality. Most – although not all – these changes were taken through Parliament (in most cases via the mechanism of a private member's bill) thanks to the support of the Labour government.

The Parliamentary Labour Party thus satisfied its liberal constituency at a time when libertarianism was in the ascendant. Without impugning the motives of genuine liberals such as Roy Jenkins (a Labour Home Secretary for part of this period) it is fair to say that it was comparatively easy for the then Labour government to support permissive legislation since the tide was running that way in any case, and they gained significant support among the young and the more progressive sections of society. That is not to say that this 'permissive legislation' was as libertarian as I may have made it appear. Stuart Hall has correctly argued that in some respects it increased the state regulation of behaviour, and rested on a strong distinction between behaviour in public and in private.[3] The distinction between public and private is one that feminists have always challenged, since one of its results has been that women have had almost no protection from husbands, fathers and lovers within their own homes. Nevertheless, despite these qualifications, it would be foolish to reject the reforms of the 1960s out of hand, and they certainly improved the lives of many men and women.

Today, by contrast, we have been for some years in a less liberal climate, and, faced with a dogmatically right-wing government, the whole political climate has shifted away from tolerance. That is not to say that the views of the majority of the population have actually moved away from liberal positions. Today, little stigma attaches to divorce or even illegitimacy; neither is there popular support for a return to more restrictive abortion laws. The main area where liberal tolerance has diminished appears to be with regard to homosexuality, where special circumstances (HIV) have fuelled prejudice, which has in turn been whipped up by religious fundamentalists both inside and outside Parliament, who have been greatly assisted by the tabloid press. (On the other hand, the abolition of the death penalty was never a popular demand, and law-and-order concerns have always attracted popular anxiety.)

In this more restrictive climate – which the Labour Party may nevertheless have misread – the feminist campaigns against pornography offer Labour a wonderful opportunity for appearing to support feminist demands without incurring political debts they will be unable to repay. The anti-porn position is consistent with their new 'respectable' image and, they hope, will draw women's votes. At the same time it will cost nothing to implement, and the constituency that apparently has most to lose from any such legislation, the producers and retailers of pornography, is not a pressure group that can wield sufficient muscle or moral force to deter a government from its intentions. Anyway, it is quite possible that the pornographers do not feel too deeply worried about the effects of any legislation such as is proposed, because much of their profit derives from material that is already illegal, or from sales in countries less restrictive than Britain.

Not only is an attack on pornography consistent with the 'law'n'order' image the Labour Party seeks, it is also consistent with a long tradition of Fabian authoritarianism. The Labour Party has traditionally been a 'broad church' and has given a home to many liberal and libertarian impulses. The Fabian strand, however, was never libertarian, and has been part of a tradition within the Labour Party which has seen progressive change coming about in society through a process of the implementation of policy plans designed by a confident professional and administrative class on behalf of the less fortunate. The Labour Party has in some respects taken over these nineteenth-century philanthropic and directive impulses. These in turn, to varying degrees, were prescriptive, directive and sometimes draconian. Sidney and Beatrice Webb, two of the most influential Fabians before and after World War I, were in favour of compulsory attendance at labour camps by the unemployed, and there was even a Fabian pamphlet recommending the sterilization of the 'unfit'. In a curious way, the anti-porn impulse is a reworking of the patronizing and protective attitude found in some sections of the Labour Party, the Fabians and the feminist movement in the late nineteenth and early twentieth centuries.[4] Typical in this regard is the refusal of the contemporary feminist campaigners against pornography to believe that any woman could possibly or reasonably disagree with them. It is no accident that they commonly cite children, and women in Third World countries (sex slaves), as the primordial victims of pornography. For them, less fortunate women are invariably positioned as victims, while they, the anti-porn campaigners, are rescuers. This is the classic nineteenth-century reforming scenario.

The meanings of pornography

Yet if the Labour Party espousal of the anti-porn cause is to some extent (by no means entirely) opportunistic, why should we object? Are not their objectives admirable: the creation of a safer environment for women; an attack on the causes of male violence? This may well be their intention, but socialist and libertarian feminists who oppose the anti-porn campaign do so in the belief that the analysis upon which the campaign – or campaigns – are based is simply wrong.

It is of interest, incidentally, that in the divisions over pornography, a new category of feminists, the 'libertarian', has been added to the rest. This is used as a term of abuse by the anti-porn campaigners – which is in itself an alarming indication of the authoritarianism that hides at the core of their thinking. In the 1970s the term 'libertarian' was used of anti-Stalinist Marxists and socialists, anarchists and community activists, and therefore implied a thoroughgoing anti-authoritarian critique both of East European socialism and of capitalist society. Then, libertarianism was on the side of autonomy and democracy, choice and self-determination. Today, for the anti-porn feminists at least, the positive connotations of this label are disregarded – to be in favour of liberty appears, so far as they are concerned, to be dangerous and even sinister!

The anti-porn analysis of pornography is incorrect and mistaken for a number of reasons. The empirical arguments will be dealt with elsewhere in this volume. These arguments are chiefly concerned with the effect of pornography on the viewer: are men more likely to assault women after they have viewed or read porn? They have less to say about the content of porn, or its construction.

A second debate is concerned with drawing a line between porn on the one hand and art on the other. The leading art historian Kenneth Clark, for example, in his evidence to Lord Longford's committee on pornography (a privately set up group which met in the early 1970s) defined the difference between art and pornography as follows:

> To my mind art exists in the realm of contemplation, and is bound by some sort of imaginative transposition. The moment art becomes an incentive to action it loses its true character. This is my objection to painting with a communist programme, and it would also apply to pornography.[5]

This is a statement of the view that while art is a reflection of the highest ideals and social values of a society, pornography is the underside: 'if art stands for lasting, universal values, then pornography represents disposability, trash'.[6] In a reworking of this opposition, which concentrates more directly on sexual issues, pornography is contrasted with erotica: erotica is the life-loving, positive expression of affirmative sexual values and erotic love; pornography then becomes the expression of negative sexual impulses, desires and acts.

All these struggles over definitions, however, seek to draw a line between what is 'good', or at least acceptable (and presumably should therefore be 'permitted' to circulate) and what is bad (and may therefore be restricted). What is on the 'wrong' side of the line is always labelled 'pornography'.

In the debate of the 1960s and 1970s in Britain, 'pornography' was the sexually explicit: words and images which acted as an incentive to action (the action of masturbation, it was assumed). In the 1980s anti-pornography feminists changed this definition, although they retained the idea of a line between acceptable and unacceptable. They redefined pornography as sexually explicit material which 'must depict women as enjoying or deserving some form of physical abuse' and 'must objectify women, that is, define women in terms of their relationship to men's lust and desire'.[7]

This definition, like all the other attempts to define pornography, fails because it clings to the illusion that pornography is a single definable entity, that it is 'a discrete realm of representation, cut off and clearly distinct from other forms of cultural production . . . the view that the pornographic resides *in* the image, that it is a question of content rather than form, of production rather than consumption'.[8] Yet, as is shown by the discussion concerning the difference between pornography and art, pornography is commonly defined in terms of its *difference* from something else.

We need to unpick the whole concept of pornography, recognizing that it makes more sense to speak in general terms of forms of cultural production of which some are sexually explicit. Some we may like and some we may criticize; however, only if we view the sexually explicit in the context of the whole range of visual and written texts will we challenge the dominant sexual ideology of our society, which does indeed want 'the sexual' to be cordoned off and separated from the rest of life – sex should be either in the bedroom or in the sex shop; it should be in a 'girlie' magazine or a centrefold, or in a special kind of 'naughty' book. If sex is seen as represented in this separate way, we are then prevented, for the most part, from perceiving how photographs in *Vogue*, for example, make use of protocols similar to those of erotic pictures, as also do works of art.

However, as Lynda Nead writes, 'to suggest that pornography needs to be examined in relation to other forms of cultural production . . . is not to move toward the position that claims that *all* of patriarchal culture is therefore pornographic',[9] although some feminists do go down this road of cultural reductionism (Titian is just tits and bums for rich men). We should, rather, be raising questions about this cordoning off of the sexually explicit, and ask ourselves why it is that sexuality is thus treated in our culture; in other cultures, after all, sexual acts were painted on the walls of tombs, represented in temple sculptures, or placed as decorations on vessels for household use.

Seen in this way, 'pornographic' works appear more complex. John Cleland's novel *Fanny Hill*, for example, was written as a parody of one of the earliest English novels, Samuel Richardson's *Pamela*, and it is much more like *Pamela* – or an even earlier novel, Daniel Defoe's *Roxana* – than it is like a contemporary video or magazine (although perhaps it has slightly more in common with a Mills and Boon novel). Of course, today's anti-porn campaigners are not really concerned with anything like *Fanny Hill*; nor, more surprisingly, are they concerned with videos and other visual material, which have much in common with contemporary porn material, yet are not sexually explicit in the same way. Any video shop will have, alongside its section of sex films, a section devoted to violence pure and simple – war movies, revenge movies, vigilante movies. If violence is male and men are violent, are not these tapes activating men's violent impulses, and might not these violent impulses be directed at women? If, as research has suggested, some convicted sex offenders have described how they were turned on by images of women knitting, are *any* images of women safe? Peter Sutcliffe, the 'Yorkshire Ripper', became obsessed with

·

a waxworks museum which contained models of women in various stages of pregnancy and people suffering the effects of venereal disease. Should similar medical exhibitions and medical books therefore be banned?

These examples demonstrate that the attempt to cordon off 'pornography' into its 'discrete realm of representations' essentially fails. It is the imagination that is 'pornographic', not the image.

Lesbians and gay men are particularly vulnerable to the effects of restrictive legislation. There are many people in positions of power who believe that homosexuality is itself essentially 'pornographic' – that it is an illegitimate, deviant and unacceptable activity in itself. It therefore follows that, for them, *any* representation of homosexuality *is* a kind of pornography – and after all, Radclyffe Hall's *The Well of Loneliness was* banned for many years, although the nearest lovers in that book get to an explicit act is the deathless sentence 'and that night they were not divided'. The general tendency of legislation relating to lesbians and gay men has been barely to tolerate such behaviour, even 'in private'. One reason that *The Well of Loneliness* caused such anxiety was that it brought lesbianism more clearly out into the open – once the veil of secrecy was torn, it was feared that more women would find out about it.

Lesbian and gay activity is therefore an especially clear example of the way in which there is absolutely no consensus in contemporary society about what constitutes the obscene or pornographic.

The anti-porn campaigners' insistence on sexually explicit images is reactionary, and simply reproduces the assumptions and ideology of the dominant culture. They argue that sexually explicit imagery is necessarily different from all other images and representations and potentially very dangerous as well. To challenge this view is not to take the opposing view of the 1960s 'sexual liberationists' who tended to argue as if simply to *show* more sex was itself progressive and liberating. Sexually explicit representations, images and texts are neither reactionary nor liberating in and of themselves. To hide them away reinforces and confirms rather than undermining their power. On the other hand, simply to legalize everything – to bring everything out into the open – does not solve the problem of misogyny and sexist representations of women. The meaning of pornographic images, like their effects, is not always clear, and may be the focus of a struggle for meaning. Again this is not to say that we shouldn't be disgusted by sadistic images of women being tortured or children being raped (although such images do not occur in pornography only but, on the contrary, in many other places as well). But pornographic images are not a simple reflection of male sexuality, nor, equally simply, do they create male sexuality. Nor is it even the case that pornography is one representation among others of 'patriarchal culture', as Lynda Nead appears to argue. That merely introduces another monolith – patriarchy – in place of the monoliths of 'pornography' and 'male violence'.

Feminists do, however, need an analysis of imagery, and of representations generally. Such an analysis ought to enable women to express anger and rejection, while at the same time it must recognize that the discourse of sex in Western culture is not monolithic but contradictory and often ambiguous. Whatever its intentions, the anti-pornography campaign gives the impression of wanting to 'save' women from 'male lust and desire'. Women in the anti-pornography discourse have no lust and desire at all. Ironically, therefore, this way of discussing the issue actually objectifies women, who are positioned as passive objects of male lust – precisely the aspect of pornography about which feminists feel so unhappy. The campaigners, in fact, re-create the fantasy world of porn, where men are always ready to perform, erections are repeatable and ejaculation is never premature. Thus the campaigns reinforce all the misinformation about sexuality which porn itself is accused of purveying.

The anti-porn campaigns constitute a form of secular fundamentalism. By fundamentalism I mean here a way of life, or a world-view or philosophy of life, which insists that the individual lives by narrowly prescribed rules and rituals: a faith that offers certainty. Revolution and liberation, by contrast, mean change and uncertainty. The search for the 'new life' can be exhilarating, but it can lead to extreme anxiety and personal collapse; by contrast, the price paid for certainty is rigidity and an incomprehension and intolerance of those who do not follow the 'true way'. Those who don't believe must be either destroyed or saved. Fundamentalism in general is also associated with restrictive attitudes towards women, maintaining a rigidly patriarchal authority over them, placing them more securely within a 'private' sphere, and carefully guarding their sexuality.

Fundamentalist methods are also used by the anti-porn campaigners. The style of the campaign, particularly in the USA, has been taken directly from evangelical Christianity, with its preacher-style harangues, its 'testimony' from women who have 'seen the light', its conversion rituals and its shock-horror denunciations.[10]

A truly feminist agenda on sex, sexuality and representation would emphasize the need for sex education for children; it would attack sexism as a representation of male power, rather than attacking sexual material as a representation of male sexuality; it would challenge the monopoly or quasi-monopoly ownership of the mass media, political censorship and the erosion of civil liberties. Feminists must – and do – attack the sexual abuse of children and the exploitation of women: these are central issues. But these issues are linked as much to ideologies of the family and employment as they are to pornography – indeed much more so. To have made pornography both the main cause of women's oppression and its main form of expression is to have wiped out almost the whole of the feminist agenda, and to have created a new moral purity movement for our new (authoritarian) times.

Carole S. Vance

Negotiating sex and gender in the Attorney General's Commission on Pornography

Larry Madigan began his testimony in the Miami federal courthouse. Dark-haired, slight, and dressed in his best suit, he fingered his testimony nervously before he was recognized by the chair. The podium and microphone at which he stood were placed at the front of the auditorium, so when the thirty-eight-year-old looked up from his typed statement, he saw only the members of the Attorney General's Commission on Pornography. They sat on the raised dais, surrounded by staff aides, federal marshals, the court stenographer, and flags of Florida and the United States. Behind him sat the audience, respectfully arrayed on dark and immovable wood benches that matched the wood paneling which enveloped the room.

'At age 12,' he began earnestly, 'I was a typical, normal, healthy boy and my life was filled with normal activities and hobbies.' But 'all the trouble began a few months later,' when he found a deck of 'hard-core' pornographic playing cards, depicting penetration, fellatio and cunnilingus. 'These porno cards highly aroused me and gave me a desire I never had before,' he said. Soon after finding these cards, his behavior changed: he began masturbating, attempted to catch glimpses of partially dressed neighbor women, and surreptitiously tried to steal *Playboy* magazines from the local newsstand. His chronicle went on for several minutes.

'By the age of 16, after a steady diet of *Playboy*, *Penthouse*, *Scandinavian Children*, perverted paperback books and sexology magazines, I had to see a doctor for neuralgia of the prostate.' His addiction worsened in his twenties, when he began watching pornographic videos. He went on to 'promiscuous sex' with 'two different women', but eventually found Christ. He concluded, 'I strongly believe that all that has happened to me can be traced back to the finding of those porno cards. If it weren't for my faith in God and the forgiveness in Jesus Christ, I would now possibly be a pervert, an alcoholic, or dead! I am a victim of pornography.'[1]

The audience sat in attentive silence. No one laughed. Only a few cynical reporters sitting next to me quietly elbowed each other and rolled their eyes, although their stories in the next day's papers would contain respectful accounts of Mr Madigan's remarks and those of his therapist, Dr Simon Miranda, who testified as an expert witness that many of his patients were being treated for mental problems brought on by pornography.

The Attorney General's Commission on Pornography, a federal investigatory commission appointed in May 1985 by then-Attorney General Edwin Meese III, orchestrated an imaginative attack on pornography and obscenity. The chief targets of its campaign appeared to be sexually explicit images. These were dangerous, according to the logic of the commission, because they might encourage sexual desires or acts. The commission's public hearings in six US cities during 1985 and 1986, lengthy executive sessions, and an almost 2,000-page report[2] constitute an extended rumination on pornography and the power of visual imagery. Its ninety-two recommendations for strict legislation and law enforcement, backed by a substantial federal, state, and local apparatus already in place, pose a serious threat to free expression. Read at another level, however, the commission's agenda on pornography stands as a proxy for a more comprehensive program about gender and sexuality, both actively contested domains where diverse constituencies struggle over definitions, law, policy, and cultural meanings.

To enter a Meese Commission hearing was to enter a

public theater of sexuality and gender, where cultural symbols – many dating from the late nineteenth century – were manipulated with uncanny intuition: the specter of uncontrolled lust, social disintegration, male desire, and female sexual vulnerability shadowed the hearings. The commission's goal was to implement a traditional conservative agenda on sexually explicit images and texts: vigorous enforcement of existing obscenity laws coupled with the passage of draconian new legislation.[3] To that end, the commission, dominated by a conservative majority, effectively controlled the witness list, evidence, and fact-finding procedures in obvious ways that were widely criticized for their bias.[4] But the true genius of the Meese Commission lay in its ability to appropriate terms and rhetoric, to deploy visual images and create a compelling interpretive frame, and to intensify a climate of sexual shame that made dissent from the commission's viewpoint almost impossible. The power of the commission's symbolic politics is shown by the response of both spectators and journalists to Larry Madigan's testimony, as well as by the inability of dissenting commission witnesses who opposed further restriction to unpack and thus counter the panel's subterranean linguistic and visual ploys.

Convened during Ronald Reagan's second term, the commission paid a political debt to conservatives and fundamentalists who had been clamoring for action on social issues, particularly pornography, throughout his term of office. Pornographic images were symbols of what moral conservatives wanted to control: sex for pleasure, sex outside the regulated boundaries of marriage and procreation. Sexually explicit images are dangerous, conservatives believe, because they have the power to spark fantasy, incite lust, and provoke action. What more effective way to stop sexual immorality and excess, they reasoned, than to curtail sexual desire and pleasure at its source – in the imagination. However, the widespread liberalization in sexual behavior and attitudes in the last century, coupled with the increased availability of sexually explicit material since the 1970s, made the conservative mission a difficult, though not impossible, task.[5] The commission utilized all available tools, both symbolic and procedural.

Procedures and bias

Appointed to find 'new ways to control the problem of pornography', the panel was chaired by Henry Hudson, a vigorous anti-vice prosecutor from Arlington, Virginia, who had been commended by President Reagan for closing down every adult bookstore in his district. Hudson was assisted by his staff of vice cops and attorneys and by executive director Alan Sears, who had a reputation in the US Attorney's Office in Kentucky as a tough opponent of obscenity.[6] Prior to convening, seven of the eleven commissioners had taken public stands opposing pornography and supporting obscenity law as a means to control it. These seven included a fundamentalist broadcaster, several public officials, a priest, and a law professor who had argued that sexually explicit expression was undeserving of First Amendment protection because it was less like speech and more like dildos.[7] The smaller number of moderates sometimes tempered the staff's conservative zeal, but their efforts were modest and not always effective.

The conservative bias continued for fourteen months, throughout the panel's more than 300 hours of public hearings in six US cities and lengthy executive sessions, which I observed.[8] The list of witnesses was tightly controlled: 77 per cent supported greater control, if not elimination, of sexually explicit material. Heavily represented were law-enforcement officers and members of vice squads (68 of 208 witnesses), politicians, and spokespersons for conservative anti-pornography groups like Citizens for Decency through Law and the National Federation for Decency. Great efforts were made to find 'victims of pornography' to testify,[9] but those reporting positive experiences were largely absent. Witnesses were treated unevenly, depending on whether the point of view they expressed facilitated the commission's ends. There were several glaring procedural irregularities, including the panel's attempt to withhold drafts and working documents from the public and its effort to name major corporations such as Time, Inc., Southland, CBS, Coca-Cola, and K-Mart as 'distributors of pornography' in the final report, repeating unsubstantiated allegations made by the Reverend Donald Wildmon, executive director of the National Federation for Decency. These irregularities led to several lawsuits against the commission.

The barest notions of fair play were routinely ignored in gathering evidence. Any negative statement about pornographic images, no matter how outlandish, was accepted as true. Anecdotal testimony that pornography was responsible for divorce, extramarital sex, child abuse, homosexuality, and excessive masturbation was entered as 'evidence' and appears as supporting documentation in the final report's footnotes.

Gender negotiations

The commission's unswerving support for aggressive obscenity law enforcement bore the indelible stamp of the right-wing constituency that brought the panel into existence. Its influence was also evident in the belief of many commissioners and witnesses that pornography leads to immorality, lust, and sin. But the commission's staff and the Justice Department correctly perceived that an unabashedly conservative position would not be persuasive outside the right wing. For the commission's agenda to succeed, the attack on sexually explicit material had to be modernized by couching it in more contemporary arguments, arguments drawn chiefly from anti-pornography feminism and social science. So the preeminent harm that pornography was said to cause was not sin and immorality, but violence and the degradation of women.

To the extent that the world-views and underlying ideologies of anti-pornography feminism and social science are deeply different from those of fundamentalism, the commission's experiment at merging or overlaying these discourses was far from simple. In general, the commission fared much better in its attempt to incorporate the language and testimony of anti-pornography feminists than that of social scientists. The cooptation of anti-pornography feminism was both implausible and brilliantly executed.

Implausible, because the panel's chair, Henry Hudson, and its executive director, Alan Sears, along with the other conservative members, were no feminists. Hudson usually addressed the four female commissioners as 'ladies'. He transmuted the term used by feminist anti-pornography groups, 'the degradation of women', into the 'degradation of femininity', which conjured up visions of Victorian womanhood dragged from the pedestal into a muddy gutter. Beyond language, conservative panelists consistently opposed proposals that feminists universally support – for sex education or school-based programs to inform children about sexual abuse, for example. Conservative members objected to sex-abuse programs for children, contending that such instruction prompted children to make hysterical and unwarranted accusations against male relatives. In addition, panelists rejected the recommendations of feminist prostitutes' rights groups like COYOTE and the US Prostitutes Collective,[10] preferring increased arrests and punishment for women (though not their male customers) to decriminalization and better regulation of abusive working conditions. More comically, conservative panelists tried to push through a 'vibrator bill', a model statute that would ban as obscene 'any device designed or marketed as useful primarily for the stimulation of human genital organs'. The three moderate female commission members became incredulous and upset when they realized that such a law would ban vibrators.

During the course of the public hearings, conservative and fundamentalist witnesses made clear that they regarded the feminist movement as a major cause of the family breakdown and social disruption which they had observed during the past twenty years. Feminists advocated divorce, abortion, access to birth control, day care, single motherhood, sexual permissiveness, lesbian and gay rights, working mothers –

all undesirable developments that diminished the importance of family and marriage. Conservatives and fundamentalists were clear in their allegiance to a traditional moral agenda: sex belonged in marriage and nowhere else. Pornography was damaging because it promoted and advertised lust, sex 'with no consequences', and 'irresponsible' sex.

Anti-pornography feminists, in their writing and activism dating from approximately 1977, saw the damage of pornography in different terms, though other feminists (and I include myself in this group) objected to their analysis for uncritically incorporating many conservative elements of late-nineteenth-century sexual culture.[11] Nevertheless, the anti-pornography feminist critique made several points which differed sharply from those made by conservatives. They argued that most, if not all, pornography was sexist (rather than immoral). It socialized men to be dominating and women to be victimized. Moreover, pornographic imagery led to actual sexual violence against women, and it constituted a particularly effective form of anti-woman propaganda. At various times, anti-pornography feminists have proposed different remedial strategies ranging from educational programs and consciousness-raising to restriction and censorship of sexually explicit material through so-called civil rights anti-pornography legislation first drafted in 1983. But a consistent theme throughout anti-pornography feminism, as in most feminism, was intense opposition to and fervent critique of gender inequality, male domination, and patriarchal institutions, including the family, marriage, and heterosexuality.

The conflict between basic premises of conservative and anti-pornography feminist analyses is obvious. Nevertheless, the commission cleverly used anti-pornography feminist terms and concepts as well as witnesses to their own advantage in selective ways, helped not infrequently by anti-pornography leaders and groups themselves. Anti-pornography feminist witnesses eagerly testified before the commission and cast their personal experiences of incest, childhood sexual abuse, rape and sexual coercion in terms of the 'harms' and 'degradation' caused by pornography. Anti-pornography feminist witnesses, of course, did not voice complaints about divorce, masturbation, or homosexuality, which ideologically give feminists no cause for protest, but they failed to comment on the great divide that separated their complaints from those of fundamentalists, a divide dwarfed only by the even larger distance between their respective political programs. Indeed, some prominent anti-pornography feminists were willing to understate and most to avoid mentioning in their testimony their support for those cranky feminist demands so offensive to conservative ears: abortion, birth control, and lesbian and gay rights. Only one feminist anti-pornography group, Feminists Against Pornography from Washington, DC, refused to tailor its testimony to please conservative members and attacked the Reagan administration for its savage cutbacks on programs and services for women.[12] Their testimony was soon cut off on the grounds of inadequate time, though other anti-pornography groups and spokespersons – including Andrea Dworkin, Catharine MacKinnon, and Women Against Pornography (New York) – would be permitted to testify at great length.

In the context of the hearing, the notion that pornography 'degrades' women proved to be a particularly helpful unifying term, floating in and out of fundamentalist as well as anti-pornography feminist testimony. By the second public hearing, 'degrading' had become a true crossover term – used by moral majoritarians, vice cops, and aggressive prosecutors, as well as anti-pornography feminists. Speakers didn't notice, or chose not to, that the term 'degradation' had very different meanings in each community. For anti-pornography feminists, pornography degrades women when it depicts or glorifies sexist sex: images that put men's pleasure first or suggest that women's lot in life is to serve men. For fundamentalists, 'degrading' was freely applied to all images of sexual behavior that might be considerd immoral, since in the conservative world-view immorality degraded the individual and society. 'Degrading' was freely applied to visual images that portrayed homosexuality, masturbation, and even consensual heterosexual sex. Even images of morally approved marital sexuality were judged 'degrading', since public viewing of what should be a private experience degraded the couple and the sanctity of marriage. These terms provided by anti-pornography feminists – 'degrading', 'violence against women', and 'offensive to women' (though conservatives couldn't resist adding the phrase 'and children') – were eagerly adopted by the panel and proved particularly useful in giving it and its findings the gloss of modernity and some semblance of concern with human rights.

Although the commission happily assimilated the rhetoric of anti-pornography feminists, it decisively rejected their remedies. Conservative men pronounced the testimony of Andrea Dworkin 'eloquent' and 'moving' and insisted on including her statement in the final report, special treatment given to no other witness. But anti-pornography feminists had argued against obscenity laws, saying they reflected a moralistic and anti-sexual tradition which could only harm women. Instead, they favored ordinances, such as those developed for Minneapolis and Indianapolis by Dworkin and MacKinnon,[13] which would outlaw pornography as a violation of women's civil rights. The commission never seriously entertained the idea that obscenity laws should be repealed; given its conservative constituency and agenda, it couldn't have.

The commission's report summarily rejected Minneapolis-style ordinances. These had been 'properly held unconstitutional' by a recent Supreme Court decision, the panel agreed, because they infringed on speech protected under the First Amendment. But the panel cleverly, if disingenuously, argued that traditional obscenity law could be used against violent and degrading material in a manner 'largely consistent with what this ordinance attempts to do', ignoring anti-pornography feminists' vociferous rejection of obscenity laws. The panel recommended that obscenity laws be further strengthened by adding civil damages to the existing criminal penalties. This constitutes a major defeat for anti-pornography feminists. But unlike social scientists who protested loudly over the commission's misuse of their testimony, the anti-pornography feminists have not acknowledged the panel's distortion. Instead, they commended the panel for recognizing the harm of pornography and continued to denounce obscenity law,[14] without coming to grips with the panel's commitment to that approach.

Even more startling were MacKinnon's and Dworkin's statements to the press that the commission 'has recommended to Congress the civil rights legislation women have sought',[15] and this comment by Dorchen Leidholdt, founder of Women Against Pornography: 'I am not embarrassed at being in agreement with Ed Meese.'[16] Over the course of the hearings, it seems that each group strategized how best to use the other. However, the vast power and resources of the federal government, backed by a strong fundamentalist movement, made it almost inevitable that the Meese Commission would benefit far more in this exchange than anti-pornography feminists.

The commission attempted another major appropriation of feminist issues by recasting the problem of violence against women. Since the backlash against feminism began in the mid 1970s, conservative groups most decisively rejected feminist critiques of violence in the family, particularly assertions about the prevalence of marital rape, incest, and child sexual abuse. Such sexual violence was rare, they countered, and exaggerated by feminists only because they were 'man-haters' and 'lesbians' who wanted to destroy the family. Acccordingly, conservatives consistently opposed public funding for social services directed at these problems: rape hotlines, shelters for abused wives, programs to identify and counsel child victims of incest. Such programs would destroy the integrity of the family, particularly the authority of the father, conservatives believed.

The commission hearings document a startling reversal in the conservative discourse on sexual violence. Conservative witnesses now claimed that there is an epidemic of sexual violence directed at women and children, even in the family. Unlike the feminist analysis, which points to inequality, patriarchy, and women's powerlessness as root causes, the conservative analysis singles out pornography and its attendant sexual liberalization as the responsible agents. Men are, in a sense, victims as well, since once their lust is aroused, they are increasingly unable to refrain from sexual aggression. It is clear that the conservative about-face seeks to respond to a rising tide of concern among even right-wing women about the issues of violence and abuse, while at the same time seeking to contain it by providing an alternative narrative: the appropriate solution lies in controlling pornography, not challenging male domination; pornography victimizes men, not just women. In that regard, it is striking that the victim witnesses provided by anti-pornography feminist groups were all female, whereas those provided by conservatives included many men.

Ironically, the conservative analysis ultimately blames feminism for violence against women. To the extent that feminists supported a more permissive sexual climate, including freer sexual expression, and undermined marriage as the only appropriate place for sex and procreation, they promoted an atmosphere favorable to violence against women. The commission's symbolic and rhetorical transformations were skillful. The panel not only appropriated anti-pornography feminist language to modernize a conservative agenda and make it more palatable to the mainstream public, but also used issues of male violence successfully raised by feminists to argue that the only reliable protection for women was to be found in returning to the family and patriarchal protection.

The pleasures of looking

The commission's campaign against sexually explicit images was filled with paradox. Professing belief in the most naive and literalist theories of representation, the commissioners nevertheless shrewdly used visual images during the hearings to establish 'truth' and manipulate the feelings of the audience. Arguing that pornography had a singular and universal meaning that was evident to any viewer, the commission staff worked hard to exclude any perspective but its own. Insisting that sexually explicit images had great authority, the commissioners framed pornography so that it had more power in the hearing than it could ever have in the real world. Denying that subjectivity and context matter in the interpretation of any image, they created a well-crafted context that denied there was a context.

The foremost goal of the commission was to establish 'the truth' about pornography – that is, to characterize and describe the sexually explicit material that was said to be in need of regulation. Pornographic images were shown during all public hearings, as witnesses and staff members alike illustrated their remarks with explicit, fleshy, often full-color images of sex. The reluctance to view this material that one might have anticipated on the part of fundamentalists and conservatives was nowhere to be seen. The commission capitalized on the realistic representational form of still photos and movie and video clips, stating that the purpose of viewing these images was to inform the public and themselves about 'what pornography was really like'. Viewing was carefully orchestrated, and a great deal of staff time went toward organizing the logistics and technologies of viewing. Far from being a casual or minor enterprise, the selection and showing of sexually explicit images constituted one of the commission's major interventions.

The structure of viewing was an inversion of the typical context for viewing pornography. Normally private, this was public, with slides presented in federal courthouse chambers before hundreds of spectators in the light of day. The viewing of pornography, usually an individualistic and libidinally anarchic practice, was here organized by the state – the Department of Justice, to be exact. The ordinary purpose in viewing, sexual pleasure and masturbation, was ostensibly absent, replaced instead by dutiful scrutiny and the pleasures of condemnation.

These pleasures were intense. The atmosphere throughout

the hearings was one of excited repression: witnesses alternated between chronicling the negative effects of pornography and making sensationalized presentations of 'it'. Taking a lead from feminist anti-pornography groups, everyone had a slide show: the FBI, the US Customs Service, the US Postal Service and sundry vice squads. At every 'lights out', spectators would rush to one side of the room to see the screen, which was angled toward the commissioners. Were the hearing room a ship, we would have capsized many times.

Alan Sears, the executive director, told the commissioners with a grin that he hoped to include some 'good stuff' in their final report, and its two volumes and 1,960 pages faithfully reflect the censors' fascination with the thing they love to hate. It lists in alphabetical order the titles of material found in sixteen adult bookstores in six cities: 2,370 films, 725 books and 2,325 magazines, beginning with *A Cock Between Friends* and ending with *69 Lesbians Munching*. A detailed plot summary is given for the book *The Tying Up of Rebecca*, along with descriptions of sex aids advertised in the books, their cost, and how to order them.

The commission viewed a disproportionate amount of atypical material, which even moderate commissioners criticized as 'extremely violent and degrading'.[17] To make themselves sound contemporary and secular, conservatives needed to establish that pornography was violent rather than immoral and, contradicting social science evidence, that this violence was increasing.[18] It was important for the panel to insist that the images presented were 'typical' and 'average' pornography, but typical pornography – glossy, mainstream porn magazines directed at heterosexual men – does not feature much violence, as the commission's own research (soon quickly suppressed) confirmed.[19] The slide shows, however, did not present many carefully airbrushed photos of perfect females or the largely heterosexual gyrations (typically depicting intercourse and oral sex) found even in the most hard-core adult bookstores. The commission concentrated on atypical material, produced for private use or for small, special-interest segments of the market or confiscated in the course of prosecutions. The slides featured behavior which the staff believed to be especially shocking: homosexuality, excrement, urination, child pornography, bestiality (with over twenty different types of animals, including chickens and elephants), and especially sadomasochism (s/m).

The commission relied on the realism of photography to amplify the notion that the body of material shown was accurate and therefore, they implied, representative. The staff also skillfully mixed atypical and marginal material with pictorials from *Playboy* and *Penthouse*, rarely making a distinction between types of publications or types of markets. The desired fiction was that all pornography was the same. Many have commented on the way all photographic images are read as fact or truth, because the images are realistic. This general phenomenon is true for pornographic images as well, but it is intensified when the viewer is confronted by images of sexually explicit acts which he or she has little experience of viewing (or doing) in real life. Shock, discomfort, fascination, repulsion, and arousal all operate to make the image have an enormous impact and seem undeniably real.

The action depicted was understood as realistic, not fantastic or staged for the purposes of producing an erotic picture. Thus, images that played with themes of surrender or domination were read as actually coerced. A nude woman holding a machine gun was clearly dangerous, a panelist noted, because the gun could go off (an interpretation not, perhaps, inaccurate for the psychoanalytically inclined reader). Images of obviously adult men and women dressed in exaggerated fashions of high-school students were called child pornography.

Sadomasochistic pornography had an especially strategic use in establishing that sexually explicit imagery was 'violent'. The intervention was effective, since few (even liberal critics) have been willing to examine the construction of s/m in the panel's argument. Commissioners saw a great deal of s/m pornography and found it deeply upsetting, as did the audience. Photographs included images of women tied up, gagged, or being 'disciplined'. Viewers were unfamiliar with the conventions of s/m sexual behavior and had no access to the codes participants use to read these images. The panel provided the frame: s/m was non-consensual sex that inflicted force and violence on unwilling victims. Virtually any claim could be made against s/m pornography and, by extension, s/m behavior, which remains a highly stigmatized and relatively invisible sexuality. As was the case with homosexuality until recently, invisibility reinforces stigma and stigma reinforces invisibility in a circular manner.

The redundant viewing and narration of s/m images reinforced several points useful to the commission – pornography depicted violence against women and promoted male domination. An active editorial hand was at work, however, to remove reverse images of female domination and male submission; these images never appeared, though they constitute a significant portion of s/m imagery. Amusingly, s/m pornography elicited hearty condemnation of 'male dominance', the only sphere in which conservative men were moved to critique it throughout the course of the hearing.

The commission called no witnesses to discuss the nature of s/m, either professional experts or typical participants.[20] Given the atmosphere, it was not surprising that no one defended it. Indeed, producers of more soft-core pornography joined in the condemnation, perhaps hoping to direct the commission's ire to groups and acts more stigmatized than themselves.[21] The commission ignored a small but increasing body of literature that documents important features of s/m sexual behavior, namely consent and safety. Typically, the conventions we use to decipher ordinary images are suspended when it comes to s/m images. When we see science-fiction movies, for example, we do not leave the theater believing that the special effects were real or that the performers were injured making the films. But the commissioners assumed that images of domination and submission were both real and coerced.

In addition, such literalist interpretations were evident in

43

the repeated assertions that all types of sexual images had a direct effect on behavior. The idea that sexual images could be used and remain on a fantasy level was foreign to the commission, as was the possibility that individuals might use fantasy to engage with dangerous or frightening feelings without wanting to experience them in real life. This lack of recognition is consistent with fundamentalist distrust and puzzlement about the imagination and the symbolic realm, which seem to have no autonomous existence; for fundamentalists, imagination and behavior are closely linked. If good thoughts lead to good behavior, a sure way to eliminate bad behavior is to police bad thoughts.

The voice-over for the visual segments was singular and uniform which served to obliterate the actual diversity of people's response to pornography. But sexually explicit material is a contested ground precisely *because* subjectivity matters. An image that is erotic to one individual is revolting to a second and ridiculous to a third. The object of contestation *is* meaning. Age, gender, race, class, sexual preference, erotic experience, and personal history all form the grid through which sexual images are received and interpreted. The commission worked hard to eliminate diversity from its hearings and to substitute instead its own authoritative, often uncontested, frequently male, monologue.

It is startling to realize how many of the Meese Commission's techniques were pioneered by anti-pornography feminists between 1977 and 1984. Claiming that pornography was sexist and promoted violence against women, anti-pornography feminists had an authoritative voice-over, too, though for theorists Andrea Dworkin and Catharine MacKinnon and groups like Women Against Pornography the monologic voice was, of course, female. Although anti-pornography feminists disagreed with fundamentalist moral assumptions and contested rather than approved male authority, they carved out new territory with slide shows depicting allegedly horrific sexual images, a technique the commission heartily adopted. Anti-pornography feminists relied on victim testimony and preferred anecdotes to data.

They, too, shared a literalist interpretive frame and used s/m images to prove that pornography was violent.

The Meese Commission was skilled in its ability to use photographic images to establish the so-called truth and to provide an almost invisible interpretive frame that compelled agreement with its agenda. The commission's true gift, however, lay in its ability to create an emotional atmosphere in the hearings that facilitated acceptance of the commission's world-view. Its strategic use of images was a crucial component of this emotional management. Because the power of this emotional climate fades in the published text, it is not obvious to most readers of the commission's report. Yet it was and is a force to be reckoned with, both in the commission and, more broadly, in all public debates about sexuality, especially those that involve the right wing.

Rituals of sexual shame

An important aspect of the commission's work was the ritual airing and affirmation of sexual shame in a public setting. The panel relentlessly created an atmosphere of unacknowledged sexual arousal and fear. The large amount of pornography shown, ostensibly to educate and repel, was nevertheless arousing. The range and diversity of images provided something for virtually everyone, and the concentration on taboo, kinky, and harder-to-obtain material added to the charge. Part of the audience's discomfort may have come from the unfamiliarity of seeing sexually explicit images in public, not private, settings, and in the company of others not there for the express purpose of sexual arousal. But a larger part must have come from the problem of experiencing sexual arousal in an atmosphere where it is condemned. The commission's lesson was a complex one, but it taught the importance of managing and hiding sexual arousal and pleasure in public, while it reinforced secrecy, hypocrisy, and shame. Unacknowledged sexual feelings, though, did not disappear but developed into a whirlwind of mute, repressed emotion that the Meese Commission channeled toward its own purpose.

Sexual shaming was also embedded in the interrogatory practices of the chair. Witnesses appearing before the commission were treated in a highly uneven manner. Commissioners accepted virtually any claim made by anti-pornography witnesses as true, while those who opposed restriction of sexually explicit speech were often met with rudeness and hostility. The panelists asked social scientist Edward Donnerstein if pornographers had tried to influence his research findings or threatened his life. They asked actress Colleen Dewhurst, testifying for Actor's Equity about the dangers of censorship in the theater, if persons convicted of obscenity belonged to the union, and if the union was influenced by organized crime. They questioned her at length about the group's position on child pornography.

Sexual shame was also ritualized in how witnesses spoke about their personal experiences with images. 'Victims of pornography' told in lurid detail of their use of pornography and eventual decline into masturbation, sexual addiction, and incest. Some testified anonymously, shadowy apparitions behind translucent screens. Their first-person accounts, sometimes written by the commission's staff,[22] featured a great elaboration of the sexual damage caused by visual images. To counter these accounts there was nothing but silence: descriptions of visual and sexual pleasure were absent. The commission's chair even noted the lack and was fond of asking journalists if they had ever come across individuals with positive experiences with pornography. The investigatory staff had tried to identify such people to testify, he said, but had been unable to find any. Hudson importuned reporters to please send such individuals his way. A female commissioner helpfully suggested that she knew of acquaintances, 'normal married couples living in suburban New Jersey', who occasionally looked at magazines or rented X-rated videos with no apparent ill effects. But she doubted they would be willing to testify about their sexual pleasure in a federal courthouse, with their remarks transcribed by the court stenographer and their photos probably published in the next day's paper as 'porn-users'.

Though few witnesses chose to expose themselves to the commission's intimidation through visual images, the tactics used are illustrated in the differential treatment of two female witnesses, former *Playboy* Playmate Micki Garcia and former *Penthouse* Pet of the Year Dottie Meyer. Garcia accused Playboy Enterprises and Hugh Hefner of encouraging drug use, murder, and rape (as well as abortion, bisexuality, and cosmetic surgery) in the Playboy mansion. Her life was endangered by her testimony, she claimed. Despite the serious nature of some of these charges and the lack of any supporting evidence, her testimony was received without question.[23] Meyer, on the other hand, testified that her association with *Penthouse* had been professionally and personally beneficial. At the conclusion of her testimony, the lights dramatically dimmed and large blow-ups of several *Penthouse* pictorials were flashed on the screen; with rapid-fire questions the chair demanded that she explain sexual images he found particularly objectionable. Another male commissioner, prepared by the staff with copies of Meyer's nine-year-old centerfold, began to pepper her with hectoring questions about her sexual life: Was it true she was preoccupied with sex? Liked sex in cars and alleyways? Had a collection of vibrators? Liked rough-and-tumble sex?[24] The female commissioners were silent. His sexist cross-examination was reminiscent of that directed at a rape victim, discredited and made vulnerable by any admission or image of her own sexuality. Suddenly, Dottie Meyer was on trial, publicly humiliated because she dared to present herself as unrepentantly sexual, not a victimized woman.

The ferocious attack on Dottie Meyer – and by extension on any display of women's sexual pleasure in the public sphere – is emblematic of the agenda of conservatives and fundamentalists on women's sexuality. Although they presented their program under the guise of feminist language and concerns, their abiding goal was to reestablish control by restricting women – and their desires – within ever-shrinking boundaries of the private and the domestic. The falsity of the panel's seemingly feminist rhetoric was highlighted by the moment when a lone woman speaking of her own sexual pleasure was seen as a greater threat than all the male 'victims' of pornography who had assaulted and abused women. The conspicuous absence of any discourse that addressed women's definitions of their own sexual pleasures, that enlarged rather than constricted the domain of their public speech or action, unmasked this agenda. Unmasked, too, was the commission's primary aim: not to increase the safe space for women, but to narrow what can be seen, spoken about, imagined, and – they hope – done. The invisibility and subordination of female sexual pleasure in the commission's hearings is a straitjacket which conservatives and fundamentalists would like to extend to the entire culture. Feminist language, disembodied from feminist principles and programs, was used to advance the idea that men, women, and society could be protected only through the suppression of female desire. In the face of false patriarchial protections embedded in shame and silence, feminists need to assert their entitlement to public speech, variety, safety, and bodily and visual pleasures.

I am grateful to Frances Doughty, Lisa Duggan, Ann Snitow and Sharon Thompson for reading early drafts and for helpful comments, criticisms, and encouragement. Thanks also to Faye Ginsburg and Anna Tsing for thoughtful suggestions and patience.

Thanks to the Rockefeller Foundation for a Humanist-in-Residence Fellowship (1987–8) at the Center for Research on Women, Douglass College, Rutgers, the State University, New Brunswick, New Jersey, which supported my research and writing.

Parts of this analysis have appeared in 'The Meese Commission on the Road', The Nation, 243, 3 (2–9 August 1986), pp. 65, 76–82 and 'The Pleasures of Looking: The Attorney General's Commission on Pornography versus Visual Images', in Carol Squiers, ed., The Critical Image: Essays on Contemporary Photography (Seattle: Bay Press, 1990), pp. 38–58. Earlier versions of this paper were presented at the annual meeting of the Society for Photographic Education, Rochester, New York, 17 March 1989; at the panel 'Gender Rituals and the Sexual Self', American Anthropological Association, 21 November 1987; and at the panel 'Contested Domains of Reproduction, Sexuality, Family and Gender in America', American Ethnological Society, Wrightsville Beach, North Carolina, 24 April 1986. Thanks to panelists and members of the audience for helpful comments.

This essay is reprinted with the kind permission of Carole S. Vance, Faye Ginsburg and Anna L. Tsing, eds, Uncertain Terms: Negotiating Gender in American Culture *(Boston, MA: Beacon Press, 1990), pp. 118–34.*

Mandy Merck

From Minneapolis to Westminster

> 3. (1) Pornographic material means film and video and any printed matter which, for the purpose of sexual arousal or titillation, depicts women, or parts of women's bodies, as objects, things or commodities, or in sexually humiliating or degrading poses or being subjected to violence.
>
> (2) The reference to women in sub-section (1) above includes men. (Location of Pornographic Materials Bill)

One hundred and twenty-two years after a British Chief Justice formulated a definition of obscenity which would be applied in the US courts for decades, an American initiative on the subject surfaced in the House of Commons. In many ways, the Location of Pornographic Materials Bill first presented in 1989 by Labour MP Dawn Primarolo seemed an unexceptional addition to current tendencies in British law. In 1982, legislation pertaining to local government and cinema exhibition introduced licensing requirements for sex shops and cinema clubs which effectively brought both under local authority control. This has been seen as a piecemeal application of the principle espoused in the 1979 Williams *Report of the Committee on Obscenity and Film Censorship*, which called for the restricted sale of potentially offensive visual representations of genital and excretory organs and functions, and acts of violence and cruelty.

Censorship law in Britain

In line with the Williams Committee's recommendation, the Primarolo bill was designed to prohibit the sale of specific representations in premises where other goods are sold. By restricting such material to locations licensed by local authorities for their exclusive sale, the bill was intended to alleviate concern over the availability of particular publications in newsagents' or shops which cater to the general public. It followed a series of campaigns opposing the trade in 'soft-core' publications (*Penthouse, Fiesta, Sunday Sport*, etc.) in local outlets and national chains like W.H. Smith, as well as wider concern over the representation of sex and violence in media varying from national newspapers to home video. These worries had already prompted a rash of legislative initiatives throughout the 1980s, ranging from the Local Government and Cinematograph Acts mentioned above to laws regulating indecent displays and video recordings, as well as two unsuccessful attempts to 'tighten' the Obscene Publications Act of 1959.

But the Primarolo bill, unlike these initiatives, introduced a new term into British legislation – 'pornography'. As Annette Kuhn observed in 1984,

> Pornography escapes legal discourse, in that it is nowhere defined in law, while at the same time both commonsense social understandings of what pornography is, and legal sanctions against it, are premised on terms whose reference is not specified representations, but the effects that representations may be thought, in certain circumstances, to produce.[1]

Historically, these effects have been legally divided into two categories – 'obscenity', which, in Lord Justice Cockburn's 1868 test, threatens 'to deprave and corrupt' its consumers, and 'indecency', which, in Lord Denning's 1976 judgement, 'an ordinary decent man or woman would find to be shocking, disgusting or revolting'.

As Kuhn and Beverley Brown[2] have argued, this distinction

(between a lesser matter of public offensiveness and a more serious – and strictly defined – crime of moral harm) reflects a liberal dispensation in British law derived from Mill and implemented in the post-Wolfenden era of the late 1950s and 1960s. Public spaces have been more readily policed (with the aim of protecting individuals from unchosen affronts) than private moral choices. But, as I have noted elsewhere,[3] both the technologies (such as home video) and the politics of recent years have redrawn the utilitarian map, with feminists and moralists alike refusing to abide by its distinction between personal choice and political jurisdiction.

In Britain this change has already manifested itself in an increasing tendency to reduce judicial discretion by formulating more precise definitions of the representations and spaces to be regulated, as well as the extension of regulation in general. Thus a 1982 statute regulating private cinema clubs defined, for the first time in British legislation, the sex film:

> Moving pictures . . . concerned primarily with . . . (i) sexual activity; or (ii) acts of force or restraint which are associated with sexual activity; or . . . genital organs or urinary functions.

The exhibition of such material now requires a licence from the relevant local authority, just as the sale or hire of video cassettes involving similar representations now requires prior certification by the British Board of Film Classification (a body which can refuse, has refused and still refuses the certification – and thus the legal distribution – of the video version of *The Exorcist*).

Vast as they are, the new legal powers conferred by these definitions are still aimed at the subject of both obscenity and indecency law – the consumer of the representation, be he reader, spectator or passer-by. I use the gendered pronoun advisedly, in respect to both judicial and popular belief that the typical consumer of pornography is male, and that the typical sex which it displays is female.

Lessons from the USA

The campaign led by Andrea Dworkin and Catharine Mac-Kinnon to protect the latter group through a series of civic ordinances is well known in the USA (but not, regrettably in the UK) and aptly documented in Donald Alexander Downs's *The New Politics of Pornography*.[4] Employing a civil rights argument first developed by MacKinnon and others against sexual harassment, they formulated a 1983 Minneapolis city ordinance defining the production, sale, exhibition or distribution of pornography – as well as any harms attributable to it, such as coercion into performance or assault – as sex discrimination and therefore actionable for damages. 'Pornography', the ordinance reads

> is the sexually explicit subordination of women,
> graphically depicted, whether in pictures or in words . . .
> women are presented dehumanized as sexual objects,
> things or commodities . . . who enjoy pain or
> humiliation . . . in postures of sexual submission . . .
> reduced to body parts . . .'

After a series of highly contested campaigns over similar ordinances in several cities, a version adopted by the Indianapolis City Council was declared unconstitutional on First Amendment grounds. Indiana Judge Sarah Evans argued that pornography could not be deemed analogous to classes of unprotected speech such as libel or 'fighting words', which 'by their very nature carry the immediate potential for injury'. Her colleague, Judge Frank Easterbrook, maintained on appeal that the ordinance 'establishes an "approved" view of women, of how they may react to sexual encounters, of how the sexes may relate to each other. Those who espouse the approved view may use sexual imagery; those who do not, may not.'[5]

In 1986 the Supreme Court, having received briefs from feminists on both sides of the question, affirmed the Indiana judgements by refusing to hear the case. But if that effectively stymied the campaign in the USA (and MacKinnon notes that a future Court could reverse the position) it offered no inhibition to a heterogeneous collection of British interest groups seeking a now fashionable feminist voice for new regulatory initiatives in the 1980s. When, in 1986, Winston Churchill Junior put forward a Private Member's bill to amend the 1959 Obscene Publications Act by automatically proscribing certain representations (of acts of 'sodomy, oral/genital connection and oral/anal connection'), the Labour MP Clare Short replied with a bill outlawing female nudity in newspapers, a measure aimed at the topless pin-ups in mass-market tabloids like the *Sun*. Neither measure passed. Churchill's bill collapsed under the opposition of civil libertarians and the arts lobby, while Short's initiative – introduced under the Ten-Minute Rule – was essentially a discussion document. But despite scabrous attacks from the tabloids, Short reported a large volume of approving mail. The Labour left began to formulate plans for a pre-emptive strike against the Conservative majority, who seemed to monopolize public concern on issues of sexual representation.

Short and her colleagues actually conferred with Dworkin about draft legislation on the subject of pornography, and a model bill worded similarly to the American ordinances circulated briefly in campaigning circles. When Dworkin objected to its retention of the 'public good' defence from the Obscene Publications Act (exempting works judged to be in the interest of 'science, literature, art or learning, or of other objects of general concern'), the alliance broke down. Nevertheless, the influence of the American ordinances survives in the abridged wording of the Primarolo bill, which defines 'pornographic material' in terms of its depiction of women 'as objects, things or commodities, or in sexually humiliating or degrading poses or being subjected to violence'. (And since this is 'only' a Location Bill, there is no public good defence.)

Primarolo's bill is unlikely to succeed in a Conservative administration, but its concerns will undoubtedly surface in the next Labour government, which promises not only a

Ministry for Women headed by Jo Richardson – a member of the Campaign Against Pornography – but also a possible manifesto commitment 'on the sale and display of soft pornography which ensures that it is not freely available in newsagents and video shops' (a recent resolution of the Labour Party Women's Conference).

Such a measure would have the support of a remarkable alliance of feminists, conservatives and left Labour politicians. In part this may be a consequence of the anti-corporatism in radical British politics, a considered scepticism about civil 'liberties' in the face of structural inequalities which animates the current debate on constitutional reform. (Britain still has no statutory equivalent of a Bill of Rights.) In part it may reflect legislative and religious traditions (both Christian and Islamic in the Britain of the Rushdie affair) which lay stress on the power of representation. What is notable about the British anti-pornography campaign, however, is its lack of grounding in the general critique of heterosexuality offered by Dworkin and MacKinnon, and its historical detachment from the broad tradition of anti-discrimination law upon which MacKinnon's legal strategy depends. (British law offers much more restricted, and ineffectual, statutes on racial and sexual discrimination. The only apposite precedent might be the prohibition of incitement to racial hatred in the Race Relations and Public Order Acts.)

Should a bill restricting pornography in the terms first mooted by Dworkin and MacKinnon succeed in Britain after failing in the United States, it would thus be something of an irony. Deborah Cameron has marvelled at how the positions of the original American debate have been adopted by a very different legal culture:

> Antiporn activists have discussed introducing some version of the Dworkin–MacKinnon ordinance and their opponents have launched a countermove whose key term is anticensorship. I call this remarkable because Britain has neither civil rights legislation nor anything like the

First Amendment. The American model, whether for regulating pornography or protecting it, is almost wholly inapplicable.[6]

The Dworkin–MacKinnon initiative

When Catharine MacKinnon first proposed her ordinance to the Minneapolis, Minnesota, City Council in 1983, she opened with an appeal to the Fourteenth Amendment of the US Constitution, 'which guarantees equality and freedom from discrimination to all citizens, including on the basis of sex'.[7] Pornography, the Minneapolis Ordinance maintains,

> is central in creating and maintaining the civil inequality of the sexes. Pornography is a systematic practice of exploitation and subordination based on sex which differentially harms women. The bigotry and contempt it promotes, with the acts of aggression it fosters, harms women's opportunities for equality of rights in employment, education, property rights, public accommodation and public services . . .

As a precedent to this argument, MacKinnon offered her own study of sexual harassment in the workplace,[8] a text which was instrumental in making such harassment actionable as a form of sex discrimination under the 1964 Civil Rights Act. This strategy had important advantages under US law, for verbal harassment had already been exempted from the constitutional protection of free speech. Furthermore, an ordinance enabling those who claimed harm from pornography to sue its 'maker(s), distributors(s), seller(s), and/or exhibitor(s)' could be seen as a measure to empower individual women, rather than the state officials whom the ordinance's authors declared to be virtually ineffectual in the criminal prosecution of rape, domestic battery and child abuse.

But this approach to pornography was a product of more than the peculiarities of American law. In a reflection on the

Dworkin–MacKinnon strategy, the gay theorist Leo Bersani draws a parallel with another practice of civil inequality, the 'legal and moral incompatibility between [male homo-] sexual passivity and civic authority' which Foucault ascribes to Ancient Greece.[9] 'To be penetrated', Bersani argues, 'is to abdicate power', and he singles out Dworkin and MacKinnon for their determination to change the 'distribution of power both signified and constituted by men's insistence on being on top'.[10]

Other feminists have commented on the cosmic pretensions of this topography ('Dworkin takes a pornographic image as a kind of world view: the law on top, men in the middle, women at the bottom') and responded critically: 'I don't see an image of a woman being penetrated in the missionary position as symbolic of a woman as a *victim*.'[11] But nothing less than a cosmology would serve what MacKinnon identifies as 'epic theory', her frankly ambitious description of an analysis of 'male power as an ordered yet deranged whole'.[12] The same ambitions (and much the same analysis) animate Carole Pateman's *The Sexual Contract*, which opens with a venerable riddle:

> An ancient belief is that the universe rests on an elephant, which, in turn, stands on the back of a turtle; but what supports the turtle? One uncompromising answer is that there are turtles all the way down.[13]

The relationship between the signification and the constitution of power is at the centre of the pornography debate, with an increasingly specified figure accused of being both a sign and a cause of women's subordination. The salience of this accusation – what MacKinnon describes as 'an entirely new theory of social causality'[14] – depends upon a critique of liberalism for ignoring sexual inequality in general, and its allegedly fundamental role in pornography's meaning and function. Not only is pornography (as the representation of sex) beyond defence or redemption, but so is sex itself – both as intercourse ('getting fucked and being owned are inseparably the same' – Andrea Dworkin[15]) and as gender ('the sexuality of male supremacy . . . fuses the eroticization of dominance and submission with the social construction of male and female. Gender is sexual.'[16])

Similar arguments have been made by radical feminists – in Britain – notably Sheila Jeffreys and Susanne Kappeler – but they could hardly be said to underwrite the analysis of pornography propounded by Clare Short or Dawn Primarolo. On the contrary, these two MPs share the American writer Susan Griffin's penchant for what MacKinnon dismisses as a liberal conceptualization of 'eroticism as natural and healthy but corrupted and confused by "the pornographic mind"':[17]

> What in the liberal view looks like love and romance looks a lot like hatred and torture to the feminist.[18]

Britain is a curiously illiberal place to stage this attack on classical liberalism. Despite the current debate about constitutional reform, the Queen's subjects – not citizens – enjoy fewer rights in regard to individual (or – *pace* Kappeler – collective) expression than most of their counterparts elsewhere in the European Community. In October 1990, the international human rights organization Article 19 drew urgent attention to recent developments such as the prohibition on broadcast interviews with members or supporters of Sinn Féin; the British Board of Film Classification's ban of the video *Visions of Ecstasy* for blasphemy; the 1989 ban on any speech or writing of a party political nature by senior local government officers; the extension of the Obscene Publications Act to broadcasting; and – most notoriously – Section 28 of the Local Government Act, forbidding local authorities and maintained schools from 'promoting homosexuality' or teaching it as a 'pretended family relationship'.

Susanne Kappeler's recent attempt to distinguish the latter – as 'a careful suppression of information produced for the sake of information' – from the government's supposed tolerance of 'the promotion of homosexuality . . . where that promotion is a commercially viable business, i.e., pornography'[19] simply flies in the face of the evidence. In sexual representation, as in so much else, Britain is one of the most restricted countries among the Western democracies, effectively outlawing photographs of any genital congress as well as the erect penis. As for specifically gay porn, as the Williams Committee wryly noted in the 1970s, in a country which permits male homosexual activity only between two adults in private, the additional presence of a photographer might in itself make the photograph illegal. This, combined with a succession of explicitly anti-gay prosecutions and judgements (in regard to the lesbian imagery on the cover of *Oz*, 1971; *Gay News* for blasphemously associating Christ with homosexual lovemaking, 1978; the National Theatre for simulating anal intercourse in *The Romans in Britain*, 1981; Gay's the Word bookshop for 'conspiring to import indecent and obscene material', 1984; Jenny White for privately purchasing lesbian videos from the USA, 1991) would hardly indicate the liberal tolerance of sexual commerce which Kappeler is so eager to condemn.

It might, however, begin to suggest why British gay men, as well as many lesbians, have begun to champion the liberal discourse of sexual freedom of which Dworkin, MacKinnon and their followers are so critical.

Future questions

If, as I anticipate, this debate intensifies, a number of key themes are likely to emerge. Among them are:

1. *The sexualization of power*: How has intercourse come to represent *the* subordinating moment in gender relations? Is this yet another effect of the explanatory power supposedly attributed to sex in modernity? (As, in Foucault's famous analysis, 'a causal principle, an omnipresent meaning, a secret to be discovered everywhere . . . as a unique signifier and as a universal signified'.[20]) Have feminists inadvertently elevated the pornographic sign to the epistemic status it

might wish to claim? Does the continuing interest in pornography represent an attempt – as Lesley Stern argued back in 1981[21] – to locate a founding principle of female subordination in the face of the political splits and reversals which have beset Anglophone feminism since the late 1970s?

2. *The question of women's consent*: Judith Vega has argued that in considering women's apparently willing participation in pornography, prostitution, intercourse, etc., Catharine MacKinnon '"solves" the problem of consent by denying its existence' . . . defining male hegemony 'as almost inescapable'.[22] In the face of MacKinnon's patriarchal characterization of all sexual desire (see also Dworkin's *Intercourse*) and Carole Pateman's argument for the difficulty 'encountered in distinguishing women's [sexual] consent from enforced submission',[23] can women ever be full legal subjects in matters sexual? How would the definition of female subjectivity vary between a more protectionist legal culture like Britain's and its US counterpart?

3. *The question of women's bodies*: Carole Pateman has challenged the feminist defence of prostitution and surrogate motherhood as legitimate contractual relationships on the grounds that both constitute direct sexual use of the woman's body, and thus '*herself* in a very real sense'.[24] This equation of the woman's body (particularly the genitalia) with the woman's 'self' similarly informs MacKinnon's arguments against pornography. Meanwhile, it remains a stubbornly central issue in legislative attempts to extend equal treatment to subjects differentiated from the male legislative norm by physiology, notably in the case of maternity rights.

4. *The question of homosexuality*: Both the American ordinances and the Primarolo bill carry paradoxical riders extending their application to men. In Britain this has been interpreted as an attack on gay pornography rather than another popular subgenre representing male heterosexual masochism. Many commentators have responded with

claims that gay sex is exempt from the both legally sanctioned dominance which informs heterosexuality and the asymmetry of its representations. More ingeniously, Leo Bersani has argued that all sex is inevitably both 'self-hyperbole' and 'self-abolition', but that only heterosexuality's 'degeneration of the sexual into a relationship . . . condemns sexuality to becoming a struggle for power. As soon as persons are posited, the war begins. It is the self that swells with excitement at the idea of being on top.' [25] Even if one accepts Bersani's description of male homosexuality as supremely impersonal, the question of lesbianism (on which he does not comment) remains. If pornography really is 'an institution of gender inequality',[26] lesbian efforts like the British *Quim* or the American *On Our Backs* must always stand accused of male identification.[27] (Radical feminism, like so many totalizing doctrines, seems cursed to discover everywhere what it most abhors.)

5. *The power of the sign*: British and American law can be distinguished by the extent to which each protects 'speech' (problematically, but importantly, equated with representation in this debate). While Britain retains common and statute law with substantial powers against libel, blasphemy and the revelation of 'official secrets', successive US Supreme Court decisions have widened the definition of protected speech under the First Amendment. Juridically, the two cultures seem to divide over the (harmful) power ascribed to speech, be it incitement, insult or disclosure. Thus the argument that pornography constitutes a form of 'group libel' would fall on fertile soil in British law. Not only does it offer wide grounds for defamation, but it founded the crime of obscenity in the seventeenth-century cluster of *libels* (seditious, blasphemous and obscene). As Beverley Brown has pointed out, these archaic crimes linked scandalous sexualities with personal reputation rather than the moral welfare of an audience:

> The old mode of libel captures some quite crucial aspects of pornography as a feminist issue – the quality of insult, the fact that it is perceived as an attack on all women as

represented by the figure *in* the image, the feeling of identification and vulnerability that many women experience in relation to pornography as if they themselves were exposed there.[28]

Throughout the contemporary women's 'movement', a common language and certain shared legal traditions have occasioned significant exchanges between British and US feminisms. Yet at the same time the two cultures have remained profoundly divided on questions of civil liberties, transcendent rights, the role of law itself. Now we are faced with the introduction of an American anti-pornography initiative which proposes itself as a civil rights measure into a British legal agenda more characteristically interested in restricting sexual representation than sexual discrimination. If this paradox comes to pass, it is difficult to believe that it will benefit British women.

Part 2

Troubled
pleasures
Dilemmas of desire

Lynne Segal

Sweet sorrows, painful pleasures
Pornography and the perils of heterosexual desire

> There have been too many times when I have guiltily
> resorted to impersonal fantasy because the genuine love I
> felt for a woman wasn't enough to convert feelings into
> performance. And in those sorry, secret moments, I have
> resented deeply my lifelong indoctrination into the
> esthetic of the centerfold.   (Harry Brod)

> Even if there were no pornography, there would be
> pornography.   (Richard Goldstein)

Sorry, secret moments suffuse our sex lives. Most acute when
sexual arousal fails to accompany the desire to make sexual
contact, such sorrow is perhaps particularly sharp-edged for
men: their failure is more often transparent, more likely to
end physical contact. Women's sexual sorrows, as discussed
in recent decades, seem both less hidden and less focused,
fanning out to encompass the dissatisfaction of lifetimes.
'With lovers like men,' Susanne Kappeler asks, 'who needs
torturers?'[1]

Some men today, and many women, see pornography as
the cause of their sexual problems. Others, more often men,
see it – or at least use it – as a possible solution to their
problems. One way or another, for both men and women,
pornography has been placed at the centre of the search for
an understanding of the pains and pleasures of heterosexual
desire. It is hard to write about pornography, so overburd-
ened with significance, without becoming excessive. Worse,

65

with some men now responding to the feminist challenge to write about the role of pornography in their own lives, it is hard to read about the topic without encountering excess – excess of confusion, incoherence or evasion.

'Pornography', Michael Kimmel tells us, introducing his sympathetically pro-feminist collection on the subject, 'is about women as men want them to be, and about our own sexual selves as we would like them to be.'[2] But can this be so? The last thing men in general (to the limited extent we can give meaning to any such notion) 'want' the women in their lives to be – whether wives, daughters, friends, work-mates, lovers or whatever – is the ubiquitously sexually desiring, universally sexually available, creature of much pornographic fantasy. In different ways at different times, it is men, after all, who have surrounded women with the innumerable sanctions precisely aimed to restrict, if not eliminate, the possibilities for them to express sexual arousal or availability. It is men also, as well as women, whose struggles over their 'own sexual selves' have led them to disparage the promiscuous, impersonal male sexuality seemingly celebrated in pornography. 'The attempt to insult sex, to do dirt on it', was how D.H. Lawrence defined and condemned pornography – though, ironically, his own *Lady Chatterley's Lover* was condemned and banned by other men as 'pornographic' throughout his lifetime. Men have always disagreed about pornography. Far from pornography proving the 'perfect vehicle' for bonding all men,[3] they have consistently fallen out over its definition, and their judgement of those who consume it.

In one of his short stories on men and their sex lives, Ian McEwan captures the scene inside a Soho sex shop:

O'Brien walked through Soho market to his brother's shop in Brewer Street . . . 'All the magazines are for sale, gentlemen'. The readers stirred uneasily like troubled dreamers . . . 'Can I help you gentlemen' . . . They scattered before him like frightened fowl, and suddenly he was alone in the shop.[4]

His observation tallies with at least some men's 'confessions' of consuming pornography:

> For me – and I'm guessing for many men who have visited porn arcades or film houses – these periodic visits are always minor traumas . . . I always feel the power of the social stigma against such experiences. Unless the people who see me have been in my situation I'm sure they'll deduce my visit to the arcades reflects my inadequacy or some inadequacy in the person I'm living with.[5]

'What is happening now', Andrea Dworkin informs her audience, this time on British television, 'is that pornography is becoming the contemporary mechanism for controlling women, and it is a control that is exercised through sheer terror.'[6] Yet many men (except when consuming it collectively as a deliberate form of male bonding) are frightened of being seen to use it. Something is amiss. What gives this particular area of popular culture, this 'inglorious and mostly despised department of the imagination',[7] one which is today predominantly produced for and consumed by working-class men, such peculiar power and significance? How has it come to occupy such a *central* place in women's fears of men and some men's embarrassment with themselves?

Men and their discontents

According to its male critics, pornography teaches men to disconnect their emotions from sexual expression.[8] This does not seem to me the most accurate of descriptions. One problem here is that those writing about pornography and its effects rarely bother to define it. It is far from easy to provide any consistent definition of 'pornography', given its shifting historical meanings and contemporary diversity. Nevertheless, looking back over the past hundred or so years of pornography, from the time when sexually explicit, sexually arousing material first appeared in any large quantities, we can see some perennial themes in the most popular forms of pornographic production not redeemed by subsequent acquisition of scientific or literary importance.

Steven Marcus lists three key features of Victorian pornography.[9] Despite significant changes in content, we still see them in many of the most popular narratives and images of commercial pornography today. The first is the creation of the ubiquitously sexually desiring, visibly sexually satisfied, female – frequently transformed from her former cold rejection of men and their sexuality. The second involves the staple of all hard-core pornography (because it is consistently banned in the more accessible soft-core), the image of the huge, hard, magical male member – always erect, forever unflagging. Finally, there is the repetition in earlier and more recent pornographies of two or more men engaged in joint sex with the one woman.

The most conspicuous of male emotions, and the anxieties they express, are surely not-so-hidden in the relentless repetition of these themes. Do we not see only too clearly here fear of female rejection, terror of phallic failure and homosexual feeling disguised as heterosexual performance? What we do not find in pornography – hence its provocation – are the acceptable male emotions associated with the approved discourses on male sexuality. Sex restrained by love and marriage, sex which is 'protective', 'respectable' and 'faithful', reverses into its opposite: sex greedy for immediate, unlimited, self-centred gratification. But would we have the pornographic representation without the accompanying authoritative discourses of and on men and their sexuality? The mirroring themes of the acceptable and transgressive discourses on sexuality suggest a dialectical relation between the two. This is well illustrated in a long and passionate, if somewhat confusing, essay on sexuality written in the early 1980s by Stephen Heath.

Heath attempts to delineate men's sexual dilemmas: 'I've suffered and suffer – it's difficult not to in our society – from "sexuality". To the point of nausea.'[10] The suffering he describes comes from men's fear of not matching up to the sexual performance demanded of them, now that sexual satisfaction is so coercively celebrated as the key to human happiness. Heath moves from chapter to chapter (despite his declared support for feminist anti-pornography arguments and campaigns) attacking not pornographic representation, but rather all scientific and cultural discourses of the last hundred years – from sexology and psychoanalysis to the diverse literary genres available to us. Their shared assumptions and discourses – whether Victorian medicine and sexology or twentieth-century literature, both high and low . . . depict a crude, imperious and promiscuous male sexuality alongside female helplessness, hypersensitivity, empathy and emotionality. It is here, as also in the anxious mirrorings of pornography, that we encounter the more basic, more fundamental 'propaganda' suggesting the ineluctable selflessness, the inevitable subordination, of woman: woman who can find her salvation only through the servicing of others. It is only in pornography, however, that this servicing is depicted as – exclusively – sexual, rather than maternal or simply menial. And it is most likely, is it not, to be the image which meshes least, if at all, with men's actual experiences of women? If so, then surely we cannot begin to address the appeal of and revulsion towards pornography without first grappling with the longings and discontents of both men and women around desire, especially as they connect with and disconnect from heterosexual encounter.

Formations of fantasy

Psychoanalytic theory offers one way of understanding what it sees as men's fetishistic need for visual proof of phallic potency, and their need for visual proof of female desire. Men's specific fears of impotence, feeding off infantile castration anxiety, generate hostility and panic towards women. Through pornography real women can be avoided, male anxiety soothed, and delusions of phallic prowess indulged, by intimations of the rock-hard, larger-than-life male organ.

Pornography, in this view, also serves men's wishful fantasy which, feeding off infantile incestuous attachment, connects them specifically to women as the maternal substitute, creating longing for the permanent possession and visible proof of female desire. The more complex pleasures of bisexuality and the capacity for identification with the 'opposite' sex, as well as the enjoyment of passivity, the eroticization of penetration and pain, are all readily available psychoanalytic explanations of men's use of pornography.

From this perspective the bizarre, fetishistic nature of pornographic material merely reflects the nature of psychic experience, of fantasy itself: where anything which connects with the object of desire can become invested with that desire; where excitement and danger, pleasure and pain, adoration and disgust, power and powerlessness, male and female, even life and death, smoothly fuse and separate out again without damage or distress – except, perhaps, to our internal psychic censors troubled by incompatibilities, not with 'real life', but with internalized moral values. Moreover, in readings true to the complexity of Freud's own thinking on the topic, fantasy is *not* thought to be reducible to wishful thinking or daydreaming about some concretely desired experience. There is no straightforward connection between the dynamics of desire in fantasy and the satisfactions sought in material reality. (It is not equivalent to Freud's daughter dreaming of her strawberries.) Rather, fantasy is its own object, in the sense that it allows for multiple identifications across differing people and positions, or for any other indulgence of the logically impossible. In the words of the leading French psychoanalysts Laplanche and Pontalis:

> Fantasy is not the object of desire, but its setting. In fantasy the subject . . . cannot be assigned any fixed place in it (hence the danger, in treatment, of interpretations which aim to do so). As a result, the subject, although always present in the fantasy, may be so in a

desubjectivised form, that is to say, in the very syntax of the sequence in question.[11]

Hence the even greater danger of basing one's politics around pornography on assumptions of fixed identities and aspirations.

When Catharine MacKinnon declares that 'fantasy expresses ideology, it is not exempt from it',[12] she is, from this perspective, astonishingly misleading (though many feminists agree with her). Ideology is precisely what most fantasy does *not* express: hence, the well-known incidence of fantasies of powerlessness from leading patriarchs, fantasies of sexual domination by black men (or women) from white racists, and rape fantasies from feminists. Such fantasies do not express ideological wobbles in political outlook, but rather have an authentic, autonomous psychic existence of some considerable complexity. (This is why the vast litera-ture on flagellation consumed by the Victorian gentry, with its variety of forms of punishment and torture frequently portraying male 'victims', did nothing to dent their confident control of empire, industry and household.) Sandra Lee Bartky writes of the 'unfortunate situation' of the feminist who has masochistic heterosexual fantasies, suggesting that such a woman is '"entitled" to her shame' over the gulf between her erotic fantasies and her feminist aspirations.[13] I would argue, in contrast, that such a woman is 'entitled' neither to shame nor to guilt, but rather to the lowering of ignorance about the nature of fantasy, and hence to the lowering of personal anxiety about the sources of sexual excitement. For pornographic fantasy has no straightforward connection with what would be presumed to be its 'real-life' enactment, unless it is a stylized 'enactment' (as in consen-sual s/m) under the fantasizer's own control.[14]

It is a strength of psychoanalytic reasoning, unlike most psychological and sociological reasoning, that it can grasp something of the reality of the autonomy and complexity of the psychic. But there is a weakness. If the penis *symbolizes* male power (and hence men's accompanying belief in its exalted value – the appearance of the penis as a fetish in pornography, alongside the devaluation or 'degradation' assumed to accompany the male gaze at the female genitalia), what, we have still to discover, *explains* male power? And here, if we wish to step outside circularity, there is another tale to tell. It is one which almost all psychoanalytic under-standings fail to acknowledge: one which must go beyond both the interpersonal dynamics of the familial and these symbolic interpretations of the phallus which remain restric-ted to its assumed dominance in sexual encounter. The wider social relations which have constructed men's power within all the institutions of public life, designated men rather than women the symbol of humanity, and everywhere shore up men's authority both inside and outside the family, are all absorbed into the symbolic meaning of the phallus. The power of men – created, maintained and also today increas-ingly challenged, within both institutional and discursive settings – has been expressed in different ways at different times. It is far from monolithic. Nevertheless, the psychic significance of boys' and girls' perceptions of sexual differ-ence, the importance attached to the penis and the devalu-ation of female genitalia, cannot in the end be explained without some acknowledgement of men's general social power in relation to women.

It is also crucial to acknowledge, as some psychoanalytic theory has done, that the powerful have always not only sexually (as well as economically) exploited the relatively powerless, but also projected sexuality itself on to those they see as least powerful – particularly the apparently dangerous, troubling and 'dirty' aspects of sex.[15] This is why it is not only women but black and working-class women and men who are mythically invested with sexuality in dominant Western discourse and iconography. The point here is that it is the dynamic interplay between power and desire, attrac-tion and repulsion, acceptance and disavowal, which eroti-cizes those already seen as inferior (and thereby gives them, in fantasy, a threatening power). It is not, as some feminists believe, the eroticizing of an object which creates it as inferior. Nevertheless, the sexualization of 'inferior' bodies does become a *sign* of difference, and a measure of the superiority of those who disown and distance themselves from such bodies. This is why any naked, eroticized display of the white male body remains taboo outside pornography and, even there, will serve to threaten other white men.

The unique importance of incestuous infantile fears and desires, cross-sex identification (present in men's enjoyment of the ubiquitous lesbian number in pornography) and homosexual attachment (present in men's pleasure in watching other penises in action) all inform the content of pornography and men's responses to it. But they do so in the context of women's social subordination, and men's far from untroubled relationship to sex.

The making of masculinities

Socialization into stereotyped sex-role attributes, beliefs and actions remains the dominant way of understanding the contrasts between men's and women's sexual interests and behaviour. And pornography, as sociologists of masculinity like Michael Kimmel argue, is seen as both an important part of this socialization into the dominant ideals of manliness – incorporating toughness, ambition, aggressiveness, confidence and success – and a vital confirmation of its achievement:

In locker rooms and playgrounds men learn to detach their emotions from sexual expression . . . Male 'sexual socialization' emphasizes how real men are supposed to have sex. Passivity is prohibited, and males must constantly seek to escalate the level of sexual activity . . . And the young woman must play the feminine role of 'gatekeeper', determining the levels of sexual intimacy appropriate to the situation. As a result neither can fully experience the pleasures of the moment.[16]

Kimmel is right to point to the interaction between the social construction of gender and the social construction of sexuality. Dominant discourses, of which pornography is but one (and one to which not all boys will have equal access), do indeed link 'masculinity' definitively to heterosexual 'drive' and 'performance'. They also link 'femininity' to 'attractiveness' and 'desirability' in the eyes of men (although the social scripts which give women the 'gatekeeper' role are surely precisely what is *not* to be found in pornographic discourses, but rather in all the other more respectable discourses of 'femininity').

What we need to ask, however, is: do all men and women 'learn' their social scripts quite so successfully, and in exactly the same way? Are the scripts themselves quite so solid as Kimmel suggests? Do the boys never encounter ideas linking 'masculinity' to 'love', 'romance' and relationships? Have the girls yet to see, and hear, Madonna's sexually assertive, if polymorphously perverse, appearance, sound, lyrics and movement? Kimmel's uniformly bleak picture of adolescent sexuality in the USA sits rather oddly beside his criticisms elsewhere of the socialization theories of much social science research as 'mired in tired formulations of "sex roles", those fixed, ahistorical containers of attributes and behaviours that are said to refer to masculinity and femininity'.[17] Certainly some young men have produced variations on the standard script, not always so distinct from girls. Here's one from Britain:

> I am 17 . . . I had fallen in love . . . I felt high and often full
> of wonder with her and then often pain and
> incompleteness when away from her. I planned and
> fantasized my way into a married future – children,
> security for ever . . . I don't remember feeling that she and
> I were separate and distinct.[18]

At least one recent study of the sex lives of North American college students suggests that the contemporary sexual orthodoxy is one where young men emphasize love and commitment in their relationships as much as young women.[19]

Kimmel's belief that 'performance anxiety' is a pervasive experience of American men is, however, affirmed even more strongly in the views of another US sociologist of masculinity, Harry Brod.[20] More firmly also, Brod blames pornography specifically for alienating men from their bodies, creating rising rates of male impotence, narrowing the range of male sexual experience and creating male self-depreciation and loss of fuller sexual satisfaction:

> Male sexual dysfunction problems ranging from
> adolescent embarrassment at inopportune tumescence to
> impotence of various sorts can be traced at least in part to
> pornographically induced obsessions with penile
> performance.[21]

Later we learn that 'imposed pornographic sensibilities' not only lessen men's potential sensual fulfilment but create 'many other aspects of estranged bodily awareness men disproportionately suffer from: heart attacks, ulcers, hypertension, etc.'.[22] 'Imposed by whom?' and 'Why?' are not questions Brod addresses.

Interestingly, Brod presents his account as 'a socialist-feminist analysis': socialist because pornography (like wage labour) turns men's bodies into machines and creates a restrictive genital, performance-driven male sexuality at odds with the realization of full humanity; feminist because pornography is linked to violence against women. Another North American male philosopher, Alan Soble, similarly claims to present a Marxist analysis of pornography. Unlike Brod, he puts forward what he calls 'a Marxist *defence* of pornography'. Unlike Brod also, Soble sees the need to address the question of the definition of 'pornography' (defining it in terms of its intention to produce sexual arousal) and is more aware of its shifting meanings and contemporary diversity. Agreeing, however, that today's pornography is largely (though far from exclusively, and certainly not inevitably) sexist and offensive, he attributes this to a variety of causes – almost all of them stemming from the productive relations of capitalism.

Using an economic reductionism that would astonish most early Marxist theoreticians, not to mention those who have addressed the relative autonomy of structures and ideological formations, Soble sees the sexual division of labour in capitalism as producing contrasting male and female sexualities:

> Male sexuality is atomistic because men participate in classical production and are excluded from women-dominated mothering, and female sexuality is holistic (no fixation partialism complex, no separation of affection and passion) because women participate in reproduction and the nurturing service industries, which are less infected and influenced by the commodity form.[23]

Men's typical patterns of labour desensitize male bodies, downgrade the tactile in favour of the visual, and produce genital hypersensitivity; women's patterns produce the opposite effects.

Standard pornography not only meshes with male sexuality but, at the same time, gives men a sense of control which is missing from the rest of their lives: from their productive, political and – increasingly, with the rise of feminism – personal and sexual lives with women. The problem with Soble's analysis, which simply inverts the feminist anti-pornography position, lies in its oversimplified, literal readings connecting men's fantasies and men's material reality. Pornography is not a means for men to *achieve* power over women, but proof that men *lack* power over women: 'pornography is not so much an expression of male power as much as an expression of their lack of power'.[24] This analysis is close to that of a few feminists. Jean Bethke Elsthain, for example, writes:

Pornography offers for voyeuristic consumption a vision
that attracts precisely because it signifies to 'public man'
what he is not – in either public or private: he increasingly
lacks the power to bend others to his will.[25]

She too cites mechanistic work, atomized social relations,
anonymous bureaucratic controls and shifts in sexual behaviour as social patterns reflected in pornography.

Both Soble and Elsthain downplay the reality that men in
general *do* still have power, relative to women. We might
agree, however, that much of pornography does suggest
male sexualities which are both anxious and defensive, in
need of reassurance through fantasies of control over others.
(We could as easily have discovered this from any other
cultural genre, from Western to thriller, from science fiction
to body-building.) It seems likely that men are *least* sure of
their power over women, and *most* fearful of women's
self-sufficiency and autonomy, precisely in their sexual
encounters with them. But nothing could be more at odds
with the feminist anti-pornography movement's understanding of the dynamics of male sexuality.

Sex as oppression
As others have noted, there is a hidden – though barely
hidden – agenda in recent feminist anti-pornography analysis: the rejection of heterosexuality as incompatible with
women's liberation. MacKinnon asserts: 'Men see rape as
intercourse; feminists say much intercourse "is" rape . . .
feminism stresses the indistinguishability of prostitution,
marriage, and sexual harassment.'[26] Finally, getting right
down to it, she argues:

Either heterosexuality is the structure of oppression or it is
not . . . And I would like you to address the question . . .
whether a good fuck is any compensation for getting
fucked. And why everyone knows what that means.[27]

Dworkin is adamant that it is, as she puts it, 'the role of the fuck' to create and maintain a social system of power over women; fucking is:

> a *literal* erosion of the body's integrity and its ability to function and survive . . . her insides are worn away over time, and she, possessed, becomes weak, depleted, usurped in all her physical and mental energies and capacities by the one who has physically taken her over . . .[28]

MacKinnon and Dworkin, like most anti-pornography feminists, insist that they speak *for* feminism. Both are equally explicit in their messianic faith that if feminism is not what they say, 'it deserves to die'.[29] It is true that since the late seventies feminism has found it hard to say anything positive about heterosexuality. If we want to understand why feminist discussion about sexuality keeps reducing down to the pornography debate, we have to understand why this is so.

Feminists who criticize pornography today mostly see themselves as rejecting the heritage of the sexual revolution. 'Sexual liberation', Susanne Kappeler argues, 'is not the liberation of women, but the liberation of the female sex-object, which is now expected to orgasm (in response).'[30] The greater sexual permissiveness of the sixties is seen by these feminists only as assisting men to exploit women. MacKinnon even sees abortion reform as removing women's last protection from men's pressure for sex.[31] Certainly, as Kappeler and others are aware, the rhetoric of sexual liberation was limited in seeing sexuality as a purely *individual* matter, ignoring men's social dominance and everyday sexism. As certainly, however, the effects of increased availability of contraception and abortion, greater tolerance of women's pre-marital sexual activities and the lessening of condemnation and punishment of single motherhood were decidedly *social*: setting a new sexual agenda for women. Once vulnerable to sacking for 'sexual misconduct', if not sent into institutional 'care' (with the 10,000 'mental defectives' guilty only of sex before marriage), or suffering death from back-street abortion, sexually active single women now exist in a world incalculably freer of the hypocrisy, dishonesty and savage cruelty of earlier times.[32]

This is why other feminists respond as I do – with despair – to feminist dismissals of 'sexual liberation', arguing instead that it is *women* who gained most from the liberalizations around sexuality in the 1960s.[33] This was despite – and in part because of – the self-serving sexism which it exposed in men's sexual conduct, helping as this did to generate women's liberation at the close of the sixties. Here, we have finally arrived at the crux of the problem which has fanned the pornography debate within feminism: *Is it, or is it not, possible for women to conceive of, and enjoy, an active pleasurable engagement in sex with men? Is it, or is it not, possible to see women as empowered agents of heterosexual desire?* Without denying the importance and significance of lesbianism, there is no doubt that many women today, like many feminists of the early 1970s, do wish to be so empowered. But while Madonna expresses their desire, and rocks the masses, feminists are widely seen as anti-sex.

Three formidable obstacles block feminist moves towards an empowering heterosexual politics, enabling the issue of men's violence against women, now condensed into the metaphor of 'pornography', to slam the door on any such pursuit. The first hurdle is the apparent rigidity of the symbolic meanings of 'sex'; the second difficulty is the slow pace of change in the social context of heterosexual relations; the final impasse is the inevitable disappointments of sex when many women, in ways somewhat distinct from those of men, seek to find within its orbit the measure and meaning of their lives.

If the main objection to pornography is that it is about the eroticization of power, there is little doubt that in this pornography reflects the meanings attaching to all dominant discourses of sex. 'Sex' symbolically, in the last instance (and, as many women complain, concretely in the first instance), still reduces to 'the sex act': a male act, a female response. Within feminism, as Jane Gallop points out, as within patriarchal or pornographic ideology, women's heterosexual desire has been theorized only negatively: 'penetration enacts the subjugation of women by men . . . there is little place for pleasure'.[34]

This is why MacKinnon and Dworkin have been able to declare that women 'live in the world pornography creates', and to deny any clear distinction between coercion and consent in women's sexual experiences with men. This is why, perhaps unexpectedly, a bias against reporting women's pleasure in heterosexual intercourse is so clearly evident in the first and classic 'feminist' sex research of Shere Hite. In this survey, so cool and neutral in tone, Hite consistently juggles with her own data, and with what women are telling her, to dismiss the significance of heterosexual intercourse for women: 'having an orgasm during intercourse is an adaptation of our bodies. Intercourse *was never meant to* stimulate women to orgasm'[35] – and this despite the fact that some women, aware of the hidden agenda, complain that they feel 'weird' because they *do* have orgasms during intercourse.[36] Reducing sexual pleasure to measurable movements of the genitals, Hite, like Masters and Johnson before her, reports that women experience stronger orgasms during masturbation, or at least outside intercourse, and she is clearly troubled by the fact that 'the majority' of her subjects insist that 'they would always prefer orgasm during intercourse'.[37] At one point Hite complains of some of the women she interviewed: 'Of course, the thirty percent of women who said they *could* orgasm regularly during intercourse often bragged about it', while elsewhere warning us that some of these women may be lying.[38]

Hite's research and reasoning have served as a model for much subsequent feminist work on heterosexuality. Although many women undoubtedly found its rejection of penetration empowering, its accompanying biases have been reproduced to form a pejorative feminist paradigm of female sexuality. For example, Anja Meulenbelt, in her later survey of sexual experience, reminded women who enjoyed fucking of men's pressure for intercourse, and challenged them as to whether they really '*wanted* to do it that way', claiming that any pleasure obtained thereby was 'emotional' rather than 'something to do with getting an orgasm'.[39] Women, especially young women, certainly *do* feel the pressure from men for intercourse, and suffer because of it, even as many older women, equally certainly, suffer from the lack of it. But strengthening women's power and desire to refuse a type of sexual engagement they do not want in favour of alternatives which they might prefer cannot be based on deceiving ourselves that we can biologically separate off the 'physical' side of having orgasms from some accompanying 'emotional' side: a separation which feminists have always condemned men – I suspect often wrongly – for being able to make.

Women and the heterosexual predicament

The attempt to separate off women's 'physical' and 'emotional' sources of pleasure has led many other feminists writing on sex (Anja Meulenbelt, Betty Dodson, Lonnie Barbach and others) to place masturbation rather than engagement with men at the heart of heterosexual pleasure and desire.[40] One reason for this seemingly odd move is the attempt to sidestep the difficulties of moving beyond or outside all the dominant representations of heterosexual desire as the desire of, or for, the phallus. Towards such an end, the first and most obvious distinction we might expect feminists writing on heterosexuality to emphasize, however, is that the phallus (as sacred sign of male power) is *distinct* from the penis (as small and fragile object generating intense anxieties). Yet this is precisely what is *denied*, with equal vehemence and passion, in both sexist pornographic *and* feminist anti-pornographic discourses.

Only in these two discourses does the 'old male cock' continue to crow immune from more recent probing – especially in the 1980s and early 1990s – which would connect the penis with every form of weakness from impotence and hysteria to sickness and disease. One text after another in recent years has embarked upon the task of 'deconstructing the phallus': turning the medical and therapeutic gaze upon the penis and its persistent premature ejaculation, impotence, loss of desire; then widening the focus to include venereal disease, testicular cancer and infertility – contemplating all the while the painful remedies men seek for their sexual disorders.

Nor are the suffering and emotion in men's sex lives, supposed until recently to be one of men's best-kept secrets, anything new. Lesley Hall, in her study of male sexuality in the first half of this century, finds the 'unmentionable subject' of male sexual dysfunction already well known, its sufferers described by one physician in 1930 as 'among the most miserable of all patients that the doctor is called upon to treat'.[41] Doctors, sex researchers and marriage advice experts were, as many remain, loath to discuss the topic, all clinging to their presumption of men's ardent and impetuous 'phallic' urges. Although Freud had written in 1908 that to many it was 'scarcely credible how seldom normal potency is to be found in the husband', and Stekel had added in 1927 that the 'percentage of relatively impotent people cannot be placed too high' (himself placing it near 50 per cent and citing premature ejaculation as modern man's most characteristic sexual practice), men's inability to use the penis as they might wish to has remained a largely private torment.[42] Men feared to consult doctors for many reasons – especially experiences of past humiliations from them.

Even men's unimaginative physical ineptitude when they did initiate sex with women was well known in the early to mid twentieth century: Balzac's image of the orang-utan trying to play the violin was invoked in several sex manuals of the day. Many men wrote to Marie Stopes in those years of their sorrow at their inability to arouse or satisfy their wives (hardly surprising when they, like their wives, often believed that any form of tactile, let alone oral, stimulation of genitals was 'shocking'): 'When I found I could not awaken the desire in her it made me feel so selfish and mean', one writer lamented.[43] It is hard not to agree with Hall's own conclusions on surveying men's chronic anxieties over the last hundred years: 'Whatever the social potency of men . . . their actual sexual potency is always dubious and open to question.'[44]

Against feminist anti-pornography discourse on the power and danger of male sexual domination, it is crucial to emphasize how the phallus as a symbol functions primarily to hide, as well as to create and sustain, the severe anxieties and fears attaching to the penis. The question is whether the public display of the fragility of the penis (as an appendage only precariously available for men to use in heterosexual engagement) can work to undermine notions of the phallus (as ubiquitous concept connecting 'masculinity' to power). At this point in history it is still not so easy to dissociate the penis from notions of the transcendent phallus. Nevertheless I agree with Jane Gallop that to insist upon the precarious nature of bodily masculinity is part of the work necessary to displace the idealized transcendent phallus.[45] It is gay men's politics and pornography which have, of course, so determinedly eroticized men's material bodies, as both active agents and passive objects of desire; bodies which, in this tragic era of AIDS, are all too readily exposed as fragile and destructible.[46] Such contradictory focus on the male body, ambivalently connecting it with both power and powerlessness (combined with assaults on the social and cultural basis of men's material power over women), is what begins to undermine the tenacity of the idealization of the phallus. What is more, in a largely unconscious way, men are well aware of this.

Only one film could not be shown in Channel 4's recent retrospective on censored films – even with cuts and parts of the screen blanked out: a harmless little film called *DICK*. The film is about men's penises and women's reaction to them. Its director, Jo Menell, was painstakingly careful to avoid showing even the hint of an erection (not one tumescent penis) to ensure that it was a film about the penis, not about sex, but it caused uproar. National Endowment for the Arts funds in the USA were threatened, and one newspaper after another deplored the horror and obscenity of 'Penises on Parade'. So strong is the taboo on displaying the penis, so great is men's anxiety about such display that even the *reviews* of the film were censored. Newspaper copy was shredded in the most liberal of American cities – Los Angeles, San Francisco and Boston. The conspiracy of silence around the penis, which the film was attempting to address, reigned supreme; though thunderous applause greeted its first showing in the USA, from its mainly feminist and gay audience.

Empowering women sexually

But what of women's bodies? If we can attempt to *dethrone* the phallus through focusing upon the penis, how might we, conversely, find symbols to *empower* women sexually? It is pornography's popular focus upon female genitalia that seems to confirm women in passive immobility: as objects, and nothing but objects, of active, phallic consumption. For women to be subjects of desire, must they not identify with a sexual agency other than the phallus? New York psychoanalyst Jessica Benjamin has attempted to grapple with this challenge, asking how a woman is to have 'a desire of her own'. The answer, she argues, will not emerge from some new symbol representing female genitalia to set beside the phallus (whether it be Irigaray's two lips continuously in contact, or Georgia O'Keeffe's central-core vaginal imagery – less imaginatively elaborated by Judy Chicago).[47] Notions of women's desire, in her view, can emerge from forms of intersubjectivity only once we see our sexual selves and their diverse sensual capacities as existing between, as well as outside and within, our bodies.[48]

Both girls and boys have (ideally) once experienced themselves as the object of their mother's active loving (or, if not, of their own fantasies of maternal love). But it is precisely her active caressing, cradling, holding and enclosing which are desexualized in dominant discourses of sex. It is the boy's defensive attempt to seek independence or to 'beat back the mother', seemingly omnipotent to the incestuously desiring son, which many psychoanalysts understand as the cause of this desexualization of the mother, alongside his identification with the father and idealization of the phallus.[49] Girls too, on this view, are seen as seeking, less successfully, to identify with the father to obtain a sense of separateness from the mother.

Benjamin argues that it is possible, at least potentially, for girls to obtain a sense of sexual agency from that first woman in their lives, the mother (as well as from the father through cross-sex identification). But this can occur only when social arrangements both within and outside the family, and the power women can be seen to have, create women not as desexualized creatures tied to reproduction and submission but as visibly sexually active in their own right. Women's sexual agency, however, will not be encapsulated within any one symbol – and this is something which the new pornography by and for women has been attempting to address.

Candida Royalle, for example, after five years acting in sex films, decided to set up her own pornographic Femme Productions. Her films, which carry many of the traditional pornographic numbers (close-ups of heterosexual and lesbian sex, including bondage – since this is high on the list of women's fantasies) emphasize sex in the context of feelings and relationships: sensuality, foreplay and 'after-play'.[50] As Linda Williams comments, pornography is one of the few genres where women are not punished or made guilty for acting out their sexual desires.[51] Her own research suggests that now more women are seeing, discussing, buying, and – just a few – producing it, pornography has been changing along the lines of distinguishing between good (consensual and safe) and bad (coercive) sex. Moreover, the more discourses there are around sex, the more the sexist oppositions between male and female, active and passive, subject and object begin to break down. Oddly, this is the most clear in pornographic s/m.

It is possible to conceive of representing woman's heterosexual desire through her actively chosen and pleasure-giving bodily interactions with men. But, we need to ask, is it yet possible to strengthen women's power and confidence to refuse sexual engagements they do not want in social contexts where many men feel entitled to demand sex? Certainly, men's attempts to impose, control and define their heterosexual engagements have often undermined women's potential enjoyment of their sexuality. This is clear, for example, in the testimonies of women who cite the 'harm' pornography has caused them. A typical report, from a woman attending the public hearings on pornography in Minneapolis, describes how, after reading *Playboy*, *Penthouse* and *Forum*, her husband develops an interest in group sex, takes her to various pornographic institutions and one night invites a friend into their marital bed:

> To prevent more of these group situations, which I found
> very humiliating . . . I agreed with him to act out in
> privacy a lot of these scenarios he read to me. A lot of them
> depicting bondage and different sexual acts that I found
> very humiliating.[52]

Only after learning karate and beginning to travel on her own did this woman feel strong enough to leave her husband.

Over and over again, what we read as women's testimony against pornography are stories of women coercively pressured into sex they do not want. But surely the harm we are hearing about cannot reside in the pornographic image, nor even in the possibilities for enacting the practices they depict – varying from straight to oral, anal, bondage and group sex. There are practices which certain women as well as men, at certain times, freely choose.[53] The harm is contained in the social context which deprives the woman of her ability to reject any sexual activity she does not want – whether with husband, lover, parent, relative, friend, acquaintance or stranger. Only the refusal to make distinctions, either between image and act or between freely chosen and coercive sex, would entail MacKinnon's bizarre logic that 'the defence of lesbian sadomasochism would sacrifice all women's ability to walk down the street in safety for the freedom to torture a woman in the privacy of one's basement'.[54] If we take seriously the question of social consent and context, we are more likely to hear MacKinnon's theatrical evocation of women's danger as serving more to confirm women's powerlessness and subordination, especially around sex, than to provide pathways towards empowering them in relation to men.

Given the slow and uneven pace of change in relations between women and men, when in public and private men remain (though less comprehensively) the likely bearers of superior economic and social power, it is not so easy, however, for women to reject men's demands – *of whatever nature*. Men are also known to be the more likely initiators of force in pursuit of their ends – especially in pursuit of sexual ends where dominant ideology has traditionally excused, if not encouraged, their more assertive behaviour.[55] A recent survey of 150 young women's heterosexual encounters in the UK, looking specifically at women's confidence in demanding safer sex practices in the context of AIDS, suggested that nearly a quarter of these women had felt pressurized into sex with men.[56] Many had found their first sexual experiences negative or limited, and although some women did express beliefs in their right to sexual pleasure, on their terms, they faced daunting obstacles putting this into practice in relationships with men. The main obstacle was women's own definitions of sex in terms of love and romance, leaving men dictating the nature of the sexual practices.

In a similar but larger study in the USA, Sharon Thompson found greater variation in the quality of teenage girls' sexual encounters with men. One group describing their sexual initiation reported little sense of sexual agency. These women did not recall masturbating before having sex with men, and sexual intercourse was something that 'just happened' to them without petting, foreplay, desire or contraception. They felt they had little sexual choice, and saw the penis as '"a big thing" that had to go into a "little hole"'.[57]

A second and smaller group of teenage girls, however, presented narratives of considerable sexual pleasure (though rarely involving orgasm, except in sexual encounters with other girls) which linked description of their own sexual desire with romantic encounters with men – holding out for kisses, foreplay, oral sex and passion. Unlike the previous group, these girls had their first heterosexual encounters with some knowledge of sexual pleasure and desire, gained from masturbation, childhood sex play, heavy petting and their mothers' accounts of sex. They had frequently obtained contraception before their first intercourse and after, if not satisfied: 'They looked for lovers with slower hands, more exploratory tongues, wiser cocks.'[58] Thompson concludes that for young women to be able to embark on sexual encounters feeling in possession of their sexuality, they need an erotic education – not just talk about and practice in exploring their bodies, but access to more complex narratives of desire: narratives of pleasure and fulfilment that do not reduce to the platitude 'just hold out for "love"'. For this is the old message which sabotages the sense of sexual confidence upon which the pleasure narratives depend, connecting girls' desire for love with the ignorance and guilt which will mean they leave the defining of sex up to boys and men.

Another more complex 'anthropological' survey, conducted by Michael Moffat in the USA with several hundred slightly older, largely suburban-bred students at Rutgers University in New Jersey, found many young women presenting themselves in written descriptions as sexual agents in ways not so different from men. Some spoke of sexual 'scoring', and the typical female fantasy of good heterosexual sex focused on male attractiveness, inspired foreplay, oral sex (initiated by both women and men) and orgasms without emotional complexities.[59] Sexual engagements were seen as good when they were intentional, emotional, mean-ingful and pleasure-giving:

> 'I feel sex, on the whole, is pretty terrific! I can get
> enjoyment from it even when not seriously involved with
> my partner. I can get more pleasure when I am . . . I don't
> know if I represent the typical female college student but I
> sure fit in with my room-mates!', one woman writes.[60]

The rise of both women's and men's reports of the enjoyment of oral sex, actively given and passively received, was promi-nent in this as in other recent sex surveys, with both sexes seeing it as a more 'egalitarian, mutual practice' for estab-lished couples.[61] In this study women explicitly promoted the value of sexual pleasure more than men, with two-thirds of the women and half of the men supporting the idea of the importance and goodness of sexual pleasure in and for itself.

Women and their discontents

Apparently unaware that pornography (according to its femi-nist critics) deprived women everywhere of sexual agency, women stressed their own right to sexual pleasure (though only 10 per cent of them were certain that they experienced it regularly). They also discussed the negative side of sexual pleasure, as well as the positive, more often than men. They wrote of difficulties reaching orgasm and, when orgasmic, noted the importance of more trusting and more experimental sexual encounters. In this study men and women alike stressed the importance of sex with affection, emphasizing 'love', 'caring' and 'commitment': 'I do not believe good sex can happen without love' was a typical comment from one senior male student, many emphasizing traditionally 'femi-nine' sexual scenarios which might include, along with the scented candles and wine, mutual enjoyment of a 'dirty movie'.[62] Moffatt concludes that despite the fact that a min-ority of male students displayed double standards or mis-ogynist attitudes, an ethic of gender equality, and emphasis on the importance of sex, was the 'new sexual orthodoxy' articulated by the majority of students.

Any feminist critique of heterosexuality is thus at odds with these women's sense of themselves as sexual agents, particularly when it is perceived (in part correctly) as feminism's rejection of the importance of pleasure and romance. How do we square a survey like this with the apparent appeal of feminist anti-pornography politics, and feminist critiques of heterosexual practice? It seems likely, as Moffatt suggests, that these young women's enthusiasm for sex and pleasure, and their sense of sexual agency, nevertheless exists alongside a reality in which women do face more problems than men. Some men wrote sadly of their lack of physical attractiveness, sexual ineptitude and lack of self-confidence, even of feeling pressured into sex, but women were more at risk of abuse and violence (16 per cent mentioned such incidents in a questionnaire compared to 4 per cent of men), had more difficulties around sexual satisfaction, and bore the brunt of anxieties around pregnancy and abortion. More significantly, here as elsewhere, social context is all-important. These women, in the liberal and ideologically more sexually egalitarian world of college, were still largely protected from the routine gender hierarchies of most public institutions, not to mention the many economic and social disadvantages which motherhood is more likely to bring. Their still confident expectations of fun and pleasure must be placed beside the more typical situations which generate many other women's disappointments with sex, and in particular disappointments with men.

When Shere Hite suggests that 98 per cent of the four and a half thousand women she interviewed for her latest survey, *Women and Love*, desire fundamental change in their relationships with men ('they have not yet found the love they are looking for' – the love they hope is yet to come) she emphasizes not so much women's lack of sexual agency, or even lack of sexual fulfilment, as their desire for greater intimacy with and emotional support from male partners.[63] Certainly there are not enough men giving women what they want. And although recent surveys in Britain suggest that most women are happy with their sex lives with men, and most younger women say they have initiated a sexual relationship, many women still feel that they have problems with men.[64] Those problems remain – as they have always been – discrimination at work, lack of adequate support, intimacy and romance when living with men, and fears of violence from men.

Because women, even more than men, still place sex and romance at the centre of their lives (hence our addiction to the powerful objects of desire in mass-market romance), it is not so hard to elicit sexual longing and discontent from women. It is all too easy to project that discontent on to the always, already tarnished target of pornography. But perhaps for women, as for men, there is no final cure for our sexual discontent and longing, with its infantile eroticization of power: the object of such longing is simply longing itself. This does not mean, however, that the search for sexual pleasure is not, potentially, a politically progressive and mobilizing force. For we certainly cannot even find the space to enjoy our wishful sexual utopias in peace without the power to reject men whose sexual demands we find coercive, irritating, or perhaps simply routinely boring. What is woefully misleading is to imagine that in eliminating pornography, we would gain that power.

Kobena Mercer

Just looking
for trouble

*Robert Mapplethorpe and
fantasies of race*

How does 'race' feature in the politics of anti-pornography?
Well, it does and it doesn't. 'Race' is present as an emotive
figure of speech in the rhetoric of certain feminist anti-
pornography arguments; yet 'race' is also markedly absent,
since there appears to be no distinctly black perspective on
the contentious issues of sexuality, censorship and representation that underpin the volatile nature of the anti-porn
debate. Although Audre Lorde and Alice Walker made
important contributions early on in the debate in the United
States over a decade ago, the question of pornography has
hardly been a top priority on the agenda of black feminist
politics in Britain in the 1980s and early 1990s.[1] If it is indeed
the case that white and black women have not been equally
involved in the anti-porn movement, or have not made it a
shared political priority, then we have to ask: What role does
'race' play in the discourse of anti-pornography which has
come mainly from white women?

'Race' as an issue in anti-pornography feminism

When 'race' is invoked to mobilize moral support for anti-
pornography positions, it tends to function as a rhetorical
trope enabling a race and gender analogy between violence
against women and incitement to racial hatred. In their
recent campaigns, Labour MPs Clare Short and Dawn Primarolo have frequently used this analogy to argue that just as
black people are degraded by racist speech and hurt by racial

violence, so women are harmed and victimized by sexist and misogynist representations which portray, and thus promote, the hatred and fear of women that erupt in all acts of male violence. It follows, so the argument goes, that just as the law is supposedly empowered to prohibit and punish incitement to racial hatred, new regulative legislation is needed to 'protect' women from the harm and danger of male violence that pornography represents. Yet the 1965 Race Relations Act, which sought to prohibit racist speech, has never been particularly beneficial to black people – more often than not it has been used against black people to curtail our civil rights to representation, and was proved to be notoriously useless and ineffective by the rise of new racist and fascist movements in the 1970s. Just as most black people know not to entrust our survival and protection to the state, one ought to question any argument, feminist or otherwise, that seeks to extend the intervention of the state in the form of prohibitionary legislation.

Indeed from a black perspective, the problem lies with the very analogy between racial hatred and male violence because it is based on a prior equation between those sexually explicit words and images labelled 'pornographic' and those acts of violence, brutality and homicide that do indeed take place against women in 'real life'. This equation – that 'pornography is the theory, rape is the practice' – is central to the radical feminist anti-pornography argument that gained considerable influence in the USA during the 1980s and is gaining ground in Britain now. One of the most worrying aspects of these developments is the strange alliance that has evolved between radical feminists demanding censorship in the name of women's freedom, and the anti-obscenity lobby of the New Right whose demands for the prohibition of sexual representations have always been part of the moral agenda of mainstream conservatism. For entirely different reasons, these two groups seek further state regulation of pornography, yet their convergence on this objective has created a wider constituency of support for a policy of cultural censorship. Where do black people stand in relation to this unhappy alliance?

While anti-porn feminists are more likely than their neo-conservative counterparts to observe that pornography itself is violently racist, one has to question the highly emotive way in which 'race' is used only to simplify complex issues and polarize opinion, as if everything were a matter of black and white, as if everything depended on whether you are simply for or against pornography and, by implication, male violence. In a theoretical defence of the radical feminist view that pornography does not merely reflect male violence but is itself a form of violence even as representation, Susanne Kappeler uses 'race' precisely in this way – not only to justify the unproven equation between images of sexual violence and actual violence experienced by women, but to elicit a moral response of horror and outrage that lends further credence to the anti-porn argument. At the beginning of her book *The Pornography of Representation*, by means of a graphic description of photographs depicting a black African man – one Thomas Kasire of Namibia – shown mutilated, tortured, and obliterated for the gratification of his white male European captors, Kappeler hopes to persuade us that, essentially, all pornography entails that women experience the same kind of actual violence as the brutal, sadistic and murderous violence of the colonial racism that resulted in the death of this black man.[2] Not only does this analogy reduce 'race' to rhetoric – whereby the black/white polarity serves to symbolize an absolute morality based on an either/or choice between good and evil – but it offers no analysis of racial representation in pornography, nor of black people's experiences of it, as Kappeler nowhere acknowledges the relative absence of black women in defining the feminist anti-porn agenda, or the fact that black feminism, in all its varieties, has certainly not prioritized the issue as a touchstone of revolutionary morality.

Each of these issues concerning race, representation and sexual politics has arisen in the very different context of Robert Mapplethorpe's avowedly homoerotic photography, which was at the centre of a major controversy in the United States during 1989 and 1990. Paradoxically, as a result of the campaign led by Senator Jesse Helms to prevent the National Endowment for the Arts from funding exhibitions of so-called 'indecent and obscene materials', Mapplethorpe's photographs have come to the attention of a far wider audience than at any point in his career before his death, from AIDS, in 1989. Although Helms's proposed amendment to NEA funding criteria was eventually defeated, the virulent homophobia that characterized his campaign against Mapplethorpe's 'immoral trash' has helped to create a climate of popular opinion favourable to cultural repression. Just as self-censorship has become routine among art-world decision-makers, so the policing and prosecution of cultural practitioners – from feminist performance artist Karen Finley to the black rap group 2 Live Crew – has also become commonplace. What is truly disturbing about these trends is both the way in which the New Right has successfully hijacked and appropriated elements of the feminist anti-pornography argument, and the way in which some feminists have themselves joined ranks with the law-and-order state. An instance of this occurred in Cincinnati in 1990 when feminist campaigners aligned themselves with the city police department to close down the touring Mapplethorpe retrospective and prosecute the museum director responsible for the exhibition, Dennis Barrie, for the violation of 'community standards'.

Mapplethorpe's black male nudes

In this context, I would like to offer a contribution to the debate on pornography that is based on my reading of Mapplethorpe's troublesome images of nude black men. Although the attack on Mapplethorpe focused mainly on his depictions of gay male sadomasochism and portraits of naked children, his black male nudes are equally, if not more, problematic – not only because they explicitly resemble aspects of pornography, but because his highly erotic treatment of the black male body seems to be supported by a whole range of racist myths about black sexuality.

To shock was always the key verb in the modernist vocabulary. Like other audiences and spectators confronted by the potent eroticism of Mapplethorpe's most shocking images, black audiences are not somehow exempt from the shock effect that Mapplethorpe's images so clearly intend to provoke. Indeed, it was this sense of outrage – not at the homoeroticism, but at the potential racism – that motivated my initial critique of the work, from a black gay male perspective. I was shocked by what I saw: the profile of a black man whose head was cropped – or 'decapitated', so to speak – holding his semi-tumescent penis through the Y-fronts of his underpants, which is the first image that confronts you in Mapplethorpe's 1982 publication *Black Males*. Given the relative silence of black voices at the time of Mapplethorpe's 1983 retrospective at the Institute of Contemporary Arts in London, when the art world celebrated his 'transgressive' reputation, it was important to draw critical attention to the almost pornographic flamboyance with which Mapplethorpe, whose trademark is cool irony, seemed to perpetuate the racist stereotype that, essentially, the black man is nothing more than his penis.

Yet, as the context for the reception and interpretation of Mapplethorpe's work has changed, I have almost changed my mind about these photographs, primarily because I am much more aware of the danger of simply hurling the accusation of 'racism' about. It leads only to the closure of debate. Precisely because of the hitherto unthinkable alliance between the New Right and radical feminism on the issue of pornography, there is now every possibility that a critique which stops only with this kind of moralistic closure inevitably plays into an anti-democratic politics of censorship and cultural closure sought by the ascendant forces of the New Right. In what follows, I explain how and why I changed my mind.[3]

Picture this: two reasonably intelligent black gay men pore over Mapplethorpe's 1986 publication *The Black Book*. When a friend lent me his copy, this was exactly how it circulated between us: as an illicit and highly troublesome object of desire. We were fascinated by the beautiful bodies and seduced by the pleasure in looking as we perused the repertoire of images. We wanted to look, but we didn't always find what we wanted to see. This was because we were immediately disturbed by the racial dimension of the imagery and, above all, angered by the aesthetic objectification that reduced these individual black men to purely abstract visual 'things', silenced in their own right as subjects and serving mainly as aesthetic trophies to enhance Mapplethorpe's privileged position as a white gay male artist in the New York avant-garde. In short, we were stuck in a deeply ambivalent structure of feeling. In an attempt to make sense of this experience, I drew on elements of feminist cultural theory.

The first thing to notice about Mapplethorpe's black males – so obvious that it goes without saying – is that all the men are nude. Framed within the generic conventions of the fine-art nude, their bodies are aestheticized and eroticized as 'objects' to be looked at. As such, they offer an erotic source of pleasure in the act of looking. But whose pleasure is being served? Regarding the depiction of women in dominant forms of visual representation, from painting to advertising or pornography, feminist cultural theory has shown that the female image functions predominantly as a mirror-image of what men want to see. As a figment of heterosexual wish-fulfilment, the female nude serves primarily to guarantee the stability of a phallocentric fantasy in which the omnipotent male gaze sees but is never itself seen. The binary opposition of seeing/being seen which informs visual representations of the female nude reveals that looking is never an innocent or neutral activity, but is always powerfully loaded by the gendered character of the subject/object dichotomy in which, to put it crudely, men look and women are there to be looked at.

In Mapplethorpe's case, however, the fact that both artist and model are male sets up a tension of sameness which thereby transfers the *frisson* of 'difference' from gender to racial polarity. In terms of the conventional dichotomy between masculinity as the active control of the gaze, and femininity as its passive visual object, what we see in Mapplethorpe's case is the way in which the black/white duality of 'race' overdetermines the power relations implicit in the gendered dichotomy between subject and object of representation.

In this sense, what is represented in Mapplethorpe's photographs is a 'look', or a certain 'way of looking', in which the pictures reveal more about the absent and invisible white male photographer who actively controls the gaze than they do about the black men whose beautiful bodies we see depicted in his photographs. In so far as the pictorial space excludes any reference to a social, historical, cultural or political context that might tell us something about the lives of the black models who posed for the camera, Mapplethorpe facilitates the projection of certain racial and sexual fantasies about the 'difference' that black masculinity is assumed to embody. In this way, the photographs are very much about sexual investment in looking, because they disclose the tracing of desire on the part of the I/eye placed at the centre of representation by the male gaze.

Through a combination of formal codes and conventions – the posing and posture of the body in the studio enclosure; the use of strong chiaroscuro lighting; the cropping, framing and fragmentation of the whole body into parts – the 'look' constructed not only structures the viewer's affective disposition towards the image but reveals something of the *mise en scène* of power, as well as desire, in the racial and sexual fantasies that inform Mapplethorpe's representation of black masculinity. Whereas the white gay male sadomasochist pictures portray a subcultural sexuality that consists of 'doing' something, the black men are defined and confined to 'being' purely sexual and nothing but sexual – hence hypersexual. We look through a sequence of individually named African-American men, but we see only sexuality as the sum-total meaning of their black male identity. In pictures like 'Man in a Polyester Suit' (1980), apart from the model's hands, it is the penis, and the penis alone, that identifies him as a black man.

Mapplethorpe's obsessive focus on this one little thing, the black man's genitals, and the way in which the glossy allure of the quality monochrome print becomes almost consubstantial with the shiny, sexy texture of black skin, led me to argue that a certain racial fetishism is an important element in the pleasures (and displeasures) which the photographs bring into play. Such racial fetishism not only eroticizes the most visible aspect of racial difference – skin colour – but also lubricates the ideological reproduction of 'colonial fantasy', in which the white male subject is positioned at the centre of representation by a desire for mastery, power and control over the racialized and inferiorized black Other. Hence, alongside the codes of the fine-art nude, Mapplethorpe seems to make use of the regulative function of the commonplace racist stereotype – the black man as athlete, mugger or savage – in order to stabilize the invisible and all-seeing white subject at the centre of the gaze, and thereby 'fix' the black subject in its place not simply as the Other, but as the object in the field of vision that holds a mirror to the fears and fantasies of the supposedly omnipotent white male subject.

According to literary critic Homi Bhabha, 'an important feature of colonial discourse is its dependence on the concept of "fixity" in the ideological construction of otherness'.[4] Just as Mapplethorpe's photographs of female body-builder Lady Lisa Lyon seem obsessively to pin her down by processing the image of her body through a thousand cultural stereotypes of femininity, so the obsessive undercurrent in his black male nudes would appear to confirm this emphasis on fixity as a sign that betrays anxiety as well as pleasure in the desire for mastery. Mapplethorpe's scopic fixation on the luxurious beauty of black skin thus implies a kind of 'negrophilia', an aesthetic idealization of racial difference that merely inverts and reverses the binary axis of colonial discourse, in which all things black are equated with darkness, dirt and danger, as manifest in the psychic representations of 'negrophobia'. Both positions, whether they overvalue or devalue the visible signs of racial difference, inhabit the shared space of colonial fantasy. These elements for a psychoanalytic reading of fetishism, as it is enacted in the theatre of Mapplethorpe's sex–race fantasy, are forcefully brought together in a photograph such as 'Man in a Polyester Suit'.

The use of framing and scale emphasizes the sheer size of the big black penis revealed through the unzipped trouser fly. As Fanon said, when diagnosing the terrifying figure of 'the Negro' in the fantasies of his white psychiatric patients, 'One is no longer aware of the Negro, but only of a penis: the Negro is eclipsed. He is turned into a penis. He *is* a penis.'[5] By virtue of the purely formal device of scale, Mapplethorpe summons up one of the deepest mythological fears in the supremacist imagination: namely, the belief that all black men have monstrously large willies. In the phantasmic space of the white male imaginary, the big black phallus is perceived as a threat not only to hegemonic white masculinity but to Western civilization itself, since the 'bad object' represents a danger to white womanhood and therefore the threat of miscegenation, eugenic pollution and racial degeneration. Historically, in nineteenth-century societies structured by race, white males eliminated the anxiety that their own fantastic images of black male sexuality excited through rituals of aggression in which the lynching of black men routinely involved the literal castration of the Other's strange fruit.

The historical myth of penis size amounts to a 'primal fantasy' in Western culture in that it is shared and collective in nature – and, moreover, a myth that is so pervasive and firmly held as a folk belief that modern sexology repeatedly embarked on the empirical task of actually measuring pricks to demonstrate its untruth. Now that the consensual management of liberal race relations no longer provides available legitimation for this popular belief, it is as if Mapplethorpe's picture performs a disavowal of the wish-fulfilment inscribed in the myth: *I know* (it's not true that all black guys have big willies), *but* (nevertheless, in my photographs they do).

Within the picture, the binary character of everyday racial discourse is underlined by the jokey irony of the contrast between the black man's exposed private parts and the public display of social respectability signified by the three-piece business suit. The oppositions hidden and exposed, denuded and clothed, play upon the Manichaean dualism of nature and culture, savage and civilized, body and mind, inferior and superior, that informs the logic of dominant racial discourse. In this way, the construction of racial difference in the image suggests that sexuality, and nothing but sexuality, is the essential 'nature' of the black man, because the cheap and tacky quality of the polyester suit confirms his failure to gain access to 'culture'. The camouflage of bourgeois respectability fails to conceal the fact that the black man, as the white man's racial Other, originates, like his dick, from somewhere anterior to civilization.

Conflicting readings of Mapplethorpe

Notwithstanding the problematic nature of Freud's pathologizing clinical vocabulary, his concept of fetishism can usefully be adapted, via feminist cultural theory, to help conceptualize issues of subjectivity and spectatorship in representations of race and ethnicity. Its account of the splitting of levels of belief may illuminate the prevalence of certain sexual fantasies and their role in the reproduction of racism in contemporary culture. The sexual fetish represents a substitute for something that was never there in the first place: the mother's penis, which the little boy expected to see. Despite conscious acknowledgement of sexual difference, the boy's castration anxiety forces the repression of his initial belief, such that it coexists on an unconscious level and finds manifestation, in adult sexuality, in the form of the erotic fetish.[6] One might say that, despite anatomical evidence, the belief symbolized in the fantasy of the big black willy – that black male sexuality is not only 'different' but somehow 'more' – is one many men and women, black and white, straight or gay, cling on to, because it retains currency and force as an element in the psychic reality of the social fantasies in which our racial and gendered identities have been historically constructed.

Yet because Freud's concept of fetishism is embedded in the patriarchal system of sexual difference that it describes, treating sexual perversion or deviation as a symptom which reveals the unconscious logic of the heterosexual norm, it is less useful as a tool for examining the perverse aestheticism of the modern homoerotic imagination which Mapplethorpe self-consciously employs. Moreover, there are limits to the race and gender analogy drawn from feminist cultural theory in the preceding analysis of visual fetishism: it ignores the obvious homoerotic specificity of the work. As a gay male artist whose sexual identity locates him in a subordinate relation to heterosexual masculinity, Mapplethorpe is hardly representative of the hegemonic model of straight, white, bourgeois male identity traditionally privileged in art history as the centred subject and agent of representation. Above all, as the recent exhibition history of his work attests, far from demonstrating the stability of this supposedly centred white male subject, the vitriol and anxiety expressed in hostile attacks on Mapplethorpe's *œuvre* (such as those of radical neo-conservative art critic Hilton Kramer) would suggest that there is something profoundly troubling and disturbing about the emotional ambivalence experienced by different audiences through the salient shock effect of Mapplethorpe's work.

In the light of the changed context of reception, the foremost question is how different audiences and readers produce different and conflicting readings of the same cultural text. The variety of conflicting interpretations of the value of Mapplethorpe's work would imply that the text does not bear one, singular and unequivocal meaning, but is open to a number of competing readings. Thus Mapplethorpe's photographic text has become the site for a range of antagonistic interpretations. Once we adopt this view, we need to reconsider the relationship between artist and audience, or author and reader, because although we habitually attempt to resolve the question of the ultimate 'meaning' of a text by appealing to authorial intentions, poststructuralist theory has shown, by way of the 'death of the author' argument, that individual intentions never have the last word in determining the meaning or value of a text. This is because readers themselves play an active role in interpreting a multivalent and open-ended modernist cultural text.

One might say, therefore, that the difficult and troublesome question raised by Mapplethorpe's black male nudes – do they reinforce or undermine racist myths about black sexuality? – is strictly unanswerable, since his aesthetic strategy makes an unequivocal yes/no response impossible. The question is left open by the author and is thus thrown back to the spectator. Our recognition of the unconscious sex-race fantasies which Mapplethorpe's images arouse with such perverse precision does not confirm a stable or centred subject position, but is experienced precisely as an emotional disturbance which troubles the viewer's sense of secure identity.

The recent actual death of the author entails a reconsideration of the issue of authorship and intentionality, and the reciprocal role of the reader, because the articulation of race and homosexuality in Mapplethorpe's art can also be seen as a subversive move that begins to unravel the violent ambiguity at the interface of the social and the emotional. To clarify my suggestion that his black male nudes are open to an alternative evaluation from that of my initial reading, I should come clean with regard to the specific character of my own subject position as a black gay male reader.

My angry emphasis on racial fetishism as a potentially exploitative process of objectification was based on the way in which I felt identified with the black men depicted in the photographs, simply by virtue of sharing the same 'categorical' identity as a black man. As the source of this anger, the emotional identification can be best described again in Fanon's words as a feeling that 'I am laid bare. I am overdetermined from without. I am the slave not of the "idea" that others have of me but of my own appearance. I am being dissected under white eyes. I am fixed . . . Look, it's a Negro.'[7] It was my anger at the aestheticizing effect of Mapplethorpe's coolly 'ironic' appropriation of racist stereo-types that informed the description of visual fetishism as a process of reduction, or dehumanization. This argument has many similarities with the early feminist critique of images of women in pornography.[8] But the problem with this view is that it moralizes images in terms of a reductive dichotomy between good and bad, 'positive' and 'negative', and thus fails to recognize the ambivalence of the text. If, on the other hand, we recognize that there is an important difference between saying that an image is racist and saying that it is 'about' racism, then we need a more reflexive approach to the ambiguities set into motion in the destabilizing moment of Mapplethorpe's shock effect.

On this view, the strategic use of visual fetishism is not necessarily a bad thing, as it encourages the viewer to examine his or her own implication in the fantasies which the images arouse. Once I acknowledge my own location in the image reservoir as a gay subject – a desiring subject not only in terms of sharing a desire to look, but in terms of an identical object-choice already there in my own fantasies and wishes – then the articulation of meanings about eroticism, race and homosexuality becomes a lot more complicated. Indeed, I am forced to confront the rather unwelcome fact that as a spectator I actually occupy the very position in the fantasy of mastery previously ascribed to the centred pos-ition of the white male subject! In other words, there was another axis of identification – between white gay male author and black gay male reader – that cut across the identification with the black men in the pictures. Could it not be the case that my anger was also mingled with feelings of jealousy, rivalry or envy? If I shared the same desire to look, which would place me in the position of mastery attributed to the author, the anger in the initial critique might also have arisen from a shared, homosexual identification, and thus a rivalry over the same unobtainable object of desire. In so far as the anger and envy were effects of my identification with both object and subject of the look, I would say that my specific identity as a black gay reader placed me in two contradictory positions at one and the same time. I am sure that emotions such as these are at issue in the rivalry of interpretations around Mapplethorpe's most contentious work. Black gay male readers certainly do not have a monopoly on the conflicted and ambivalent structures of feeling they create. My point here is not confessional, but to use my own experience as a source of data about the complex operations of identification and desire that position us in antagonistic and contradictory relations of race, gender and power, which are themselves partly constituted in representations. In revising my views, I have sought to reopen the question of ambivalence, because rather than simply project it on to the author (by asking whether he either perpetuates or challenges racism) one needs to take into account how different readers derive different meanings not only about race, but about sexuality and desire, in Mapplethorpe's work.

The perverse aesthetic

The whole point about the use of textual ambivalence in the modernist tradition is to foreground the uncertainty of any one, singular meaning – which, in the case of Mapplethorpe's double transgressions across race and homosexuality, is a risky business indeed. This is because the open-ended character of the images can provoke a racist reading as much as an anti-racist one, elicit a homophobic reading as much as arouse a homoerotic one. A great deal depends on the reader and the social identity she or he brings to the text. The same statement – the black man is beautiful, say – retains the same denotative meaning, but acquires different connotational values when enunciated by different groups of subjects: the same sentence, uttered by a white man, a black woman, a black man or a white woman, would inevitably take on a qualitatively different 'sound'. Similarly, once we situate the network of relations between author, text and reader, in the

contingent, context-bound circumstances in which Mapplethorpe's work currently stands, then we can examine the way
in which the open-ended structure of the text gives rise to
antagonistic readings that are informed by the social identity
of the audience.

Without returning to a naive belief in the author as a
godlike figure of authority, it is necessary to argue that it
really does matter who is speaking whenever artists, because
of their sexual, gender or racial identity, are assigned 'minority' status in the arts and in culture at large. Once we take
the biographical dimension of Mapplethorpe's work as a gay
artist into account it is possible to reinterpret the black male
nudes as the beginning of an inquiry into the archive of
'race' in Western culture and history, which has rendered
black men into 'invisible men', in Ralph Ellison's phrase. As
Mapplethorpe put it in an interview shortly before his death,
'At some point I started photographing black men. It was an
area that hadn't been explored intensively. If you went
through the history of nude male photography, there were
very few black subjects. I found that I could take pictures of
black men that were so subtle, and the form was so photo-
graphical.' An awareness of the exclusion of the black subject
from one of the most valued canonical genres of Western art –
the nude – suggests that it is both possible and necessary to
reread Mapplethorpe's work as part of an artistic inquiry into
the hegemonic force of a Eurocentric aesthetics which historically rendered invisible not only black people but
women, lesbians and gays and others before the radical
social transformations of the modern and postmodern
period.

By virtue of a perverse aesthetic of promiscuous intertex-
tuality, whereby the overvalued aura of the fine-art nude is
contaminated by the filthy and degraded form of the commonplace stereotype, Mapplethorpe transgresses on several
fronts to make visible that which is repressed and made
invisible in the dominant, and dominating, tradition of the
West against the rest. In the contemporary United States, for
example, black males constitute one of the 'lowest' social

identities in the late-capitalist underclass: disenfranchised, disadvantaged, disempowered. Yet in Mapplethorpe's studio, some of the men who in all probability came from this class are elevated on to the pedestal of the transcendental aesthetic ideal of the male nude in Western culture, which had always excluded the black subject from such aesthetic idealization on account of its otherness. Mapplethorpe's achievement as a postmodern 'society photographer' lies in the way he renders invisible men visible in a cultural system – art photography – that always historically denied or marginalized their existence. One can see in Mapplethorpe's use of homoeroticism a subversive strategy of perversion in which the liberal humanist values inscribed in the idealized fine-art nude are led away from the higher aims of 'civilization' and brought face to face with that part of itself repressed and devalued as 'other' in the form of the banal, commonplace stereotype in everyday culture. What is experienced in the salient shock effect is the disruption of our normative expectations about distinctions that imply a rigid separation between fine art and popular culture, or between art and pornography. Mapplethorpe's transgressive crossing of such boundaries has the effect of calling into question our psychic and social investment in these cultural separations.

Changing political climates

If I am now more prepared to offer a defence rather than a critique of Mapplethorpe's representations of race, because of the changed ideological context, it is because the stakes have also changed. I am convinced that it was not the death of the author so much as the cause of his death that was a major factor in the timing of the Helms campaign against the NEA. Almost all the discourse surrounding the furore noted that Mapplethorpe died of AIDS. The new-found legitimacy of political homophobia and the creation of new folk devils through the mismanagement of the AIDS crisis has proved fertile ground for the spread of popular authoritarian tendencies across the left/right spectrum. Yet the Mapplethorpe/NEA crisis in the USA was often perceived, like the Rushdie crisis in Britain, simply in terms of a straightforward opposition between censorship and freedom of artistic expression. This model of a crude binary frontier is unfeasible because what was at stake in the conflicting readings of Mapplethorpe was not a neat dichotomy between bigoted Philistines and enlightened cultured liberals but a new configuration of social actors, some of whom have engaged in unexpected alliances which have transformed the terrain of contestation.

In many ways the right's success in organizing a popular bloc of public opinion on issues like pornography derives from these new alliances. Just like the alliance formed between radical feminist anti-porn activists and the local state legislature in the form of the Dworkin–MacKinnon-drafted Minneapolis Ordinance in 1984, or the appropriation of the feminist argument that pornography itself is violence in the official discourse of the Meese Commission in 1986, the Helms campaign has highlighted some significant developments in popular right-wing politics. In his original proposal to regulate public funding of art deemed 'obscene and indecent', Jesse Helms went beyond the traditional remit of moral fundamentalism to add new grounds for legal intervention on the basis of discrimination against minorities. Helms wanted the state to intervene in instances where artistic and cultural materials 'denigrate, debase or revile a person, group or class of citizens on the basis of race, creed, sex, handicap or national origin'. By means of this rhetorical move, he sought to appropriate the language of liberal anti-discrimination legislation to promote a climate of opinion favourable to new forms of coercive intervention. In making such a move, the strategy is not simply to win support from black people and ethnic minorities, nor simply to modernize the traditional 'moral' discourse against obscenity, but to broaden and extend the threshold of illegitimacy to a wider range of cultural texts. As the moral panic unfolds, more and more cultural forms transgress or come up against the symbolic boundary that such prohibitionary legislation seeks to impose. Consider the way in which parental warning labels on rap and rock albums have become commonplace: the Parents' Music Resource Centre that helped to initiate this trend in the 1980s has also inspired prosecutions of rock musicians on the grounds that their cultural texts do not simply 'deprave and corrupt', as it were, but have actually caused violence, in the form of suicides.

Under these conditions – when, despite its initial emancipatory intentions, elements of the radical feminist anti-porn movement of the 1980s have entered into alliance with neo-conservative forces – it is not inconceivable that a reading of Robert Mapplethorpe's work as racist, however well intended, could serve the ends of the authoritarian trend supported by this new alliance of social actors. The AIDS crisis has also visibly brought to light the way in which homophobia can be used to draw upon conservative forces within minority cultures. In black British communities, the anti-lesbian and gay hostility expressed in the belief that homosexuality is a 'white man's thing', and hence, because of the scapegoating of gay men, that AIDS is a 'white man's disease', has not only helped to cement alliances between black people and the New Right (for example, in the local campaign on 'Positive Images' in Haringey, London, in 1987) but has had tragically self-defeating consequences in the black community itself. Men and women have been dying, but the psychic mechanism of denial and disavowal in such fear of homosexuality has been particularly apparent in many black responses to AIDS.

Yet these contradictory conditions have also shaped the emergence of a new generation of black lesbian and gay cultural activists in Britain and the United States. Their presence is seriously important not only because they contest the repressive precepts of authoritarian politics in both white society and in black communities, but because their creativity points to new ways of making sense of the contemporary situation. Black lesbian and gay artists such as Isaac Julien, Pratibha Parmar, Michelle Parkerson and Marlon Riggs in film and video; or Essex Hemphill, Cheryl Clarke, Barbara Smith and Joseph Beam in writing and critique, or

Sunil Gupta, Rotimi Fani-Kayode or Lyle Harris in the medium of photography, have widened and pluralized the political and theoretical debates about eroticism, prohibition, transgression and representation. In films such as Isaac Julien's *Looking for Langston* (1989) some of the difficult and troublesome questions about race and homosexuality that Mapplethorpe raised are taken on in a multifaceted dialogue on the lived experience of black gay desire. In his photographs, Rotimi Fani-Kayode also enters into this dialogue, not through a confrontational strategy but through an invitational mode of address which operates in and against the visual codes and conventions his work shares with Mapplethorpe's. But in this hybrid, Afrocentric, homoerotic image world, significant differences unfold as such artists critically 'signify upon' the textual sources they draw from. In the hands of this new generation of black diaspora intellectuals rethinking sex, such 'signifying' activity simultaneously critiques the exclusions and absences which previously rendered black lesbian and gay identities invisible, and reconstructs new pluralistic forms of collective belonging and imagined community that broaden the public sphere of multicultural society.

Such radical changes in black queer visibility were unthinkable ten or fifteen years ago, and one would hope that their emergence now suggests new possibilities for an alternative set of popular alliances that seek to open up and democratize the politics of desire. In the event that the legislation sought by those opposed to whatever can be called 'pornographic' is ever successful in Britain, it is far more likely that it will first be brought to bear on independent artists such as these rather than on the corporations and businessmen who own the porn industry, edit the tabloids or sell advertising. To propose to outlaw something the definition of which no one seems to agree upon is hardly in the interests of anyone seeking not just the protection of our existing civil rights and liberties (few as they are in Britain) but the necessary changes that would further democratize and deepen new practices of freedom.

Anne McClintock

Gonad the Barbarian and the Venus Flytrap

Portraying the female and male orgasm

Pornography is a realm of contradiction. I recall with chagrin how, as a nineteen-year-old *naïf* leaving South Africa for the first time, I strode into a German magazine store to see, finally, what porn for women looked like. Since I knew that beyond South Africa's realm of the censors lay a bounty of undreamed-of sins for women, I imagined I had simply begun in the wrong place. Certainly, a number of grey-suited men were leafing idly through images of spreadeagled women, but the section for women's porn somehow eluded me. When I explained my quest to the woman at the counter, she looked as though I had dropped in from Planet Claire, and I awoke, embarrassingly late, to the knowledge that the denial of female desire is no pathology peculiar to South African life, but a global erasure. Later, someone handed me a copy of *Playgirl*, singularly shrivelled fruits for such a long wait.

A few years later, still searching for clues to the history of my elementary mistake, I sat at *Show World*, Manhattan's four-storey, boys-are-us sex emporium in the heart of the tottering combat zone. I was a stranger in a country not for me, an illegal alien without a visa for pleasure, and I protected myself against the hurt of my exclusion by feigning a studied anthropological poise. Yet where were the brutish howls, the heady odour of male power, the whiff of abuse? I could as well have been looking at the nursery of a maternity ward during breastfeeding: the men were slumped low in their chairs, slack-jawed and still, mouths wet with longing, a spectacle of glazed and infantile enthralment. The vaguely mocking dancer, on the other hand, moved powerfully through her routine. When her spot was over, she pushed through the chairs to me, and held out her hand: 'It's good to have a woman here,' she said. 'We need more women to come. Women need more pleasure.' I was unaccountably honoured, and left with my preconceptions in ruins. Have women been forbidden the world of commercial sex because men's need for women is there so nakedly on display?

A couple of years later I sat in a porn palace, the only woman amid scores of masturbating men. With an effort I ignored my neighbour's thigh juddering against mine, and tried to attain the double vision required of women watching men's porn. Without warning, the male lead began, in manly rebuke, to club his partner across her face with his penis, and at once the porn palace broke into a roar of glad baritone cries. I was jolted into trauma, any arousal doused by this barrage of male hostility, and I left in disarray.

These memories crisscross my encounters with pornography, and I tack with difficulty across my own ambivalence. Until recently, porn was a boys'-own affair. For decades men consumed the stuff in vast quantities, but kept an adamant silence about what it meant to them. Michael Kimmel's book *Men Confront Pornography* disturbs that silence, voicing almost all the contradictions that have riddled the porn furores: porn is vile, but even Nazis should be allowed to air their views. Porn is vile, and smut should be snuffed willy-nilly. Porn is the last celebration of sexual freedom. Porn is a how-to guide that makes sexism sexy and turns injustice into a sexual thrill. Porn is private. Porn is everywhere.[1]

If, reading Kimmel's book, I expected a volley of virile defensiveness, I was startled instead by the tone of male insecurity and sexual distress that scores it. Women are seldom privy to how much men are unmanned by desire. In a fine essay, Tim Beneke voices the 'chronic, fearful, humiliated stance' towards women that pervades men's sexual longing. Men are everywhere snugly in power – in armies and boardrooms, parliaments and churches – yet on the evidence of this book, men's power over women seems invisible to them, and they feel women's sexual allure to be an affront meriting revenge. Timothy Beneke notes, for example, that one-third of men surveyed by *Men's Health* agreed that women should be charged with sexual harassment simply for looking sexy – convicted for *looking* sexy?[2]

Many of the essays in Kimmel's book are marked by confessional sincerity and sympathy with women's unease in the sometimes vengeful land of straight male porn, yet the writers also argue that the reigning fantasy in male porn is not rape, but women seducing men. Porn, they claim, offers men a dream vacation from sexual scarcity, staging the delirious spectacle of erotically demanding women who 'freely surrender their power of rejection'.[3] Porn theatres are the body shops of society where men beat their egos back into serviceable shape. But is it any wonder, then, that women voice unease at the spectacle of our sexual agency and desire managed on male terms for male affirmation?

I lost patience at times with a cloying self-pity indulged in by some of the contributors to Kimmel's book. Sure, men don't get enough sex: but then neither do women. Men have privileged access to the global emporium of porn and prostitution – not to mention that hardy perennial the double standard. Women's desire, by contrast, has been crimped and confined to history's sad museum of corsets, chastity belts, the virginity cult and genital mutilation. Alongside women's erotic malnourishment, men's sexual scarcity looks like a Roman banquet.

A major contradiction emerges in the defence of the pornographic status quo: some defend porn as educational; others claim that it is pure fantasy. Yet I am as unconvinced by the argument that porn inhabits a remote land safely behind the green door of the mind as I am by the argument that porn is practice for rape. There is every reason for a critique of hard-core violence – not because it is the direct cause of assault and rape, but because it can sanction violence in a world where male rage is already catastrophic.

None the less, the Women Against Pornography position strikes me as theoretically misbegotten and strategically unsound. Criminalizing porn slams the door on lesbian and gay commercial sex, turns masturbators into one-armed bandits, the imagination into a no-go zone, and sex workers into criminals. In the censorious world of British porn, moreover, there is every evidence that where sexual reciprocity is censored, sexual violence prevails. By contrast with European and US porn, the wretched sex shops of Soho offer a sorry spectacle of male rage and frustration, while women's porn is resolutely snuffed.

Demonizing porn as a genre offers too easy a scapegoat for women's ills, and does little to alter the real conditions of women's lives. Indeed, the generic boundaries of porn are unstable: soft-core and couples' porn is closer to soaps and romances than it is to hard-core violence. Most porn is notably less violent than many box-office and late-night TV thrillers, not to mention the slime-time of the horrorzines and slasher movies, where the iconography of body-terror and the craze for carnage offer a fix of violence every few minutes – Hieronymus Bosch for an MTV generation.

Most problematically, the anti-porn movement has shown scant concern for the women and men who work in the sex industry. Take Back the Night Marches have been rife with racism and indifference to the class privilege of the women marchers. Would WAP and MAP sleep easier if sex workers were back on their knees cleaning corporate toilets, wiping the bums of the corporate sons, helping the middle class to keep a clean routine? To their disgrace, WAP in New York teamed up with the boys at The League of New York Theater Owners and Producers and the 42nd Street Redevelopment Corporation, taking money and office space to help 'clean up' Times Square and coerce sex workers out of sight, out of mind and out of pocket.

The social context of male pornography well-nigh guarantees its sexism, but there is no reason why the commercial staging of sexual pleasure should be inherently sexist. Porn is phallic if the penis is the judge and jury of desire, but this need not be true of all porn. If porn objectifies the human form for pleasurable consumption, so do ballet, boxing, TV snooker, music videos and advertising. Televising the Olympics fragments and displays the human body for commercial pleasure; yet our culture finds it more acceptable to pay to watch bodies disciplined for conflict than bodies entwined in erotic delirium.

So much has been written on the question of pornography (as if it were one thing), and so little on the myriad types, texts and subgenres that make up porn's kaleidoscopic variorum.[4] Instead of closeting porn behind the law, where male power proliferates out of reach of feminist intervention, we might do better to explore the myriad contradictions within pornography's changing regimes of pleasure and power. The anti-porn rhetoric of outrage and the sex-object argument has jammed any truly subtle analysis of porn's patterns of power, pleasure and profit. There is ample evidence that male porn stages male submission, female dominance, intricate identity and gender crossings, the validity of female desire, and myriad forms of inversion and contradiction. Far greater attention to the paradoxes and nuances of such identifications is called for.

Chronicles of the clitoris

How many slang terms are there for the clitoris? Count them on your fingers: the blank balance sheet of our society's concern for women's pleasure. None the less, the clit has a history – an obscured and contradictory history, certainly, but a history nevertheless.

The female orgasm is as much a social construction as it is an anatomical matter. In 1492 Christopher Columbus, blundering about the Caribbean in search of India, wrote home to say that the ancient mariners had erred in thinking the earth was spherical. Rather, he insisted, the world was formed like a woman's breast, with a protuberance upon its summit in the unmistakable shape of a nipple, towards which he was slowly sailing. 'Oh my America, my new-found land!' In

1559 another Columbus, this one baptized Renaldus, trumpeted his discovery of an Edenic spot as marvellous as Christopher's, only somewhat more modest in size: the female penis, or clitoris. Intoxicated by the Adamic power of christening their respective Edens, neither Columbus, it seems, paused to consider whether the Caribs, or women, might have had first claim to knowledge and naming.

In an important book, *Making Sex: Body and Gender from the Greeks to Freud*, Thomas Laqueur offers compelling evidence that two contradictory models of sexual difference have dominated male, Western accounts of sexual history.[5] He argues that from the Greeks until the end of the eighteenth century, it was a commonplace of medical anatomy and the 'one-sex model' that women had the same genitals as men. The giants of Renaissance medicine, for example, saw the vagina and uterus as nothing more than the penis and balls turned outside in, and gave them the same names. The only difference was that women's genitals hid snugly inside, while men's hung out in the cold. The female and male body reflected each other in a common mirror, desire in men being relieved by rubbing the penis, desire in women by rubbing the clitoris. Certainly, the female was an imperfect copy, her body chillier and danker, her seed thinner, but it was only a question of degree. The vagina was simply a penis that had taken cover from the cold.

In the one-sex model, a women's erotic pleasure was as vital as men's for, as any dolt knew, a woman could become pregnant only if she had an orgasm. So, for two millennia at least, the clitoris enjoyed an amorous devotion only befitting the 'precious jewel' of women's sexual delight. And since women's orgasm erupted deliciously from the clitoris, her 'female rod' and 'great joy', no one who wanted an heir wasted their time pursuing such a will-o'-the-wisp as the 'vaginal orgasm'. There, however, lay the rub. In a one-flesh world, all sex was potentially homoerotic. Avicenna, for one, gave voice to an undertow of anxiety that coursed through the one-sex model: if women were unsatisfied by men, they might remain in the thrall of desire, but turn to 'rubbing with other women'.[6] Not for nothing was the clitoris nick-named 'the scorner of men'.[7]

By the end of the eighteenth century, however, Laqueur argues, the one-sex model began to metamorphose into the two-sex model. Men of science now tirelessly showed how unlike each other female and male genitalia were. Women's orgasm was seen to be irrelevant to conception, the vagina acquired a name of its own, and the clitoris was banished. The era of the passionless woman was born, and a great amnesia descended on humanity. Gone were the days when Roman and Renaissance matrons were coaxed luxuriously into fruition with tasty banquets, hot baths and deft handi-work. Women's delighted moanings and orgasmic flutter-ings were hushed, stifled under a quickly spreading chloroform of constructed ignorance. William Acton summed up the sentiments of the age when he said: 'Women are not much troubled by sexual feeling of any kind.'

Most importantly, it was changes in the politics of gender, not changes in anatomical knowledge, that shaped the sexual body. Nature replaced tradition as the guardian of social difference, and gender became writ in the blood and the bones. Women were figured as shackled to their flesh, destined every month to ride the crazy, crimson rollercoaster of menstrual unreason. Such a creature could not be trusted with political power, for sexual difference was nature's simple way of telling us that women belonged in a different sphere. As one man put it grandly: 'What was decided among the pre-historic protozoa cannot be annulled by an act of parliament.'[8]

Then, in 1905, Freud decreed, with breathtaking boldness, that the 'immature' clitoral orgasm had to be replaced by the 'mature' vaginal orgasm. The privileging of the superior 'vaginal orgasm' was no more than a figleaf of Freud's imagination, covering over the scandal of a clitoral pleasure that was not dependent on the penis, or reducible to a reproductive teleology. Clitoral eroticism, like homo-sexuality, stood outside the Victorian reproductive economy and the teleology of racial evolution. For Freud, the penis owed its 'extraordinary high narcissistic cathexis' to its 'organic significance for the propagation of the species'. The clitoris, by contrast, could not be assigned 'any teleological purpose'. Thus the little girl's 'incredible phallic activity' in clitoral masturbation had 'to be got rid of'. Women who couldn't have the proper orgasms were declared frigid – living proof that women didn't want sex anyway – or condemned to a lifetime of fakery. Marie Bonaparte, Freud's protégée, underwent an agonizing and entirely fruitless operation to move her clitoris closer to her vagina in order to attain the 'normal' orgasm.

Freudian sexual theory and scientific sexology emerged at much the same time as women began to push against the doors of male privilege, insisting on greater social and sexual power. Men of science mustered their forces to retain monopoly over the sexual regime, bowing to feminist pressure by recognizing female desire while containing this desire within a revamped marital morality under the tutelage of imperial Nature.[9] The new sexology was born, and the era of the marriage manuals arrived.[10]

Early-twentieth-century sex manuals acknowledged that marital sex involved the needs of two persons, but, as it turned out, these needs remained remarkably consistent with the needs of men. The orgasm ordained by Nature for women was vaginal, aroused by penile thrusting, and properly occurring simultaneously with the man's. Conveniently for men, 'simultaneous orgasm' was orchestrated by the penis, which retained its primacy as the organ of sexual pleasure for both sexes. Clitoral eroticism, at odds with the logic of penile satisfaction and racial reproduction, was stigmatized as immature and best repressed. Rebellious clitorises were tamed by neglect, by therapy or, in especially stubborn cases, by surgery.

In the eyes of the sexologists, imperial Nature had endowed husbands with a rampant and spontaneous sexuality, while women's sexuality lay dormant until aroused by men. Nature allotted men the task of initiating women into their proper desires. As Van de Velde grandly proclaimed:

'The wife must be taught, not only how to behave in coitus, but, above all, how and what to feel in this unique act.'[11] At least for the time being, it seemed, the one-sex model was enjoying a renaissance. Nature guaranteed the symmetry of heterosexual coitus: there was one canonical sex, and that sex was male.

But the new sexology was rife with contradictions. A presiding paradox of the sex manuals was their insistence on *teaching* an *instinct*.[12] The vaginal orgasm, putatively a natural 'instinct', had to be *learned* (and by most accounts the vagina appeared to be a sluggish and diffident pupil), while the unnatural clitoral orgasm had to be unlearned.

Then, to compound the contradictions, the Kinsey reports appeared. Kinsey precipitated a national furore by discussing females as autonomous sexual beings, and contending that the clitoris was the anatomical seat of female orgasm. In 1957 Masters and Johnson followed suit with their corroboration of the 'scientific discovery of the female orgasm', but gamely tried to show that the penis need not surrender its primacy after all: empirical evidence, they suggested, showed that penile thrusting, if done correctly, could cause sufficient friction of the skin over the clitoris to excite an orgasm.

Such damage management could not conceal the fact that an irrevocable fissure had appeared in what Irigaray called the 'old dream of symmetry'. As Paul Robinson, for one, noted acidly, Kinsey represented 'the absolute nadir of phallic consciousness' by casting 'doubt on the importance of the penis for the sexual pleasure of the female'. Masters and Johnson, likewise, earned Robinson's ire for relegating 'the clitoral–vaginal distinction to the dustbin of history'. Noting that Masters and Johnson's 'masturbatory bias' was 'linked to their feminism', Robinson warned his readers that by celebrating female masturbation Masters and Johnson had, 'at least theoretically, liberated women from their sexual dependency on men'.[13]

In the 1970s, in the anxious aftermath of the Kinsey and Masters and Johnson sex reports, male porn began to dramatize openly the contradiction between the autonomy of female clitoral pleasure and the primacy of the male phallic regime. Until the 1960s porn had remained a highly organized, but largely secret, all-male subculture. In the late sixties porn began to move from the semi-licit, seedy porn theatres and to play not only to the 'raincoat brigade' of furtive middle-class men, but now also to 'respectable' gender-mixed audiences in large, legitimate theatres. At the same time, feminists denounced male power as political rather than natural, and insisted vocally on the autonomy and difference of female sexual pleasure. Men could no longer make porn without taking into account the complications of women's desire; henceforth female sexuality, in particular the clitoral orgasm, would haunt male pornography as a central problematic.[14]

The Devil in Miss Jones

In 1972 Gerard Damiano produced and directed *Deep Throat* and *The Devil in Miss Jones*, unleashing a media storm and an international scandal by showing full erections and intercourse in a regular theatre. Both films were threshold events, marking the moment in the industrial capitals of Europe and the USA when women began, however uncertainly, to consume male porn in public. *Deep Throat* opened at the New Mature World Theater in the summer of 1972 to a rave review by Al Golstein, who gave it a 10 on his 'Peter Meter'. The media uproar and the lawsuit that followed transformed this low-budget ($25,000) film into a box-office extravaganza: in the first year it grossed over a million dollars, as a quarter of a million people jammed theatres to see it. At the same time, the media hype exposed to public scrutiny and increasing feminist criticism the asymmetry of female and male sexual pleasure and privilege. Women began to interfere critically in the public consumption of male porn, rocking notions of an ungendered sexual spectator and disavowing the idea that a man's and a woman's eroticism is one, and that one is the man's.

Both *Deep Throat* and *The Devil in Miss Jones* are structured around the contradiction between clitoral pleasure and the male inability to imagine female pleasure outside a phallic regime. The clitoris presides uncertainly over both films as their invisible yet governing sign. Indeed, both films dramatically underscore that which Jacques Lacan all too casually dismisses as 'the fairly trivial opposition between clitoral orgasm and vaginal satisfaction' – not so trivial after all.[15]

The Devil in Miss Jones opens, in violation of erotic expectations, with Gloria's languid suicide in a bath. Luxuriantly self-absorbed in pleasuring her body, as if in preparation for the pleasure of the male spectator, Gloria slits her wrists instead and slips into the solitude of suicide, beyond the edicts of male chronology and desire. Suicide signals a refusal, and the scandal of autonomy. In suicide Gloria refuses to consecrate her body to the sovereign male authority of God, and assumes her right to dispose of her flesh as she pleases.

At the same time, the film sets out to discipline her transgression before the tribunals of male decree. The second scene finds her standing in the antechamber between heaven and hell, before Abaca, the Doorkeeper, the male alphabet, beginning and end. Abaca intones the sentence of eternal damnation, containing the sin of her autonomy in the male letter of the law. 'It's the one thing', says the Doorkeeper, 'that they cannot forgive.' But Gloria's suicide has interfered with male chronology: having lived a life of unblemished chastity, she was expected to go to 'the other place', and now there is an excess of time. Gloria begs Abaca to let her earn the wages of eternal damnation by being 'filled, engulfed, consumed by lust' for the remaining interval before her scheduled rendezvous with hell. Abaca agrees, and she crosses the threshold into what Steven Marcus has called the land of 'pornutopia'.

True to the cult of the male expert – and the edict that female sexuality be awakened and managed by a male tutor – Gloria finds herself standing before The Teacher, who grandly initiates her into heterosexual desire, female sexual obedience and phallic worship. Yet at once a paradox appears in the cult of male sexual pedagogy. The moment when the Teacher orchestrates Gloria's desire is also the moment in which his penis becomes the object of her pleasure and her judgement. Licking and sucking his disembodied cock, Gloria arrogates to herself the power of desiring and judging: 'I must have that power,' she demands, and for the remainder of the film she is the dominant and presiding figure.

'Teach', as Gloria soon mockingly calls him, and the other nameless and inconsequential men she fucks, are rendered merely functional to her pleasure. Contrary to the anti-porn nightmare vision of female disempowerment, *The Devil in Miss Jones* reverses traditional polarities. Georgina Spelvin, the actress who plays Gloria, applauded the film as 'presenting a situation in which a woman uses men solely as a means of sexual gratification'. Spelvin, who lives openly as a lesbian with her lover Claire Lumiere (her co-actress in the lesbian scene), found Gloria a powerful and sympathetic figure who 'experiences a complete reversal in which she makes everything around her an object of her own sexual gratification'.

Hard-core male porn is the only genre where the penis is flagrantly on display – no part of the body is more taboo in our culture than the penis as the public object of female judgement. Thus the presiding contradiction of hard-core heterosexuality is that the penis becomes an object of critical female scrutiny at the very moment when male power is putatively most potent. For women who watch hard-core porn, as Cindy Patton has noted: 'being constructed as the owner of the penis produces a curious sensation of transgression'.[16] Positioned as both owners and judges of a man's penis, women become, by extension, owners and judges of other penises, a position of spectacular power seldom accorded them in our society. Arguably, this is one reason why women have been so jealously barred from the consumption of porn; perhaps it is also a reason for the often hyperbolic efforts in male porn to have a woman genuflect before the ejaculating cock. At the moment when the penis is most ostentatiously exhibited for public scrutiny, the female is figured as doing obeisance, on her knees, her eyes closed, submerged beneath the visual logic of male pleasure. In *The Devil in Miss Jones*, for example, when the Teacher cums in the early pedagogical scene, Gloria places herself uncomfortably beneath him, his erection hanging over her head in pyrotechnic display.

The male cum-shot is an overdetermined contradiction in heterosexual porn.[17] Emerging first in gay porn, the shot became *de rigueur* in straight porn during the seventies. At one level, the cum-shot represents the primacy of the male orgasm at the moment when women began to consume male porn and demand their right to orgasmic satisfaction. In earlier stag movies, jealously guarded from female consumption, male sexual privilege was guaranteed and unproblematic. It was only with the insistence of feminist demands that the display of the cum-shot became necessary to figure the now precarious centrality of male pleasure. Yet in so doing, the shot at the same time paradoxically represents the express failure of the phallic logic of the 'simultaneous orgasm', and the asymmetry of female and male sexual pleasure.

The cum-shot in heterosexual porn is a paradox, for it is a masturbatory shot occurring in the context of heterosexual merging. For men who watch themselves cum when they masturbate, orgasmic pleasure is linked to the spectacle of ejaculation. At the same time, the cum-shot is potentially homoerotic: men who time their orgasms to the cum-shot identify vicariously with the spectacle of another man's pleasure.

Timothy Beneke has argued that some men are unmanned by the loss of boundary that sex entails, and learn to manage these dangerous crossings with rituals of detachment or violence. Men speak to their penises in the language of work or war, and address them by name: 'John Thomas', 'Dick' and 'Peter'. Sex with a woman entails an unnerving confusion of body boundaries and an unmanning confession of need for women, which may be warded off by strategies of detachment or domination. On the other hand, porn offers men the rare, taboo pleasure of identifying with women –

while gender boundaries are maintained by the male mon-opoly over the boys'-own world of the 'combat zone'. But when women disturb that monopoly, interfering in porn as consumers and critics, the boundaries blur. The cum-shot restores gender decorum: the cum on the woman's body *marks* her as separate, different, out-there. The male with-draws at the moment of orgasm, to preserve his detached and bounded sexual identity.

In its hyperbolic narrative closure, the cum-shot distracts visual attention from the inevitable subsidence of the male erection after sex. If the erection guarantees male advantage and difference, the flaccid penis suggests the impermanence of this power. The cum-shot offers a premature foreclosing of the threatening moment of subsidence and *in*difference: a closure unnecessary before women became viewers. It is important to emphasize, therefore, that the cum-shot is not an essential or ahistorical phenomenon but only one con-structed strategy in the panoply of gender power.

The cum-shot (called in the industry the 'money shot', because men are paid more for the shot, and consumers get their 'money's worth') most perfectly conveys the sexual alienation of contemporary society. In a pause-button, fast-forward culture of repetition and replay, the freeze-frame replaces the warm touch. As Linda Williams puts it: 'Pleas-ure is figured as an orgasm of spending': the movie, the mag, the peepbooth, the VCR and video all cost cash, and the advantage to capital is that the deferment of fulfilment renews 'the consumer's willingness to pay for that which will never be owned'.[18] In the hand-shandy of the pornographic peepbooth, men in solitary cubicles masturbate to 8mm films spliced together without beginning or end in an infinite loop of narrative time. The spectator cranks a machine with one hand and himself with another, posting coins every half-minute or so into carnal cash registers that devour money at the same rate as the average minimum wage, a solitary penile servitude to the dollar. Reach out and touch yourself.

If sexology and the marriage manuals attempted to contain female desire within the symmetry of the simultaneous orgasm and vaginal eroticism, *The Devil in Miss Jones* dramatizes the failure of the heterosexual regime to contain the difference of clitoral pleasure. Alternating rhythmically between autoerotic scenes where Gloria silently pleasures herself, languid, solitary and self-absorbed, and group scenes in which she volubly confesses her desire for men, the film ultimately stages the failure of sexual symmetry by staging the failure of a purely phallic heterosexuality to satisfy the woman.

Feminist film theory has argued widely that the subject of the gaze is male, and that looking is equated with the male position. Yet the double exposure or double vision characteristic of much female consumption of images cannot easily be equated with the sanctioned position of male gazing, nor reduced to a phallic logic. If, until recently, most male porn has been framed for male pleasure, the camera's I-for-an-eye is fluid and mutable. Identification in porn can be multiple and shifting, bisexual and transsexual, alternately or simultaneously – although context can limit or prohibit the degree of transgression. Lesbians and gays can consume heterosexual porn, and vice versa, by adopting intricate and shifting patterns of identification across gender and orientation. Where in feminist film and porn theory, moreover, are women of colour? In that brave, nowhere space so adroitly captured in the famous title *All the Women Are White, All the Men Are Black, But Some of Us Are Brave*? Analyses of 'the male gaze' have for the most part ignored the different ways in which women and men of colour negotiate their desires around the magisterial forms of the white male imaginary.

The pornographic imagination shifts libidinously: I am the watcher/the watched; I am the pleasurer/the pleasured. The masturbatory imagination is incoherent: bits of memory, trauma, pleasure, anger, recalled for pleasure. Porn is the theatrical performance of sexual risk, ritually staging pleasure and danger under remote control. The pace of porn – the swerves in scene, the switches of persona, the rehearsal of variety within the structure of compulsive repetition – mimics the floating, chaotic structures of masturbatory fantasy, an obscure logic about which we know very little.

Much straight male porn is structured about the paradox of staging the fluidity of desire and identity while still guaranteeing heterosexuality. The darkness and privacy of porn theatres allow heterosexual men to see each other's erections in abundant close-up without having to name homoerotic desire for what it is. Women are there to guarantee heterosexuality in a world populated by penises. Similarly, the 'girl–girl' genre of male porn typically includes a male voyeur. The brim of a hat, a male shoulder, a hirsute hand guarantees heterosexuality in scenes where the spectacle of women pleasuring themselves might threaten promiscuously to confuse gender boundaries. In the *ménage-à-trois* scene in *The Devil in Miss Jones*, for example, the women kiss with laughing complicity, their tongues touching and entwining, negotiating themselves around the man's disembodied penis, which stands like a sentinel between their kissing tongues. The man is little more than instrumental to their play, there only to guarantee heterosexuality in a scene dominated by female desire.

This scene is immediately paralleled by one where Gloria has sex with two men. Again, in reversal of stereotype, the scene is remarkable in that Gloria is in full control of the situation: she issues instructions, she controls the pace, she tells the men how to please her, her commanding voice governs their homosexual pleasure. 'Can you feel his cock against yours, can you feel it?' she asks. Just as in the previous lesbian scene the penis guaranteed heterosexuality, so does Gloria's voice guarantee heterosexuality in a scene where cock rubs cock, and the male cum-shot is against another man's penis. In both scenes, in violation of dominant conventions, it is the woman who is in control, and if anybody is objectified and rendered instrumental to another's pleasure, it is the men.

If *The Devil in Miss Jones* opens with female autonomy and the crime of will, it ends with Gloria's anguished confessions of heterosexual dependency. Alone in 'hell' with an impotent man, she rubs her clit furiously and futilely: 'I can't do it by myself. Damn you, help me. I can't do it by myself,' she moans. Thus at one level the film seems to rebut the ominous lessons of the Kinsey and Masters and Johnson reports, foreclosing the threat of women escaping heterosexuality into clitoral autoeroticism and dramatizing once more the primacy of the penis for female satisfaction. But Gloria, not the man, now commands the position and power of desire. The man, on the other hand, is impotently locked in the solitary confinement of selfhood, his existential meanderings dismissed brusquely by Gloria as 'a silly waste of time'.

In this way the film reverses the conventional distributions of sexual desire, while at the same time struggling to retain heterosexuality. Its failure to do so satisfactorily is specifically figured as a failure to resolve the contradiction between female clitoral eroticism and the primacy of male phallic desire. In its very attempt to resolve the contradiction between clitoral and penile pleasure, the film renders unstable both heterosexuality and the gendered imbalances of sexual desire and power on which heterosexuality depends.

It is worth noting that nowhere in the film is Gloria shown visibly having an orgasm. The contradiction for male porn is that to portray a 'vaginal orgasm' means rendering the penis invisible inside the woman, while at the same time obscuring the vagina. Yet to portray a clitoral orgasm, excited by hands or mouth, is to refuse the primacy of the penis. Female orgasm is thus displaced on to the face in the visible gamut of ecstatic grimaces that have little to do with the varied ways in which women really come. By contrast, the spectacular shot of a woman cumming and ejaculating in *Clips*, the video produced by the California lesbian video group Femme Fatale, usefully debunks the notion that a woman's orgasm is somehow 'unrepresentable'; it is unrepresentable only on male terms.

The fundamental question of *The Devil in Miss Jones* is the question that Al Golstein, editor of *Screw* magazine and host of the TV show 'Midnight Blue', asked of Linda Marchiano: 'Do you come when your clit isn't being worked on?' Marchiano answered: 'I have an orgasm every time I get screwed in the throat.' The calculated absurdity of her answer exposes the absurdity of Golstein's question. At the same time, Marchiano's answer demonstrates that in a world where men still have to ask that question, all too often women will have to fake both the answer and the orgasm.

From image to industry

Far from being simply a free-speech or private-fantasy issue, porn is a giant, high-profile, multi-billion-dollar international business that draws on the most sophisticated electronic systems, vast personnel divisions, teams of technicians, secretaries and market analysers, fleets of transport vehicles, and global distribution networks. Porn flourishes in an advanced commercial society, with highly developed technology and marketing, cheap reproduction of images, a climate of sexual scarcity, and deeply entrenched class, gender and racial inequities. Anyone entering the porn debates would do well to get to know the industry, and what better way than by listening to the professionals themselves?

Yet most notably absent in the porn debates are the voices of the women and men who work in the industry. All too often, feminist analyses of porn are dominated by theories of image and identity. Scant interest, by contrast, has been shown in porn as a commerce, and the voices of the sexperts have been muffled to a murmur. If sex workers are mentioned at all, it is most often as icons of female degradation. Catharine MacKinnon, for one, cites Linda Marchiano's *Ordeal* as the representative case against pornography: 'Almost everything that needs to be said about pornography can be said about Linda Marchiano, because everything people think about it, they think about her.'[19] Not only is this a non sequitur, but MacKinnon irresponsibly collapses the diversity of all sex workers' experiences into the ahistorical, essential narrative of one woman's ordeal. Worse, she flagrantly distorts Marchiano's account in order to bolster her anti-porn diatribe. Honesty might have compelled MacKinnon to acknowledge that Marchiano was abused, enslaved, tortured, battered and raped – not by the director of *Deep Throat*, nor on the set of *Deep Throat*, but by her husband, Chuck Traynor, in the 'privacy' of their marital nightmare. Marchiano has insisted that the making of *Deep Throat* was profoundly paradoxical: 'To me it would be at once a low point and a salvation.' As she puts it:

> Compared to men like Bob Wolf, Gerry Damiano was Cecil B. De Mille . . . The first day of shooting everyone was in a good mood . . . For the first time in many months I began to feel better . . . The crew members were all in high spirits, telling jokes, playing pranks, goofing on the director and, somehow, despite all this taking some pictures. Something was happening to me, something was strange. It had to do with the fact that no one was treating me like garbage. And maybe it was just the chemistry of being part of a group. For the first time in many months, I was thrown in with other people, other people who weren't perverted and threatening. I became part of a group. I began to ease up . . . *I was laughing along with the rest of them.* And no one was asking me to do anything I did not want to do. [original emphasis][20]

Marchiano records that it was precisely her unaccustomed gaiety and new-found confidence on the porn set that prompted Traynor to beat her so viciously and relentlessly that night in the motel room: 'The presence of other people diminished him and diluted my fear of him. It gave me courage.' What is important here is that while Marchiano became involved in porn only through Traynor's coercion, it was the making of *Deep Throat*, her fame and renewed confidence that finally empowered her to escape her abuser. As she sums it up: 'But the truth is this: Linda Boreman and Linda Traynor never managed to get away from Chuck; it took a Linda Lovelace to escape.' Such nuances are entirely lost in MacKinnon's wilfully one-dimensional account, and pornography *as a genre* is scapegoated for what was in actuality sustained *marital* battery.

Popular myths that porn is produced by sinister, cigar-chewing humanoids who wear nothing but towels round their middles and spend their time groping the talent off-camera are woefully out of date. Most decriminalized porn in Europe is produced by professional camera crews biding their time to get into the mainstream. As one sex worker says: 'Unprofessional attitudes get in the way of making money and would not be tolerated.' Criminalizing porn only drives the business underground, where it remains brutally managed by men.

Arguably, the most damaging aspect of mainstream porn is its jealous exclusion of women as directors and consumers. More men than I care to count have insisted that women are not excited by erotic images. But arguing that a quirk of anatomical design has left women numb to erotic images is both implausible and reactionary. If some women react to male porn with sharp anxiety, it is because they feel disempowered by a sexual world colonized for male desires and bewildered, perhaps, by a momentary gender confusion and secret, uneasy arousal. Now, however, women are beginning to stage and speak pleasure on our own terms. Femme Productions makes sex videos for women and couples, lesbian and bisexual porn continues to proliferate, and a hard-core porn magazine for women is soon to appear in Britain.

Evidence of women's increased power as porn consumers is pouring in. Women have been targeted as the largest growth area for porn; it is estimated that they now account for 40 per cent of all X-rated video rentals, and a *Redbook* magazine survey confirms that nearly half the women surveyed regularly watch porn films. Another poll estimates that two out of three women in Germany and France watch video porn regularly. At the same time, female porn workers need no longer be ventriloquists' dummies for male fantasies about female pleasure. Sex workers are organizing internationally for the decriminalization of sex work, for better working conditions, and for the removal of gender, class and racial inequities.

The arrival of video has turned porn into a sure-fire coin-spinning venture as never before, and with it has come a historic opportunity for women. With the cheaper, potentially less threatening and more private world of home erotic videos, a new era is upon us. But Cindy Patton's question remains to be answered: Can both women's and men's pleasure be represented simultaneously in heterosexual couples' videos? Or will men still hold the remote control in the living-room?

Creating women's commercial sex complicates the notion of porn as a world absolutely colonized for the male gaze. None the less, celebrating women's pleasure does not mean denying or subduing the penis. Rather, it simply means insisting that the penis take a more modest place in a far more generous world of sexual diversity. At the same time, quarrels over the hierarchical primacy of 'proper' female orgasms should make way for recognition of the polymorphous variety of women's multiple pleasures, which are not reducible to a single male phallic economy. Gay men – particularly now, in the era of safe sex – have, moreover, been pioneers in expanding the pornutopia of male pleasures to include anal, oral and other eroticisms into a far greater diversity of sensual delirium than five minutes of gunga-da-gung.

Recently, I watched performance artist and ex-go-go dancer Tornado challenge male spectators at the Harmony, a strip theatre in New York. I watched Annie Sprinkle, post-porn-modernist, stage male voyeurism and female control of sex work at the Kitchen. At the Three Dollar Bill Theater I saw performance after performance of lesbian singers, poets and performers, sex professionals, and members of PONY (Prostitutes of New York) enrapture an aroused and jubilant crowd of women. It's been a long wait, but it's been worth it. If women organize instead of agonize, we can alter the shape of the industry on terms more suitable to our own uncharted pleasures. At last we can expand our historical experimentations in female sexual pleasure, and demand more power to come.

Elizabeth Cowie

Pornography and fantasy
Psychoanalytic perspectives

The use of the term 'pornography' to describe obscene representations is comparatively recent. It was only in the nineteenth century that a body of material became organized as a category – pornography – and the term was applied where before there had merely been disparate works and collections of obscene materials, usually literary rather than visual.

Pornography is fundamentally a term within a discourse of regulation, whether criminal – as in prosecutions for obscenity – or regulatory – as in the 'X' or 'over 18' rating system for films, regulations on the display of pornographic magazines in newsagents, or the various codes of practice adopted by the television companies and broadcasting authorities. What these seek to regulate is not sexual arousal as such, but an improper form of sexual arousal which would bring harm, by nineteenth-century criteria, to the person who consumes pornography, including the harm arising from masturbation. Or, by twentieth-century criteria, it is a sexual arousal which would bring harm to others, in particular to the women and sometimes children who are represented as the objects of male arousal. In the latter the harm is seen as either direct – for the women, and especially the children, who posed for the images – or indirect, as a harm arising as a result of and subsequently to the man's enjoyment of pornography.

However, this assumes first that the images of pornography – which, by any definition, involve very varied kinds of scenario – 'represent' male sexual attitudes and desires:

that the two are the same. Second, it assumes that consuming such representation not only may 'teach' men these attitudes but also will teach them to expect or to re-create the same scenarios in actuality. With the rise of the notion of 'consenting adults in private' the issue of the harm to the consumer has receded, and explicit sexual representation alone is no longer a qualification for censorship. Instead, scrutiny and proscription are now centred on the kind of practices represented, and especially where violence is implied or actually present. Yet the force of such representations cannot be understood without considering the nature of pornography as sexual fantasy, and the nature of the relation of fantasy to the social relations of sexuality.

The sexual, desire and the image

The debate on pornography presents a series of knots of confusion. First, there is the confusion which arises in the attempt to distinguish between permissible sexual imagery and 'pornography', where the permissible imagery is variously claimed as 'erotic' or 'art' or 'socially redeeming' in contrast to 'pornography'.[1] Second, there is a confusion about sexual arousal – not the fact that it occurs, but what produces it. Is it provoked by the visual content as such – that is, in a kind of pure denotation – or is it stimulated by the scenario of presentation, by the *mise en scène* and implied narrative, and hence by the connotation? Finally, there is a confusion around the issue of sexuality itself. This is rarely addressed as such but instead tends to be assumed as a natural phenomenon or essence which can nevertheless be perverted or distorted.[2] As a result, sexuality is never a mere biological fact; rather, it is also a social concept, the object which poets, moralists, comedians and all the rest of us talk of. It is constructed by the social discourses of a community or society. Central to this construction is the opposition permitted/forbidden or proper/improper. In Western society this has most often assumed the form of an opposition between 'natural and unnatural', in which 'unnatural' is variously produced, depending on the protagonists of the argument, by man's capacity to sin, by inherent evil, by inadequate parenting or sexual abuse in childhood, by a distortion produced by the unnatural demands of capitalism, or by the hierarchical relations of power between men and women. This gives rise on the one hand to the demand to free sexuality from its imposed constraints, and on the other to the demand for the necessity of certain controls, or even for an increase in such controls.

It is a paradox that while sexual relations are pre-eminently the object of social control in human societies sexual desire is often taken to be something beyond social organization or rational control. The realm of the sexual is seen as *par excellence* the realm of the irrational, the anarchic – the realm of the senses. However, the opposition control/beyond control arises only once 'control' is imposed – which, one might argue, following Lévi-Strauss, is the moment of the emergence of human society as such. The 'beyond control' is then desire, including or especially sexual desire. It is defined by what it is not – namely, socially organized sexuality. It is what our parents never had; it is the forbidden – because we are too young, or whatever. Desire here is most truly itself when it is most 'other' to social norms, when it transgresses the limits and exceeds the 'proper'. The result is a hotchpotch, formed only by its status as the forbidden; it is characterized not only by the now more conventionally acceptable transgression of barriers of race or class, but by the transgression of the barriers of disgust – in which the dirty and execrable in our bodily functions becomes a focus of sexual desire.

In the case of pornography, what is presumed is an instinctual or automatic natural human response of sexual arousal which is produced by the visual or verbal imagery as a kind of reflex response, and which therefore – Pavlov-style – may be natural or conditioned. It is often this so-called non-intellectual aspect which is seen as most dangerous and has come to be associated in particular with the visual image. The majority report of the US Attorney General's Commission on Pornography exempts the written or printed word from all prosecution on the grounds that 'the absence of photographs necessarily produces a message that seems to necessitate for its assimilation more real thought and less almost reflexive reaction than does the more typical pornographic item. There remains a difference between reading a book and looking at pictures . . .'[3] But it is this presumption of a stimulus–response which blinds us to the complex signifying process set in play by what is termed 'sexual imagery'. Sexual arousal is a matter not of nature, but of signification. What arouses is already a highly coded entity. Sexual arousal is not merely a bodily affair but first and foremost a psychical relation. However, this signifying process is not a set of contents – of socially learned conventions of sexuality; rather, it is what psychoanalysis has termed fantasy.

Sexuality is constructed in and for the human subject, but this is neither a deformation of a prior natural sexuality nor a 'writing' on the infant as if it were a *tabula rasa*. It is not learned as a set of roles. Sexuality is constructed by seduction. That is, the infant experiences its pleasures as coming to it from outside – as the breast which comes and goes – or as something which the child puts into the outside, its shit. The voice and image of its carer, the sounds and sights of the world, come to it from outside – they 'penetrate' it. Out of the most natural, biological events emerge polymorphous pleasures which thereby exceed the biological function. Feeding becomes the pleasure of sucking the breast distinct from the satisfaction of a full tummy. As a result, the 'experience of satisfaction' is separated from the object which satisfies, and the latter is represented as a sign. For the baby, the 'breast' becomes the object of desire – as giving the experience of satisfaction – but it is so not as itself but as a signifier of the *lost* object which is the *satisfaction* derived from suckling the breast, but comes to be desired in *its absence*.

This is the emergence of autoeroticism, for the sexual drive is separated from the non-sexual functions such as feeding, which are its support and indicate its aim and object. The feeding still nourishes the child, but the experience of satisfaction in feeding has been split off through the function of representation – the breast stands for a possible satisfaction – and thus moves into the field of fantasy, and by this very fact starts existing as sexuality. The psychoanalyst Jean Laplanche has described this as the 'propping' of the sexual drive on what he terms 'the vital order': that is to say, it emerges from the strictly biological – feeding as a kind of self-preservation, and hence a drive to self-preservation – as a separate and distinct drive whose object is not survival but satisfaction, pleasure.[4] Hence for psychoanalysis sexuality is not the upsurging of an instinct, a programmed response, but arises in the emergence of fantasy. As a result sexuality is characterized as a desire for pleasure, rather than simply the satisfaction of biological sex.

Sexual fantasy and sexual images

The emergence of desire is the emergence of fantasy. It is in this sense that Freud posits sexuality – but not simply genital sexuality – as the basis for all wishes. Fantasy is the support of desire, not a particular object of desire. Desire arises first of all in relation to a wished-for satisfaction, not in relation to an object. The object does not cause the desire; rather, desire finds the object as a signifier for another, lost object. Moustafa Safouan notes that 'instead of being co-opted to an object, desire is first co-opted to phantasy'.[5]

Fantasy itself is characterized not by the achievement of wished-for objects but by the arranging of, a setting out of, the desire for certain objects. It is a veritable *mise en scène* of desire, a staging of a scene. In so far as this involves a set of actions, a set of events, the staging implies a resolution, a consummation of the scene in some particular act implied by its setting out. Here we can see the inexorable drive of narrative, with its beginning, middle and end. Yet there is an inherent conflict between the wish for the staging of desire, and the consummation which ends the story or fantasy. The delays, diversions and obstacles in a story are all means to postponing the ending. They mark a pleasure in the happening and continuing to happen of the scene, of how the consummation will come about, not the act itself, which immediately moves it into having happened, when it will fall back into loss, the past. The story's conclusion, with the couple married, or the orgasm graphically achieved, finally ends the fantasy. Alternatively, rather than this deferral of the orgasm, of the resolution, there is an endless repetition, with the same scene or series of scenes reproduced over and over again, and in which the variation is subordinate to the repetition. (Such repetition is also characteristic of narrative in general, though it may be more disguised, and the variation more pointed.)

Fantasy as a *mise en scène* of desire is the setting out of the lack, of what is absent, rather than making it present or having it: desire itself coming into existence in the representation of lack, in the production of a fantasy of its becoming present. No doubt there is orgasm along the way, with reading punctuated by the climaxes of masturbation. Richard Dyer has noted the pleasures of the male gay pornographic cinema where spectators may find partners for the viewing among other members of the audience, enabling a complementary climaxing between spectators and screen performers.[6] However, what must be emphasized is not the climax as the obvious image of pleasure, but the desire to desire which pornography represents. It is the wish to be aroused and the wish to fantasize a scenario of sexual activity which pornography serves, so that the climax is a kind of interruption, albeit one which also maintains the system. The pleasure of sexual fantasy and pornography is desired for itself, not as a simple means to physical sexual gratification. It is the continuing imagining of a possible sexual satisfaction which drives desire. Even where the body flags and the penis refuses to rise, the *wish* for sexual desire is there.

The assumption of the image which arouses, as if a simple content of anatomy stimulates desire, effaces the complex system of signification involved and the complex fantasy implied. This is the case even with the most stereotyped pornographic image – say of the woman laying prone, her genitals exposed to the camera, her hand suggesting the gesture of masturbation – which nevertheless figures a scene of fantasy. This is not an image of pure denotation, with a corresponding automatic stimulus–response. The image is already part of a complex system of signifying the sexual and a complex process by which the woman's body, for many men, comes to be the sign of their desire. It is already a connotative system, signifying the possibility of sexual satisfaction for the man. The woman's naked body and the delineation of her genitals as fragmented images present at the very least 'the object which satisfies' or 'the object through which I am pleasured', just as the breast had done. (Such part-images are successors of the early part-objects – the breast, etc. – while also functioning as substitutes.) However, the subject of the satisfaction – the spectator – is absent from the image, implying a scenario in which that subject would come to be present – a scene which might be variously imagined but could include the man putting his penis into the woman's sex thus displayed. This involves both a bodily pleasure, now genital in contrast to the polymorphous sexuality of the infant, and a psychical pleasure in refinding the object of satisfaction.

The image of the woman's genitalia thus stands for something else, the man's pleasure, which is why it is a sign.[7] At the same time it offers a fantasy scenario in time – of the woman there ready for me, a woman waiting to be pleasured, *already* excited and desiring, a scene into which the spectator can step. If the gesture of the woman masturbating herself is also there, this clearly is not taken to exclude the male spectator. Rather, it demonstratively affirms the woman's sexual arousal; it is a sign of her desire, but suggests that she has not yet climaxed, leaving scope for the man. The scene narrates a situation of lack – the sexual climax – which will be supplied by the man, in fantasy as he completes the scene with his penis and even quite literally, in his own masturbation.

It is also a kind of voyeurism of the most childish kind, of the order 'I'll show you mine, if you show me yours', which is also 'I want to see your sex because I want you to see mine', whereby the display of the woman sexually stands in for and is equivalent to the man's wished-for display of himself sexually, including as a display for *someone else*. The woman's 'shameless' display of herself provokes an identification in the spectator transitively, just as a small child cries when it sees another child crying. It is an identification with the exhibitionism of the scene. This works, therefore, across the difference of biological sex, and it also shows why women may find such images stimulating.

A more sadistic voyeurism may be involved as well – of the gaze which penetrates the woman who is splayed for view, victim to the spectator's look. Nevertheless this also implies the correlative, just as in the earlier example of voyeurism, of a reversibility whereby the eroticism arises in the being exposed in one's sex to the gaze of the other. The inclusion of a male figure in the scene offers not only a surrogate with whom the spectator may identify but also an other to whom one may exhibit oneself.

Changing positions

The pornographic image, then, is a signifying system and a fantasy scenario. What is portrayed is not the object of desire but a scenario in which certain wishes are presented. Moreover, the subject of the fantasy may take up more than one position within the scenario. This can be seen clearly in the primal scene, a scene posited by psychoanalysis as the child's earliest attempt, through fantasy, to imagine its parents when they are together at those times when the child is excluded.[8] It is projected as a scene of pleasure between the parents, with the child looking on – a scene of parental coitus, but imagined without full knowledge of the sexual functions. The child obtains pleasure from the fantasy by satisfying its voyeuristic wish to see what its parents do when it is not there. It models this scene on the basis of its own sexual wishes for the parents, to be pleasured by them – in the broadest, polymorphous sense. But it is also a scene of aggression where the child imagines itself usurping the place of one or other parent: replacing the mother with the father, or the father with the mother. Moreover, the scene of the parents' lovemaking may itself be construed as aggressive: either as the father's aggressive penetration of the mother, or as the mother's violent appropriation of the father's penis. This represents the child's aggressive wish to penetrate the mother, or father, to be back inside, and it also punishes the mother or father for his or her relationship with the other parent to the exclusion of the child. Also present is the passive wish to be penetrated, to be the object of the other, just as the child had so recently been in its carer's arms.[9] At the same time the child fears parental retribution for its aggressive wish to usurp their position with each other, so that its identification with the parent who is the victim in the child's scenario also represents its own punishment. (Analytic evidence from children and adults suggests that the child imagines a scene of anal intercourse and hence one in which, whether boy or girl, it can be penetrated and, since the anatomical difference is not yet understood, the girl just as easily as the boy fantasizes 'doing things' to the parent, just as things are done to it.)

A fourth position is implied by the child imagining a look which sees it looking, which discovers it in the act of forbidden looking. It is not a position which the subject of the fantasy can occupy; rather, the subject submits to it. It is the gaze of the superego, of conscience and shame, which is always so easily co-present in our best scenarios, and brings them to an end. It is a look which poses the spectator as such, and may be posited by the representation itself, as attempted in certain kinds of avant-garde film, so that the audience is shifted from the illusion of the scene to the realization of its construction, including its construction of their desire.

Whether the fantasy is a daydream 'thoughtlessly' composed, or an adult sexual fantasy, each, as in the 'original' or primal fantasy, visualizes a scene which presents a variety of positions which the subject of the fantasy may take up, whether he or she is also represented in the scene or not. The figures in the scene stand for positions of desire: to love or be loved from this place, to pleasure or be pleasured from this position. The public, published forms of fantasy, visual or literary, whether pornographic or not, offer this same scenario of fantasy. The spectator identifies not with the figures, whether objects or subjects of desire within the narrative, but with the different positions of desire. Hence a man may identify with the woman's pose of self-display in so far as it signifies the wish to be found lovable in one's sex, an identification with a passive wish, rather than an identification with the woman and her body as female. However, the fantasy scenario does not offer the spectator a set of multiple choices of positions of identification; rather, it constitutes a particular array, textually orchestrated as a limited set of oppositions, which the spectator must enter, and hence psychically be able to enter, or else the scenario will 'fail' for him.

Active and passive desire in fantasy

Active and passive therefore constitute two distinct forms for any of the positions within the scenario, of a doing and being done to, the child caressed, pleasured by the other, and the child pleasuring itself through the other. The position of the mother may be either active – taking in the father's penis – or passive – receiving it. It is in relation to this reversibility of active and passive in the fantasy scenario that the 'seduction' or 'rape' fantasy can be understood, for it involves the placing on to the other of the active part in the scene, which is equivalent to making the other active, to having the other pleasure one – a highly active role for the subject of the fantasy who seeks to control the actions of the other, to have it done to one in this way not that, where one's own pleasure is also the desire of the other. The substitution of rape for seduction arises in the attempt to disavow the subject's own active desire, so that the looked-for sexual activity is received in the form of an imposition from outside; the woman resists valiantly but is overcome, so that despite herself she is pleasured – which is the aim of the fantasy. For feminists this is one of the most difficult fantasies, but it is also very common amongst women, and not only among heterosexual women. In C. Bailey's 'Ride My Bitch II', two women, Liz and Carol, drive around the USA 'looking for women to fuck'. They pick up a hitchhiker, Iris, who then invites them in for supper. Soon their intentions towards her become clear.

> Here again was the roughness that Iris longed for yet feared. She made as if to protest, but Carol was quick, pinning her face down across the table-top. Iris struggled, but Carol twisted her arm behind her back, effectively taking command. Iris could feel Carol enjoying taking command. Iris could feel Carol enjoying the roughness, and whimpered, more grateful than afraid. Liz stripped away her pants, then there was a long pause in which Iris felt not at all degraded as the two women coveted her greedily.[10]

Even more difficult is Pat Califia's account of 'The Surprise Party' in which a 'self-possessed butch gets arrested and repeatedly and ritually fucked by three policemen' and likes it – 'But I'm a lesbian, her public persona objected. This doesn't have anything to do with that, the wiser voice replied.'[11]

Such accounts offend the rational mind as well as moral norms, for how can women desire rape when it is the most extreme instance of male domination and violence against them? But precisely because of this it can be used, in fantasy, to represent the most extreme of sexual desire, projected on to the active other whose very violence and insistent demand are but an inverse representation of the subject's own desire to be pleasured. It is a profoundly passive fantasy, and apparently found as commonly in men as in women; in its benign form it absolves the subject from the guilt and responsibility of his or her desire, which appears to come from outside, apparently imposed, but in which the subject will be pleasured. As an *active* desire it also includes wishes of penetrating or devouring the other, and hence produces a fear of damaging the other. If, however, the wish is turned round from active to passive, its *force* remains, but the risk – of damage to the other and his or her retribution – is avoided. Of course the woman does not want to be raped in reality, but the fantasy may be the basis for her relations with men, so that in order to have sex she needs to say 'No,' by which she will mean 'Yes, but only because you "force" me to have what I really want.' The woman must therefore co-opt the partner to her fantasy, which may not be easy, for it requires a complementary wish in the man to 'give her the pleasure she denies wanting', whereas he may actually wish to take the pleasure he wants, and punish her for her refusal of desire for him – her 'No, I don't want sex/you'. Then it becomes real rape, and not at all what one wants.

Repression, guilt and sadomasochism

Freud saw the reversibility of the sexual drive and its turning round on itself from active to passive, together with repression, as important transformations of the drive, which arise as a result of the subject encountering some prohibition of its desire. However, this turning round in which Freud saw the emergence of sadism and masochism is subsequent to the emergence of the active form of the drive out of an original 'passive' or 'self-reflexive' form. As a result, sadism and masochism are not simply 'perverse' forms of the active and passive, but distinct transformations.[12] Wishes are always liable to prohibition. In a process adults call weaning, the child loses the breast for ever. It is denied access to its parents' bodies as sexual objects. It discovers 'reality', that realm or reason by which its heartfelt desires are shown to be impossible – 'No, you can't fly; only birds and aeroplanes can.' And it must give up its wishes for its parents, mother or father, and internalize this repression, or risk the loss of the parents' love (the Oedipal complex resolved by the accept-ance of castration, as psychoanalysis describes it). Without assenting here to the excesses of repression to which family structures give rise, it is possible to recognize that some form of limitation of the child – of ordering, and hence of repression – is a corollary of human social organization. As a result, instead of pursuing the wish in reality, one may pursue it in fantasy.

Where the wish relates to a prohibition, however, the effects of repression will nevertheless make themselves felt; so that where a wish has undergone repression, a fantasy may provide a satisfaction – not by presenting a scenario for the achievement of the wish but, on the contrary, by enacting the failure and frustration of that wish or even its reversal into its opposite, becoming a fantasy of pain rather than pleasure. It is this which Freud describes in his account of the fantasy 'A Child is Being Beaten'.[13] This phrase sums up the minimal fantasy scene which Freud found several of his patients, both male and female, presenting as childhood memories in analysis. The fantasy was always felt to be pleasurable, whether accompanied by masturbation or not.

Freud shows that the fantasy consists of three phases, each involving a different subject position. In the first, the fantasy is 'My father is beating a child, whom I hate'; thus, 'My father loves me, since he is beating the other child' but also 'I am making my father beat the other child to show he loves me', in which the subject erases the other, rival child from the father's affections. It is thus egoistic, identifying both father/self-love and father/self as beater of the other child, and hence a form of sadism, yet one which arises from an earlier, passive wish: to be loved by the father. For this to become transposed into 'A child is being beaten', with its third-person syntax, Freud proposed a second phase: 'I am being beaten by my father'; while the first phase may be remembered through analysis, this second is wholly unconscious and can only be inferred from analysis. The implicit incestuous desire of the first phase is subject to repression in the second, to produce a reversal: 'No, my father does not love me (you), for he is beating me (you).' The beating is not only the punishment for the incestuous wish but also the 'regressive substitute for that relation, and from this latter source it derives the libidinal excitation which is from this time forward attached to it'.[14] Guiltiness and punishment are thus attached to the sexual desire: to be punished is to have had the forbidden sexual relation, for why else would you be punished? Between the two phases there is a move from sadism to masochism, although the first phase is not yet properly sadistic, or erotic, inasmuch as it is pregenital. In the third phase, the consciously remembered fantasy 'A child is being beaten' once more appears sadistic – these other children are being beaten while I look on – however, Freud sees this as sadistic in form only, for he argues that the satisfaction obtained is masochistic: nothing more than substitutes for 'All the many unspecified children who are being beaten by the teacher are, after all, the child itself.'[15] The fantasy escapes repression by the disguise of the third-person syntax. Out there, there are children being beaten – as I should be for my forbidden wishes. The stake, the effectiveness, of this third phase of the fantasy is the interchangeability of the subject and the other children being beaten. The active wish for the father is not superseded in the final version but overlaid.[16]

As a result, fantasy is highly mediated by the defensive processes set in play by the introduction of repression. It is in this process that the adult sadomasochistic fantasy scenarios can be located – a pleasure not so much in being beaten as in what this beating represents, a forbidden transgression. But this is also only a version of an interchangeability between active and passive.[17] We cannot assume, therefore, that the man watching the porn film showing scenes of violence identifies only, if at all, with the male (or female) figure who conducts the violence. The wish for a passive position in the sexual relationship, even without the attendant masochistic fantasy, is extremely common in male sexual fantasies.[18]

A fantasy is therefore a kind of palimpsest, a layering of multiple positions in a specified relation of oppositions. This may involve wishes and positions which, logically, cancel each other out – the wish to have something and not to have it, or the wish to be punished for one's wish. Fantasy is therefore not only the realm of pleasurable wishes but also a domain of anxiety: fear of punishment by others for one's forbidden wishes. The fantasy of rape may also constitute a fantasy of punishment in which the sexual aggression of the other is a punishment for sexual desire. There is a split between a good sexual other of desire and a bad sexual other who punishes so that 'one asks for rape' by having sexual desires. Fantasy may also involve aggressive wishes which have been projected on to others, producing a fear of attack from outside. Public forms of fantasy, too, involve the exploration of such fears, and the wishes and projections which gave rise to them.

Fantasy and the Other

There is, however, not only the subject's wish for pleasure, which may be an active or passive wish, but also a wish to pleasure the other person, to give pleasure and hence be the object of the other's desire. The child wishes to be what its mother or carer wants, a passive wish which becomes the active wish to give the mother, or other, what he or she wants. Sexual pleasure is contingent on some kind of 'being or having for the other', which at its crudest can become the fantasy of having the penis for the woman, which signifies being loved by her. Here, most clearly, pleasure is related not to a biological upsurge but to a psychically constructed relation to the other in which desire is contingent on the other's desire. This need not be any real person's desire, and indeed the difficulty of harmoniously realizing one's wishes with a sexual partner is one of the major reasons for the success of pornography, of ready-made scenarios which figure wishes without the danger of being found 'not good enough' encountered in actual sexual relations. That this is not only a phallicism in which the penis is centred as the means to the woman's pleasure is borne out by the success of cunnilingus with both men and women. Here, too, can be found the motive for the oft-noted feature of pornography to become an investigation of the women's sexual pleasure, the attempt to discover the 'truth' of her desire in which to know what she wants is also to be it, to have what she wants.[19] But the man never really discovers this truth, is never really certain that he is what she wants – hence the need endlessly to repeat this investigation of the woman's desire. From this can arise a fantasy complementary to the woman's fantasy of rape, whereby the man really knows she wants what he has, despite her protestations, and will find pleasure in spite of herself in his sexual activities on her. He shows her what she always wanted all along, which is also himself; hence the fantasy is also an affirmation that he is the desired object. Here it is more a fantasy of seduction than of rape. But much less benignly, such a fantasy is readily susceptible to aggressive wishes to punish the woman for failing to desire him. The woman's lack of desire ceases to be a challenge to overcome so as to bring her to desire, and becomes something to be punished.

The reality of fantasy
Fantasy is clearly a separate realm from reality, but it also exists only in so far as reality circumscribes it. Freud referred to fantasy as a 'kind of "reservation"' which was 'separated from the real external world at the time of the introduction of the reality principle', to which the subject can resort.[20] It is a place in which the subject 'remodels' reality to its own liking. For Freud, both neurosis and psychosis are a rebellion on the part of the id against the external world and result from its unwillingness, or perhaps incapacity, to adapt itself to the exigencies of reality. In psychosis, however, the reality is remodelled; whereas in neurosis, there is an avoidance or flight from reality. Freud says:

> Neurosis does not disavow the reality, it only ignores it; psychosis disavows it and tries to replace it. We call behaviour 'normal' or 'healthy', if it combines certain features of both reactions – if it disavows the reality as

little as does a neurosis, but if it then exerts itself as does a psychosis, to effect an alteration of that reality. Of course, this expedient, normal, behaviour leads to work being carried out on the external world; it does not stop, as in psychosis, at effecting internal changes. It is no longer *autoplastic* but *alloplastic*.[21]

Freud therefore saw as 'normal' the subject's attempt to realize some part or all of a fantasy, to make reality fit the fantasy – for example, in the wish to become successful, liked, rich, famous, etc. But this remodelling of reality in relation to one's fantasy must take some account of reality, of reality-testing, in order not to fall into psychosis. As a result, its realization rarely 'matches' the fantasy; it rarely provides the satisfaction looked for in fantasy, even though someone's success may exceed even their wildest dreams. There is something in desire, Freud said, which escapes satisfaction. 'Reality' here is of course the social world of conventions, norms and prohibitions, as well as the reality of the desire of the other to whom one addresses a demand for love and sexual satisfaction. It is the maintenance and definition of these norms for social reality that feminism is concerned with, but this is not achieved by simply policing fantasy and its public circulation. It is necessary to maintain fantasy *as* fantasy, not allowing it to become the basis for social norms. Thus accepting the reality of women's fantasies of rape in no way implies accepting rape as a social practice, as if it were a real 'answering' to those fantasies.[22]

Such a confusion is present, however, in the legal position on rape. In the British criminal justice system the accused is assumed to be innocent until proven guilty beyond reasonable doubt. As a result, the nature of the woman's consent is necessarily central to rape as a crime, yet the male-dominated legal system has focused 'the problem of rape' as the problem of the innocent man falsely accused. Consequently, the claim of 'an honest belief' in the woman's consent is accepted, and this 'honest belief' need not be either reasonable or corroborated by other evidence or witnesses. The woman's testimony of rape, too, does not require corroboration, yet the judge is required to 'warn the jury of the danger of convicting solely on the basis of the evidence of the complainant'.[23] The rationale for this is that women, it is said, may fabricate sexual assault out of jealousy, spite, or revenge, or because they are prone to tell lies and fantasize.[24]

Until recently in British law a woman's sexual history could be presented by the defence as relevant both to her credibility and to the issue of consent – the implication being that since she had slept with other men, her testimony that she refused consent in this case was less trustworthy. Changes in norms of sexual relations and feminist pressure have forced the courts to disallow such information, so that the notion of an 'innocent' victim versus a woman whose sexual experience implies that any man's attentions are welcome is no longer at issue.[25] What continues, however, is the courts' expectation that the woman should be clear about her intentions, so that *she* is made responsible for what the man may believe about them. In other words, the law continues to maintain the norm that the man can never be sure whether a woman means yes or no – that is, whether she desires him or not; it remains wedded to a norm of male sexuality contained in the man's fantasy of seduction: she never really knows she wants it. The courts demand that the woman ensures the man understands her intentions. What is not demanded is that the man takes responsibility for his own assumptions, or that the norm of male behaviour in these circumstances should be that unless clear assent is received, the man should assume the woman does not want sex.

Disavowal, playing and fantasy

Freud emphasized that the role of fantasy for adults is the same as the function of play for children – in both large amounts of emotional energy are cathected, while nevertheless sharply separated from reality. Fantasy, and especially public forms of fantasy – films, stories, plays, television – in the main replace childish play for adults. As a result, adults rarely 'play out' their fantasies in real enacted scenarios, although an increasingly popular leisure activity is such re-enactment, whether it is the battles of the Roundheads and Cavaliers in the English Civil War or the old-time West of the United States of America. Similarly, there is a playing out of sexual scenarios, although here there is often either the replacement of the sexual act by the play-acting as such, or a deferment of the sexual act by a lengthy foreplay of a 'scene-setting'. Fantasies are actualized, but remain 'play-acted', and this is the recurrent defence made by those engaging in consenting sadomasochism, as well as by the besuited businessmen who pay women to dress them up as schoolgirls, servants, etc. Pat Califia has argued that:

> The key word to understand S/M is *fantasy*. The roles, dialogue, fetish costumes, and sexual activity are part of a drama or ritual. The participants are enhancing their sexual pleasure, not damaging or imprisoning one another. A sado-masochist is well aware that a role adopted during a scene is not appropriate during other interactions and that a fantasy role is not the sum total of her being. The S/M subculture is a theater in which sexual dramas can be acted out . . .[26]

Pat Califia's account is very close to the description of fantasy in psychoanalysis – in her emphasis on S/M as a scene, as a form of theatre with its role-playing and hence interchangeability of roles, together with her recognition of the 'unreality' of fantasy as distinct from its seriousness, and her notion that fantasy involves not so much an object of desire as a scenario of activities which depend upon the partner's participation. Her defence of S/M rests on the sexual pleasure obtained, the fact that it is always very clearly *play* – 'Even a minor accident like a rope burn can upset the top enough to mar the scene' – and on the interchangeability of roles – 'You can always switch your keys . . .' This apparent interchangeability is in fact a set of fixed oppositions of positions, compulsively replayed. Nor is the scenario 'freely chosen', since an anodyne scene of foreplay would hardly substitute. Choice, consent and the free will to engage in s/M are all emphasized by Pat Califia, yet she also makes a powerful confession of the compulsive quality of her fantasies:

> Three years ago I decided to stop ignoring my sexual fantasies. Since the age of two, I had been constructing a private world of dominance, submission, punishment and pain. Abstinence, consciousness-raising and therapy had not blighted the charm of these frightful reveries.[27]

It is this compulsive element in fantasy which must also be recognized, for fantasy does not constitute an unlimited field of variability in the imagination but is more typically an endlessly repeated scene, carefully dressed up each time in new clothes. Of course, sexuality itself partakes of just such a compulsive nature.[28]

Fantasy is also a form of disavowal, that process for which Freud saw fetishism as a paradigmatic example. In each case a disagreeable reality is replaced by an agreeable substitute; however, in the case of disavowal what is replaced is a disagreeable knowledge, whereas in fantasy it is a disagreeable constraint on a wish. Disavowal thus joins the process of fantasy, for it is in order to retain a wish that the disagreeable knowledge is renounced. Disavowal involves some form of affirmation of the knowledge, and its rejection – 'I know, but all the same, I believe the opposite.' Freud saw fetishism as paradigmatic of disavowal in so far as it is the refusal to know the difference of the woman – the mother's lack of a penis – and the replacement of this 'lack' by some form of substitute. However, he modified his initial assumption that fetishism is a successful defence by the man against castration anxiety, and came to argue that it more characteristically appears in conjunction with castration anxiety, so that 'The two contrary reactions to the conflict persist as the centre-point of a splitting of the ego.'[29] As a result, Freud saw this 'holding of two contradictory knowledges' as occurring much more widely than in fetishism alone, although this was the example he always returned to for his discussion of the concept. Women, therefore, may disavow just as much and just as easily as men. Indeed, Freud's controversial theory of female penis envy implies disavowal on the part of the woman in her refusal to recognize her lack or castration; instead she continues to believe in – or to expect – her possession of the penis.

The substitution that arises in fetishism proper is a feature of disavowal in general as well as of fantasy, as Freud notes when distinguishing psychosis from neurosis, for both of which fantasy is:

> the store-house from which the materials or the pattern for building the new reality are derived. But whereas the new, imaginary external world of a psychosis attempts to put itself in the place of external reality, that of neurosis, on the contrary, is apt, like the play of children, to attach itself to a piece of reality – a different piece from the one against which it has to defend itself – and to lend that piece a special importance and a secret meaning which we (not always quite appropriately) call a *symbolic* one. Thus we see that both in neurosis and psychosis there comes into consideration the question not only of a *loss of reality* but also of a *substitute for reality*.[30]

The objects and elements in the fantasy scenario may be present not for what they are but for what they are not – as substitutes in a process of defence. Fantasy cannot be taken at face value. Psychoanalysis shows that it is a complex realm of subterfuges and satisfactions as well as terrors. It is this complexity, and the understanding of fantasy which psycho-analysis offers, which must be taken into account in discussions of pornography.

My thanks to Anne Bottomley, who read an earlier version of this article, and to Lea Jacobs for discussing the issues with me.

Part 3

The personal as political

Problems with anti-pornography feminism

Mary McIntosh

Liberalism and the contradictions of sexual politics

Liberalism is not enough

The crusade against pornography and its efforts to strengthen legal controls challenge us to rethink what we mean by the slogan 'the personal is political'. If we accept that there is a feminist critique of pornography, if we accept that women's liberation requires a transformation of patriarchal culture, why not campaign to have sexist pornography legally banned? Now of course, there are many problems about defining the category to which this critique applies and about how any new law would actually work, which are discussed in other essays in this collection. But the niggling suspicion remains that those of us who oppose further censorship are libertarians, left over from the 1960s era of 'if-you-dig-it-do-it', who do not recognize the social implications of 'private' individual actions.

It is a paradoxical fact that these campaigners have chosen the liberal arena for their political campaigns, as Beverley Brown has pointed out.[1] When they claim that pornography causes the identifiable public harm of sexual violence against women, they implicitly accept that there is a private sphere which should be free from state control, provided no one else is harmed. Since the causal claim is so implausible in the crude form in which they have expressed it (that individual men who are directly exposed to pornography are more likely to abuse women sexually[2]), many of us have been quite happy that the battle is pitched in this arena, and to fight it under the banner of civil liberties. We have, perhaps, been

155

relieved that they have not pressed the much more challenging argument that feminists cannot treat the personal questions of sexuality as part of a separate sphere that has no connection with the wider politics of women's oppression. Yet that is the position that most of them would support. Indeed, in their more reflective moments they see this separation of personal and political as the greatest failing of those of us who oppose legislation on pornography. For instance, Catharine MacKinnon and other leading crusaders against pornography have contributed to a book called *The Sexual Liberals and the Attack on Feminism*,[3] which takes a principled position against liberalism.

Again, it would be easy to attack the argument of writers like MacKinnon by focusing on its crudest excesses. Their basic position is that every aspect of society is so structured by male supremacy that abstract concepts like choice, consent, equality and freedom are all suspect, as far as women are concerned. This argument has, indeed, a grain of truth, but since they place sexuality at the centre of women's oppression and see it as a practice whose function is to subordinate women to men, some of them recommend withdrawing from sex altogether. One group writing in the book, calling themselves Women Against Sex, say that 'sex has to stop before male supremacy will be defeated', which suggests a gloomy prognosis for feminism. It would be easy, too, to quote Catharine MacKinnon's statement:

> [The women's movement] knew that when force is a normalized part of sex, when no is taken to mean yes, when fear and despair produce acquiescence and acquiescence is taken to mean consent, consent is not a meaningful concept[4]

and to point out that this undermines the whole of anti-rape campaigning by merging it with a campaign against intercourse in general. But there remains a nub of argument that must be taken seriously, which lies in their recognition that every aspect of society is interconnected with every other.

The notion of the private as against the public sphere is problematic for feminism, given that we recognize this as a historically developed distinction that was highly gendered in its origins. In the ideology of the emergent middle class, the division of the world into private and public was linked with the flowering of the bourgeois domestic sphere as women's domain and the elaboration of formal organizations and associations as men's. The family home became the model of private life, separated from work and commerce, proudly independent and with its own front door to mark its boundary. The notion of the privacy of family life has been used to justify policies of non-intervention in child abuse and wife-beating. It has often made women lonely and isolated and obliged them to shoulder heavy burdens of care and responsibility. Feminists have wanted to bring these things out into the open and to say that, far from being a sphere of freedom and autonomy, the private family can be a state-protected patriarchy.

The liberal image is of the family as a primordial, even natural, social form which an increasingly predatory state seeks to control through education, social security rules, social work and psychiatry, in the interests of economic efficiency, population policy and social hygiene. Against this, feminist theorists have pointed out that the family is by no means natural, that household forms vary from one society to another. The dominant form in our society is of an economically independent, self-supporting little nuclear unit geared to providing at least one efficient full-time worker for the labour market and to rearing a few more for the future. This is a form that particularly suits a capitalist society. Its privacy and independence are not so much a bulwark against state intervention as a product of state policies that were designed to establish such ideas as the breadwinner and 'his' family, the dependent housewife and parental responsibility. All of this means that the 'rights of privacy' that are so favoured in liberal thought are highly problematic from a feminist point of view.

The right to freedom of speech depends upon a distinction

between words and deeds that is hard to sustain. That words – and visual images – are powerful in underpinning social institutions is an insight that is not confined to feminism. Social thought over the last two decades has laid great stress on culture and ideology. There has been a recognition that social power at the level of the state is sustained not only by law and force but also by an elaborate system of ideas that make it seem normal and incontrovertible. There has been a growing awareness that racial oppression is to be found as much in the way dominant discourses assume white men as their subject and cast black people as strange and 'other' as in employment discrimination or physical racial attacks. The power of the mass media to whip up issues of public concern and define the political agenda has become more and more apparent. Feminism has brought this sort of concern to bear on understanding women's oppression and there has been a flowering of feminist film studies, literary and art criticism and cultural analysis.

In a more positive and practical way, feminists have sought to transform culture: to get anti-sexist books into schools, to publish new magazines for women, to create our own art and writing, humour and drama. Clearly, we have believed in the power of words and images and in the importance of cultural politics. But if the pen is indeed mightier than the sword, should it not be subject to the same controls, licensing and non-proliferation treaties?

In apparent contradiction, though, the term 'liberal' has often been associated with 'reformism' – an orthodox approach to social change through democratic processes and legislation. Feminists have often been ambivalent about orthodox politics and about invoking the state in support of women's interests. On the one hand there has been the view that women are ignored in the political process, denied proper citizenship, and our concerns are treated as 'merely personal'. The project, then, should be to transform official politics to take us into account and to assert a continuity between the politics of everyday life and the politics of party and Parliament. On the other hand, the state has been criticized as irredeemably patriarchal, its apparatuses staffed by men and its policies designed to sustain the institutions that oppress women. The project, then, should be to liberate women, to remove state controls from areas that affect our lives, like divorce or abortion: 'Not the Church, not the state: women should decide their fate.'

Should women be within the state hierarchies, at risk of co-optation, or mobilizing at the grass roots and sniping from strategic positions outside? Should we demand state maintenance for divorced mothers and their children, or should the men be made to pay? Should we be working within mixed political parties or in women-only organizations? Should we run our own anti-sexist nurseries and women's health centres, refuges and self-defence classes, or campaign for the state to change its ways? Such questions exercised the women's movement during the 1970s. On the whole, the conclusion has been the pragmatic one: there is no general answer; there may be occasions for an engagement with orthodox politics and legislative reforms, but there are also occasions for a more subversive politics of demonstrative actions, self-activity and everyday life.

There are, then, serious problems with the liberalism which had led feminists to assert that 'the personal is political'. On the other hand, 'the political' is not identical with making demands on the state. So the fact that the personal, the sexual, the cultural and – our concern in this book – pornography are 'political' does not necessarily mean that they should be the subject of legislative control. I shall argue, indeed, that the appropriate politics is one of subversion – a kind of cultural guerrilla warfare – because pornography is an inherently contradictory phenomenon.

The social construction of sexuality

To work out strategies for feminist sexual politics, we need to understand more about how sexuality and sexual behaviour are formed, how sexual desire – apparently such an individual matter – is shaped by the social context. The anti-pornography campaigners are acutely aware that men's sexual behaviour is influenced by the culture around them, but they usually have very simplistic ideas of the processes involved. Diana Russell, for instance, says:

> My theory, in a nutshell, is that pornography (1) predisposes some men to want to rape women or intensifies the predisposition in other men already so predisposed, (2) undermines some men's internal inhibitions against acting out their desire to rape, and (3) undermines some men's social inhibitions against acting out their desire to rape.[5]

The other 'causes of males' proclivity to rape' that she mentions are 'male sex-role socialization, sexual abuse in childhood, peer pressure and portrayal of women in the mass media'.[6] Her analysis applies 'the laws of social learning . . . about which', she says, 'there is now considerable consensus among psychologists'. In other words, her analysis of sexuality involves men who have no self-reflection and whose engagement with the cultural complex is completely passive and unselective. So contradictions within that culture become internalized simply as a 'proclivity' that is held in check by internal and social inhibitions. There is no room here even for men to look around them and recognize a wider cultural terrain, and certainly none for such ideas as the 'thrill of the forbidden', perversity, transgression, subversion.[7]

Many anti-pornography crusaders, especially in Britain, are inclined to turn to Russell for their theory. It is a theory in which men are not subjects, except in the sense of 'subjects' in laboratory experiments. At the same time there is a completely opposing theory, most tellingly expressed by Andrea Dworkin, that men are indeed the dominant subjects, the collective subject of 'male sexual domination'. For Dworkin, sexuality is so much a part of this social order that it is no longer conceived as individual or personal at all. She says:

Men control the sexual and reproductive uses of women's bodies. The institutions of control include law, marriage, prostitution, pornography, health care, the economy, organized religion, and systematized physical aggression against women (for instance, in rape and battery) . . . The ideology of male sexual domination posits that men are superior to women by virtue of their penises; that physical possession of the female is the natural right of the male; . . . The metaphysics of male sexual domination is that women are whores . . . One does not violate something by using it for what it is: neither rape nor prostitution is an abuse of the female because in both the female is fulfilling her natural function.[8]

Here we have a vision of patriarchy as a seamless social totality. But again, as with Russell, there is no sense that there may be contradictions within that totality, and that this may pose problems for a feminist sexual politics. Dworkin rejects the idea that the Marquis de Sade was a dissident or a deviant – though she reports the many occasions when he was pursued and imprisoned by the authorities: for her he is 'Everyman'. She takes no account of the fact that pornography is banned, seized, burned, kept shamefully under the bed – by men. Nor does she recognize that, far from being considered as an acceptable part of the system, clients and ponces, as well as prostitutes themselves, are hounded and criminalized:

In the male system, women are sex, sex is the whore . . . Buying her means buying pornography . . . Wanting her means wanting pornography. Being her means being pornography.[9]

So women, too, are completely caught up within this totality. There is no room here for the actual sex worker – only for the 'whore' of men's imagination. Dworkin says: 'The word *whore* is incomprehensible unless one is immersed in the lexicon of male domination',[10] but because her image of society is totalitarian, her solution is utopian: 'We will know that we are free when pornography no longer exists. As long as it does exist, we must understand that we are the women in it.'[11] So she rails against the injustice of being labelled a 'vile whore', but does not engage with the actual politics of prostitution or of women who are 'whores' in a more than metaphorical sense. There is no room here for subversion or destabilization, let alone reform or amelioration.

We need a theory of the social construction of sexuality that is somewhere between what might be called the 'liberal' view that it lies outside the social altogether and the 'totalitarian' view that it is a determinate aspect of a homogeneous social whole. For this purpose, we can turn to the 'social constructionism' that has been developed by lesbian and gay theorists in an effort to explore the development of the contemporary gay identity. From its origins in my (now very dated) 1968 article 'The Homosexual Role',[12] this work has been concerned to understand the part played by stigmatization in the historical – and, indeed, the individual – formation of this identity. It starts from the recognition that although homosexual behaviour probably exists in all societies, it is not universally interpreted as being a speciality of a particular type of person: the homosexual. There has been much debate about when this identity emerged in Western cultures, with the most popular candidates ranging from the late seventeenth to the late twentieth century. What is clear, though, is that there are many complex processes at work but that the stigmatization and punishment of individuals who were beginning to be identified in this way had an important part to play. Doctors, sexologists, psychiatrists, the police, recurrent scandals and moral panics all helped to develop the contemporary notion of 'the homosexual'. So too, of course, did homosexual subcultures and apologias which gradually took root and offered a variety of defensive and offensive strategies.

Now, there are some useful features of this body of theory which may be helpful in understanding heterosexuality as well. One is a clear recognition that the social patterning of sexual behaviour varies from one society to another – so some societies are 'rape prone' while others are 'rape free', as the anthropologist Peggy Reeves Sanday has shown.[13] Another is that although current sexual conceptions are immensely powerful in affecting our identities and behaviour, they do not by any means determine them. Thus there are people who resist classifying themselves as either homosexual or heterosexual and many more who, though they adopt one identity or the other, are nevertheless bisexual in their behaviour, resisting the exclusive sexual orientation that is implied in the social label. Similarly, many heterosexual men do not act out the current hegemonic notions of masculinity; and many heterosexual women resist dominant ideas of feminine passivity, despite Catharine MacKinnon's claim that women's lives are 'seamlessly consistent with pornography'.

A third useful feature of social constructionism is its awareness that the actual social patterning of sexual behaviour is not the same as the culturally and morally approved patterns of behaviour. Just as homosexuality grew up alongside a new emphasis on normative heterosexuality, tied into marriage, procreation and family, so prostitution exists as a separate and specialized institution only because promiscuous, impersonal sex-for-money goes so much against the moral norms and because women are expected to be more monogamous and less sexually active than men.

The inherent contradiction of pornography

It can be argued, also, that pornography represents another non-normative, disapproved phenomenon which has become institutionalized in the form it has precisely because sexual explicitness is so strongly stigmatized. Pornography as a term, and as a phenomenon, is relatively recent in Western history.[14] It would not be a great oversimplification to say that it developed along with middle-class morality in the nineteenth century. As this morality of prudery and sexual restraint displaced both aristocratic licentiousness and the rules of thumb of earlier Christian teaching and rural custom, so a separate space, outside the pale of the new respectability, was created for everything that prudery condemned. It was very typical of the Victorian period to create a deep chasm between respectable and non-respectable, and the image of the Madonna and the Magdalen was often used to divide women in these terms. In the cities prostitution flourished as never before, but was also more sternly punished and stigmatized. Bourgeois morality projected on to prostitutes (as well as the working classes and 'savages') many of the desires it sought to suppress, so it is perhaps not surprising that the term pornography literally means 'a description of prostitutes or of prostitution'.[15]

According to Walter Kendrick, one of the first uses of the word pornography, in anything approximating to its present sense, seems to have been to refer to all those pictures and artefacts unearthed in the excavation of the Roman city of Pompeii which were thought too obscene to be displayed in public and were conserved in a separate collection in the National Museum in Naples – the 'secret museum'. These images were found all over the town, and there were erect stone phalluses at many Pompeiian street corners, but the museum cataloguers of 1866 chose to identify rooms painted with sexual scenes as brothels and to call the locked room in the museum the 'pornographic collection'.

The people excluded from the locked room were women and children and the uneducated in general. When an illustrated catalogue was printed in 1877, it was in an expensive edition which only the wealthy could afford; the genitals were miniaturized or blurred, and the whole text was larded with erudite Greek and Latin quotations – 'the decent obscurity of a learned language'. In this way pornography was born as a genre available to bourgeois men who could declare that their interest was scholarly. So, from the start, the definition of pornography was a highly gendered and class-bound one.[16]

During the course of the nineteenth and early twentieth centuries, the definition of pornography developed and changed with shifts in the boundary of what should be available in public, and particularly what should be available to the most 'vulnerable' and 'corruptible' members of society. In England and Wales, this boundary was succinctly defined in 1868 when Lord Justice Cockburn formulated the test of obscenity to be applied to the 1857 Obscene Publications Act:

> A tendency . . . to deprave and corrupt those whose minds are open to such immoral influences, and into whose hands a publication of this sort may fall.

Ironically or not, this test was first formulated in a judgement against a political tract, in which the Protestant Electoral Union exposed the prurient questions that Catholic priests were said to ask women in the confessional. From the start, then, pornography and regulation were an inseparable couple, and censorship was part of a paternalistic form of patriarchal domination that had its heyday in the Victorian era.

During the twentieth century it became established that scientific and literary merit could outweigh 'obscenity', and the courts were required to take into account the work as a whole, rather than to select out particular passages. The Obscene Publications Act of 1959 says:

> For the purpose of this Act an article shall be deemed obscene if its effect . . . is, if taken as a whole, such as to deprave and corrupt persons who are likely, in all the circumstances, to read, see or hear the matter contained or embodied in it . . . [The defendant shall not be convicted] . . . if publication of the article in question is justified as being for the public good . . . in the interests of science, literature, art or learning, or of other objects of general concern.

Subsequent appeal rulings have further established that shock or disgust by itself does not indicate obscenity, since works which provoke such feelings might actually *discourage* depravity.

The general line of development from the mid-nineteenth century to the present day is that the obscene becomes identified with a particular genre: pornography – that is to say, writing or pictures (and later videos, and so on) that are produced with the purpose of sexual arousal and have no 'redeeming' value. The assumption was that to set out intentionally to produce sexual arousal is despicable, but if the main objective of the work is artistic or scientific and the possibility of sexual arousal is only incidental, then these higher purposes may justify publication. The courts thus undertook to make aesthetic judgements, apparently unaware that class prejudice and aesthetics go hand in hand. The 'educated man' – and nowadays, indeed, the educated woman – can have erotic images packaged with arts and sciences; the uneducated should either do without or make do with the popular press, where they come wrapped up with 'news'. Pornography itself flourishes either as the illegal or restricted 'hard core' or the permitted borderline of available 'soft core'. In both cases it is entirely defined by the laws of obscenity, with the hard core transgressing and the soft core trimming its sails with great precision to stay within the law.

Pornography, then, represents a contradiction within bourgeois Christian morality, in that it exists only because it is condemned. Pornography and censoriousness are an inseparable couple. Until feminism entered the debate, all definitions of pornography depended upon this, and an essential ingredient of pornography was the desire to shock, to cross the boundaries, to explore forbidden zones. Repressive sexual morality always tends to foster and feed its own worst enemies in this way. Struggles over the censorship of pornography have been paradoxical because to defend pornography in public would be at the same time to recognize the morality which defines it as pornographic.

You can't get there from here

Where, then, is the space for a feminist sexual politics in all of this? Feminism has tried to intrude completely new considerations into this long-established contradiction. It has wanted to sidestep the whole question of the boundaries of sexual decency, through which censorship has defined pornography, and to focus instead on the sexually oppressive content of pornography. Some feminists have even wanted to introduce new legal controls on pornography (to extend or replace the existing ones – it is never quite clear). There are many problems with this. One is that since pornography is political, it involves political censorship. Another is that it involves making a political alliance with the forces of bourgeois Christian morality. But even more important is that in accepting the *concept* of pornography, it by definition accepts that morality.

When there is a deep-seated patriarchal contradiction like this, the appropriate feminist strategy cannot be to take one side or the other, but to seek to transcend the contradiction. This calls for a politics of subversion, not of reform. The crusade against pornography has been both utopian and reformist, in that it has imagined a society in which women are free from sexual violence and sought to usher it in through legal constraints on men. It has seen pornography as a branch of patriarchal ideology, whereas I have argued that, far from being the socially approved blueprint for sexual behaviour, pornography is the repository of all the unacceptable and repressed desires of men (even if only for sexual expression outside marriage).

The argument of this essay is that the 'personal' of sexuality is indeed political – that feminists should have a great deal to say about pornography, as about the rest of cultural representations, but that our politics has to take the form of transgression. Transgressive cultural politics can take a variety of forms. In recent years, 'gender-bending' dress – coupling heavy boots with black lace, for instance – has been used by some young women to challenge their elders. Making feminist 'pornography' and declaring ourselves as sexual beings is not simply something that we do for our own pleasure, using such freedom as we have gained; it is also a way of undermining all the oppressive things that sexuality has meant for women in the past. And feminist humour and poetry have immense power to subvert existing discourses by uncovering their contradictions and hinting at new meanings. Through such humour, through creating feminist 'pornography', through outrageous dress – if we can bring ourselves to do it – we can weaken the hold both of Mrs Grundy and of her delinquent sons.

Delightful visions

*From anti-porn to
eroticizing safer sex*

Today, I believe in promoting 'every sort of hedonism and perversion under the sun' – particularly to help bring about the end of the Aids crisis – but this was not always so.

When I was a student, and struggling to make sense of my feminism, I organized a week of women-centred events at a local arts centre. The week, called 'Delightful Visions', consisted of lunchtime jazz, late-night films, debates and the play *Masterpieces* by Sarah Daniels. This is an anti-pornography piece making frequent connections between porn and rape, and culminating in a disturbing monologue about snuff movies as justification for a woman (disturbed by pornography) apparently pushing a man under a train. 'Delightful Visions' was a financial disaster – hardly surprising, given the difficulties most women students in Oxford at that time (1986) had with the word feminist, let alone debating the complexities. Yet we (the cast and crew) spent an enjoyable time looking at lots of pornography, rehashing the porn debates and trying to make some statements. The only one I felt at all comfortable with was that there should be a division between erotica and pornography – we just couldn't work out where or how. It was obvious to us that pornography was central to the oppression of women – to think otherwise would have been anti-feminist.

Recently I found myself back in Oxford, and facing the Student Union Women's Committee. This time I was there as an Aids worker promoting erotic safer sex material. It's easier now for the students to use the word feminist, but it's still hard to hear more than the 'party line' on feminism. After my encounter with the massed anti-porn ranks of the student feminists, I finally joined Feminists Against Censorship (FAC), frustrated by the inability of the 'party line' to allow for the diversity of women's sexuality. Nearly five years of Aids work have enriched my awareness of sexuality and, in particular, the dangerous ways in which important issues are avoided in many feminist debates.

And so from the personal history to some politics of Aids. AIDS[1] (Acquired Immune Deficiency Syndrome) is a medical condition first noted as a new phenomenon in 1981. In the first decade of the crisis extensive research has identified a principal causative agent – Human Immunodeficiency Virus, or HIV – and confirmed the major routes of transmission: blood-to-blood contact, anal and vaginal intercourse, and from mother to foetus.

Sexual transmission is established for penetrative inter-course, and continues to be debated for oral sex (both fellatio and cunnilingus). The vast majority of other sexual activities have no proven cases of transmission. Essentially, HIV can be isolated, in sufficient quantities for transmission, from the blood, semen, and vaginal/cervical secretions of an HIV-infected person. One of these infected fluids has, in effect, to enter another person's bloodstream for transmission to occur. This cursory overview of the facts about HIV and AIDS is simple and easily understood. What is complicated in Aids work is not the facts but translating facts into action – for example, behavioural change – and the ways in which Aids is represented.

Representation is central to any description or critique of the Aids crisis. The effects are manifest in the attitudes and consequent policies towards people living with and affected by HIV/AIDS, the possibilities for behavioural change and prevention of transmission and, quite simply, the possibilities for gaining accurate information.

Representations of people living with HIV or AIDS swing variously between the moral degenerate with only him- (usually) self to blame, the leper, the powerless victim or sufferer and 'the most tragic of all' – the innocent victim (usually a heterosexual non-drug using woman/a child/a person with haemophilia). Rarely are we given any sense of the reality of a woman or man living with a life-threatening disease caused by an infectious agent. Whilst the most vitriolic 'God's punishment for wickedness' messages are now heard less regularly, there remains a general tendency to link HIV acquisition with lifestyle, and consequently with guilt, in both media representations and, tragically, many health education messages.

In addressing the question of representation of Aids in respect of censorship and pornography, our focus is clearly on measures taken to prevent the sexual transmission of HIV. There are also questions of representation regarding drugs use (in particular, the incessant use of the word 'addict', which makes it harder for occasional users to gain accurate information), but this does not fall within the scope of this essay.

There are two important themes when considering women, censorship and the Aids crisis:

- the silence and self-censorship which ignore women's sexualities;
- the censorship of sexually explicit materials prompting safer sex.

World Aids Day, 1 December 1990, took as its focus 'Women'. What should have been a marvellous worldwide opportunity to explore the diverse ways in which we are affected by the epidemic turned, all too often, into discussions about pregnancy, childbirth, women as carers and occasionally as cheap health educators (putting condoms on reluctant male lovers). Very few events, projects or media reports dared to address Aids in the way it affects the majority of women – as sexual beings with desires and needs. World Aids Day 1990 was a typical missed opportunity, which instead enabled Aids (as a topic) to become 'safe' for the general public (whoever they are). We can all rally around 'women and children' and safely shift the focus away from unpalatable homosexuality.

Yet such silence on our sexuality is not just politically motivated by the right. Even the inspiring ACT UP[2] NY book *Women, Aids and Activism* does not list desire, erotica or pornography in the index (pregnancy gets fifteen listings). The less inspiring leaflet on *Women and Aids* produced by Reading Borough Council began its listing of issues for women with 'acupuncture and earpiercing'. There is some lack of perspective here – fucking, not earpiercing, is most likely to result in HIV transmission. Yet the erotic self and the desire to express our sexuality are often negated and left out of discussions. On the few occasions when our sexuality is addressed, coercive sex is often assumed – how to say 'No' to him (usually), never how to say 'Yes', or 'I want', or 'How about . . .' Of course, our sexual orientation is assumed to be heterosexual. According to epidemiologists gathering data on HIV cases, there are now three categories of humans: homo/bisexual men, heterosexual men, and heterosexual women.

In his seminal [*sic*] work *Policing Desire – Pornography, Aids and the Media* Simon Watney brilliantly explores the connections between censorship, homophobia, sexuality and the representation of Aids in general and the effects of the epidemic on gay men in particular. His work clearly exposes the spurious methods used to deny potentially life-saving interventions for gay men. In this context censorship of sexually explicit material is not just dangerous, it verges on the murderous. So too with interventions for women. Although depressingly few, there *are* health education initiatives promoting erotic safer sex for women, and here once again censorship rears its ugly head. Perhaps the long-standing denial of our active sexuality just makes positive sexual images too hard to stomach. The extraordinary contortions resulting from the fear of being sex-positive not only present unattractive options, they also frequently lead to inaccurate information, as is clearly shown in the example cited by Cynthia Chris.[3] The excerpt is from a pamphlet by the American College of Obstetricians-Gynecologists:

> Limit your partners . . . the safest kind of sexual
> relationship is one that is mutually monogamous. If either
> you or your partner has sex with other people keep in mind
> that with each sex partner, the chance of getting infected
> rises.

Not only does this suggest that sex is somewhat unwholesome and undesirable, it also avoids essential information – we are ordered to keep in mind our rising chance of becoming infected, but not guided on how to avoid this. Furthermore, as Edward King shows, commenting on the UK Health Education Authority message, such morally contorted messages are just plain wrong:

> Many of the government's high profile national safer sex
> campaigns have advised people to 'stick to one faithful
> partner, or use a condom', rather than recognising that the
> need for safer sex is universal, and that being in a
> relationship does not obliterate the chances of previous
> infection, or of infection during sex outside the primary
> relationship.[4]

I noted earlier that what is most difficult with Aids work is not the facts but their representation, and translation into action. Facts are twisted and omitted in the various representations of Aids, and I must now turn to the problems of enabling behavioural change and developing prevention initiatives.

Health education to prevent HIV is, of course, far more than just transmitting facts. Nevertheless, the accuracy of these facts is clearly essential. As I have said, the major routes of transmission are clearly understood, yet debate still continues on, in particular, the efficiency of transmission during oral sex. There is clearly a need here to accelerate the research (curiously, research tends to neglect these fundamental concerns in favour of more lucrative ones) and simultaneously for messages to be sufficiently explicit to address what is already known. Frequent references to 'protected' or 'unprotected' sex appear to assume that sex is always intercourse. Appealing to the reality of individuals' sex lives is not just acknowledging that monogamy isn't the sole answer, it is also exploring the kinds of sexual activities people actually engage in with their one or several partner(s), and discussing them clearly and explicitly. This fudging and avoidance of direct descriptions have been particularly pointed in relation to women. In the USA one hundred cases of alleged woman-to-woman transmission of HIV have been reported to the Center for Disease Control (CDC)[5]. Whilst these statistics lead to significant debates, what has become evident is how little information exists, even within the lesbian community, about the types of sexual activities women are engaging in with one another (quite apart from the taboo subject of lesbians having sex with men). Without information about the practices, there can be no possibility for health education initiatives assessing their risk and promoting safer sex. This in turn is then complicated by the debates about efficiency of transmission methods.

Ensuring accuracy of facts is essentially a matter for research, and should be eminently possible given adequate funds. More complicated in prevention is developing ways of communication to enable behavioural changes. Theories of health education stress the need for promotion – emphasizing the positive aspects of adopting healthy behaviour, rather than dwelling on the fearful consequences of unhealthy behaviour (for example, the message 'non-smokers taste better' is more effective than 'smoking kills').

Astonishingly, many safer sex interventions for women tend towards anti-sex. Within some lesbian communities the acknowledgement of the Aids crisis has led to the development of 'safer sex' guidelines which sterilize sex practically out of existence – latex is inappropriately everywhere (irrespective of chosen fetish). There are other approaches which simply deny some sexual activities, and thus the diversity and complexity of sexual experience. The fact that non-penetrative sex is safer has led to some feminist claims that HIV justifies the long-standing claim that non-penetrative sex is 'better and more fun for women than penetration'. Unfortunately this argument tends to leave out 'some', so that those women who enjoy penetration (by penis, hand or sex toy) are presented as either unreconstructed or perverted.

Despite these extremes, there is a core of health promoters/educators seeking to prevent HIV sexual transmission within a holistic context of sexual health. This holism is rooted in the belief that sex is fundamentally good, and sexuality, sexual acts and sexual behaviour form continua. Sexual ill-health (including HIV infection) and pregnancy are small elements in a spectrum which recognizes 'that sexual activity is mainly a recreational activity'.[6] The imperative of promoting a holistic vision of sexuality is not just due to the theoretical desirability of a sexually balanced population, but because 'only an individual who has the strength to say yes to sexuality, has the strength to say no to risky sexual behavior – to make the choice'.[7] We cannot seek to prevent one sexual disease without addressing the roots of sexual dis-ease.

Within these contexts the practice of HIV prevention is, of course, complicated. The following extended example may serve to indicate some of the many difficulties inherent in promoting and eroticizing safer sex.

In the summer of 1989 I was working for Oxford's City Council and Health Authority as Aids Liaison Officer. Through discussions with OXAIDS' (the local Aids Service Organization – ASO) student co-ordinator, Edward King, we identified the need for a prevention initiative focused on students at the university and polytechnic. A particular concern was the constant focus on condoms as the only 'answer' to Aids (an approach which is factually inaccurate and ignores the diversity of sexual expression). We aimed, therefore, to present an extensive, erotic series of non-penetrative sexual options and to discuss sexual activities rather than gender preference – in particular to acknowledge the spectrum of sexual desire, and the fact that many students might not be self-identifying as anything other than heterosexual.

For many students, university or polytechnic brings with it

their first room of their own, and consequently the practical possibilities for increased sexual activity. We therefore designed a durable double-sided A2 poster to decorate their new walls. The front has a sexy photograph (fully clothed) of either a single woman, a single man or a man and woman (to cater for different preferences) with the slogan 'Take A Course In Safer Sex', and the back gives detailed information about safer sex. The text for the leaflet was developed initially by a women's and a men's writing group.[8] An agreed text went out for consultation with the appropriate authorities: City Council, Health Authority, OXAIDS, student unions and several groups of students. This process was lengthy, complicated and extremely painful. The tension between keeping to the initiative's objectives and incorporating the needs of the focus groups and stake-holders frequently brought us up against potential censorship. Eventually the final draft was delivered to the printers in summer 1990. The next I heard of it was during a 9.30 p.m. phone call to a Terrence Higgins Trust colleague. The poster had apparently been leaked to the right-wing group 'Family and Youth Concern' (FYC), who alerted the *Evening Standard*. This somewhat premature press launch (the poster wasn't even finished) led to a rushed distribution to all students and some nifty media liaison by OXAIDS. The subsequent independent evaluation of student reactions showed a positive and welcoming response, and very little offence caused.

The initiative sought both to be inclusive – addressing women and men simultaneously – and to respect gender differences (we had initially considered two separate posters). It was to facilitate this process that we worked in separate gender groups and then negotiated to develop a final draft. Negotiation is a somewhat gentle term for the debates that ensued. Whilst we respected each other's 'Women Talk . . .' and 'Men Talk . . .' sections of the poster, it was remarkable how different our core texts were and how difficult we found it to develop a common approach, let alone text. The women were ridiculed for being too 'touchy, feely' (for lines like 'Sex is . . . warm, sensuous, cuddles; flirting, teasing, fun times'), whereas the men were accused of being too blunt and removed (focusing on acts with no indication of any relationships). The men's apparent failure to have women's needs on their agenda, and vice versa, was striking to us all. We all perceived ourselves as pro-sex and relatively aware of the '-isms', yet the underlying differences in approach to eroticizing safer sex were profound. One potential conclusion could be that Simon Watney and his ilk are grossly sexist – as proposed by feminists such as Tamsin Wilton.[9] Other feminists vigorously oppose this view. It was not the sexism of the individuals we were confronting, but rather the societal differences of gender and sexuality. Ultimately the men were gently bullied into submission and we moved on to the next battleground.

Inevitably the poster was referred for consultation to the major stake-holders – the producers, OXAIDS, and my employers, the City Council and the Health Authority. The public health physician welcomed the medical accuracy and the specific focus. The Labour-run City Council had always supported the principle of this initiative, but there was a fair dose of self-censorship, anticipating the tabloids' baiting of any Labour support for sexual minorities, let alone sexually explicit literature. OXAIDS also had its concerns. Voluntary organizations often feel at the mercy of their current and future funders, and self-censorship then comes into play. There is a frequent fear that explicit sexual work may endanger funding – and indeed it often does:

> The government should cease funding the Terrence
> Higgins Trust, the AIDS charity, because it spreads homo-
> erotic propaganda among people below the age of
> homosexual consent, a pro-family pressure group said
> yesterday.[10]

Interestingly, this attack came hot on the heels of a contrary accusation, which illustrates the difficult balancing act most ASOs have to perform:

> There are major problems which continue to beset non-government Aids service organisations, ranging from serious shortages of funds, to equally serious shortages of vision and courage.
>
> For example, the Terrence Higgins Trust is evidently failing in its responsibilities to gay men at a time when there is no other national organisation which understands or represents our interests.[11]

These styles of censorship, potential and real, are well recorded elsewhere. The most interesting reactions to the poster were those of the women students. Our most important consultations – we felt – were the three months spent meeting representatives of our focus groups. We consulted a range of student groups: student union officials, lesbian and gay groups, black groups, Christians and the Student Union Women's Committee. In general at these consultations the intervention was welcomed, and helpful stylistic amendments were made. The only significant change was from our 'street' language – most students requested medical language for body parts.

The consultation with the Students' Women's Committee was the most unnerving. The poster was placed on the agenda after a discussion of their latest Campaign Against Pornography (CAP) project. There was a tense silence as the women read the draft. They objected that the use of the front – and, indeed, any – photographic image was oppressive to women, and suggested that a line drawing would be less objectifying. They considered that the leaflet content would become a source of ridicule amongst male students, who would approach it as a 'wank leaflet' (the argument that 'wanking is safe' was not well received). Yet most depressing of all were not individual arguments but the all-pervading horror. The sexual explicitness itself was taken as oppressive. To integrate the women's comments, we would have had to return to vague language avoiding any erotic feeling or description of specific sexual acts. We had not anticipated this all-pervasive erotophobia, nor these 'unholy alliances'.

We were hearing from women students what we had expected from the 'moral right'.

Anyone producing sexually explicit literature can pretty much rely on the far-right 'family' groups to object. We had anticipated their response when the initiative became public, yet had not expected a provincial printer to accelerate that process. From whom, and how, FYC received a copy of the poster before OXAIDS did is unclear. What is clear is their prurient fascination for the very topics they claim to despise. In their attacks on the Terrence Higgins Trust in May 1991, their objections are followed by lurid descriptions of the degrading/deplorable/disgusting material:

> We find this deplorable, particularly as the letter comes
> with a selection of posters showing the naked male body
> in bondage poses, emphasising the genitals.[12]

Responding to 'Take A Course In Safer Sex', FYC spokesperson Valerie Riches complained: 'It encourages every sort of hedonism and perversion under the sun. It's just disgraceful!'[13]

The basis for objecting to such sexually explicit material differs – for the student feminists it degrades women, whereas for FYC it degrades everyone by promoting perverted practices. The consequent demands of both groups are that such material should not be disseminated or should be withdrawn. The efficient and intelligent work of the OXAIDS worker, who essentially dared the media to align themselves with the far right, manoeuvred us out of that position. However, the potential harm of such a minority group is hard to overestimate.

Throughout this project we frequently had to recall that the most important reactions to the poster would be those of the students, the people for whom it was designed. The reaction of the Women's Committee was therefore a significant concern. We were fortunate in having an external evaluation conducted by a university student (James Ray, St John's College). The evaluation did not seek to calculate behavioural change (this being a long-term, not an immediate, objective) but rather the students' reaction to the initiative. Overall, the response was favourable:

> General reactions to the poster were that it was 'informing' and 'amusing'. A very small proportion (1–4%) found it 'offensive', 'shocking', or 'obscene'. Nine out of ten students had read the leaflet, half more than once. One third still had a copy of the leaflet [poster] at the time of evaluation.
>
> Women (43%) more than men (16%) thought of the leaflet as a source of information for developing a wider sexual repertoire and were more positive about experimentation and non-penetrative options.
>
> However, twice as many men found the material 'erotic' and 'helpful'. The majority did not feel uncomfortable about the leaflet and over half recognised that its purpose was not to promote sexual activity per se.[14]

The evaluation results were particularly telling in that significantly more women identified an increase in information from the poster. This apparently justified our suspicion that it was a minority of women who would be offended. Furthermore, oppositions to explicitness may have been due to an initial denial of the need for information on HIV/Aids in general.

After working slowly through this one example, and the frequent bursts of censorship it was subjected to, it is worth reflecting on why it was difficult for women to accept an erotic safer sex message. The evaluation showed that a fair proportion of women found it acceptable and informative, yet the initial rejection of the material cannot be ignored. Self-censorship is clearly one element, but one which derives from the more fundamental lack of history of positive sexual expression.

The most effective erotic safer sex initiatives have been in gay communities where there is a strong tradition of enjoying sexually explicit material. The initiatives generated by, for example, Deutsche Aids Hilfe and New York's Gay Men's Health Crisis appropriate the framework and discourse of gay porn and integrate, naturally, safer-sex techniques and fantasies. There is a community language of desire and fulfilment which can carry the message. For men who have sex with women, although few initiatives have yet been undertaken, the genre of 'straight' pornography exists. Although little HIV education has been done with this medium, there are at least community expressions of sexual desire. And indeed, initiatives by women sex workers to educate the clients of the heterosexual sex industry exist and are increasing.

Sadly, there is a general lack of sexually explicit material directed at women. At least for lesbians, erotica is increasing, especially considering the size of the community (for example, the Sheba collective collections *Serious Pleasure* and *More Serious Pleasure*, and the occasional magazine *Quim*), and within it 'safer sex' messages (appropriate or not) are integrated. However, women who have sex with men (whom even the Health Minister, Virginia Bottomley MP, identifies as being at high risk of HIV acquisition) are most alienated from any organized community sexual expression. Perhaps it is not so strange that attempts to eroticize safer sex for women are met with hostility. After all, there have not yet been many attempts to eroticize *sex*. It is well known that health promotion of any kind which integrates with existing community values and perceived needs is the most successful. Where these do not exist, we are constructing a programme without foundations. This clearly brings us back to the concept of holistic sexual health. Without a fundamental appreciation of the recreational, raunchy, enjoyable and diverse spectrum of sex, a virus in particular, or sexual ill-health in general, cannot be tackled.

And so we find ourselves back to basics: the need to explore our sexual selves, to affirm our sexual worth and to identify our sexual desires. In a sex-denying culture, which constantly ignores our sexualities, this is no simple task for women. The urgency of the Aids crisis, the challenge of making changes in our intimate, private, hidden sexual lives, might just provide an opportunity to start this process.

The student women and the Students' Women's Committee have received a poorer image here than is fair. After my dismay at their reaction to the poster, I encouraged them to invite Feminists Against Censorship to speak. They hired a small room, and it was packed. Elizabeth Wilson and Sue O'Sullivan did not receive a hostile reception, but it was not all-embracing either. Some of the women were intrigued to hear Sue O'Sullivan speaking of the diversity of desire, the spectrum of sexuality and her fear that CAP campaigns might be a way of diverting attention away from women's appreciation of their own sexuality. They asked her to return and expand on this.

Together we planned a workshop and called it 'Women Talk Sex'. One Sunday afternoon we found ourselves in a student common room clutching a bag of sex toys and a bag of porn, and surrounded by forty eager, nervous young women. Given a safe space and some fairly straightforward information (for example, how women's genitals are arranged), the women began to talk about their desires, their needs, their fears, the practices they like, the words they don't understand, how to ask for what they want, and on and on and on. We have since run four of these workshops, and they are constantly inspiring. We impart health advice – including advice about HIV – with latex demonstrations, as appropriate, but most of these workshops resemble 'consciousness-raising groups', never health lectures. The groups are starting to develop a momentum of their own, and are perhaps a small step for some women towards developing shared sexual expressions.

It is tempting, and generally misguided, to try to snatch benefits from the horrors of the Aids crisis, yet there may be some (albeit minor) positive and lasting effects. These small gains cannot justify or diminish our immense – and continuing – losses of individuals and communities, but this should not stop us from welcoming the positive. There are a few tentative advances in the UK alone: levels of sensitivity to the health needs of gay and bisexual men are improving in some centres; some areas have developed more compassionate and rational drugs policies; some terminal care facilities have improved, and the involvement of patient advocacy groups in decision-making is slowly starting. Where attitudes to sex are concerned, we shall see such positive and lasting effects only if the extraordinary struggles forced on us by the Aids crisis begin to encourage a more holistic vision of sexuality. Aids presents the possibility of a justification for the sex-negative – the 'not only is sex embarrassing, messy, immoral and perverted, it also kills' – line. It offers opportunities for the 'politically correct sex mafia': never penetrative (with anything), and the 'family' lobby: always within a loving, monogamous relationship (i.e./e.g. marriage). Or it can offer us the potential to respect the complexity of human sexuality, to welcome and enjoy our erotic selves, to embrace and celebrate the diversity of sexual desire and, from such a position of strength, make the healthy choices we want.

Many thanks to Tanneke Zeeuw for bullying me, keeping me awake, correcting my English, then word-processing the text – and remaining anti-porn throughout.

Carol Smart

Unquestionably a moral issue

Rhetorical devices and regulatory imperatives

I have been intrigued for some time by the rhetorical power of the feminist anti-pornography, pro-censorship lobby. I want, therefore, to explore issues of form more than content of speech or, perhaps more accurately, how form dictates a certain cluster of meanings which may not be the 'intention' of the speaker.

Rather than arguing whether or not activists like Catharine MacKinnon or Andrea Dworkin are *really* sexual conservatives, my focus will be the form of argumentation they use and the power that this form exercises in feminist circles. I shall argue that this form of argument uses powers of persuasion and logic which are already too grounded in specific meanings about sexuality to be wrenched out of their overdetermining historical context. I shall also suggest that as a consequence of insisting on a distinction between politics and morality, with feminist arguments being presented as addressing politics and traditional anti-feminist positions being presented as imbued with a given sexual morality, we have become blind to the moral underpinnings of much of the feminist response to pornography. It is precisely this (denied) underlying morality which gives strength to the rhetoric of feminists like MacKinnon and Dworkin.

A moral issue?

One of the major strengths of feminist analyses has been their insistence that pornography is not 'outside' power. Thus pornography has been recast in terms of power relations between men and women, between multinational corporations and women, and between the state, law and women. In taking (hetero)sexuality out of the sphere of the natural, many feminists, adopting quite different theoretical stances, began to see pornography as a form of deployment of power. Not all may agree that it represents a simple deployment of power by men against women, but at least the issue of power, and hence politics, became central. Once the issue of power was addressed, doubts were cast on the liberal moral argument that only the public sphere should be the realm of legitimate political (legal) intervention, leaving the private free of any form of investigation (analytical, legal or otherwise). The conservative moral argument had been less of an obstacle to the development of a feminist stance on matters of sexuality. The form this moral argument took in the 1960s and 1970s was so clearly pro-monogamous heterosexuality and anti-women's sexual autonomy (let alone lesbianism) that feminists were able to deconstruct this rhetoric and reframe it as a form of anti-feminist politics.

So the argument went that (all?) moral positions are merely politics in disguise, and while these liberal or conservative politics obscure the oppression of women, feminist politics reveal not only the truth of oppression but how its obfuscation occurs. It may be that we have taken the force of the critique too far and have come to imagine that, because feminism speaks of politics, it is not imbued with a wide range of values on the question of sexual morality. In observing the mote in our opponent's eye, we may have become blind to the beam in our own. But this is perhaps an unhelpful analogy, because it sees morality as a sort of ideological blemish on the purity of politics's vision and thus perpetuates the feminist aversion (which is perhaps beginning to wane) to addressing questions of morality. But my point is that much feminist work in the field of sexuality has seen questions of morality as automatically meaning the reintroduction of reactionary politics. This makes an error on two levels. First, it equates morality fixedly with a narrow Judaeo-Christian, Victorian version of sexual morality, or as a ruse for something equally problematic. Secondly, and ironically, it imbues assertions of politics with a moral superiority (because they at least are clear and open about questions of power) whilst seemingly embracing a politics without morality. Traditions of moral philosophy may not have been informed by feminist thinking, but does this mean we reject all questions of morality quite so smoothly? Even more importantly for my discussion here, have we deceived ourselves in thinking that because we are talking of (sexual) politics we have transcended (sexual) morality?

To pursue this line of argument, I want to consider two speeches (which later became articles) by Catharine MacKinnon. The first is entitled 'Not a Moral Issue',[1] the second is entitled 'On Collaboration'.[2] The former article deals in detail with the separation of morality and politics. MacKinnon argues:

> Obscenity law is concerned with morality, specifically morals from the male point of view, meaning the standpoint of male dominance. The feminist critique of pornography is a politics, specifically politics from women's point of view, meaning the standpoint of the subordination of women to men. Morality here means good and evil; politics means power and powerlessness.[3]

This argument is part of a specific strategy to distinguish between criminal laws based on issues of obscenity (good and evil) and civil laws based on issues of civil liberties and harm (politics). Thus MacKinnon and other feminists (who are not necessarily pro-censorship) are distinguishing between the feminist objection to pornography and the traditional moral objection that all sex outside marriage is dirty, representations of sex are smut, and so on. MacKinnon goes on to argue that disputes over what constitutes obscenity have always been fights between men over the best means to perpetuate the male system of power over women. Thus debates between liberals and conservatives which dominated the question of pornography in the 1960s and

1970s are interpreted as questions between men. The feminist insistence on politics is seen as avoiding the trap of perpetuating this form of debate.

My point is not that we can never distinguish politics from morality on an analytical level (although I am not sure that an amoral politics would be desirable in practice), but that, in having made this initially useful distinction, much feminist discourse has ignored the way in which fairly traditional moral ideas and rhetoric have entered feminist speech. It is as if we have come to assume that whenever a feminist speaks, what comes out is politics, not morals, no matter what she is saying. The distinction between politics and morality has absolved us of the need to be rigorous about moral issues, because morality was seen as a diversion and merely a question on the reactionaries' agenda. Perhaps as feminists we have just tended to assume that the espousal of feminist politics definitively embraces good rather than evil (taking MacKinnon's definition of morality). However, as debates over abortion, new reproductive technologies, pornography and sexuality in general have deepened, it seems we are now increasingly having to recognize that not enough has been done to deconstruct the implicit moral agenda of some feminist thought. Instead of transcending moral questions, feminism has failed, until recently, to address them sufficiently reflexively.

It is to this largely unreconstructed or undeveloped element in feminist thought which much of the anti-pornography, pro-censorship rhetoric appeals, *whilst publicly disavowing questions of morality*. Thus, whilst the content of the speech denies the traditional moral dimension, the form speaks directly to this traditional, unreconstructed moral paradigm. It may not be a deliberate strategy, but it has very serious consequences. I shall now give some consideration to examples of the form of rhetoric deployed in the pro-censorship lobby.

Speaking from the heart?

A vital strategy of the pro-censorship lobby has been the personal testimony, a form of argument which appears to be powerful in both mainstream politics and marginal pressure-group politics. I stress that it only *appears* to be successful in mainstream politics, because we should be aware by now that a broad and complex sociopolitical context all but determines which personal testimonies will be heard and when. Yet, in spite of the fact that it is not always successful, many campaigners have realized that you do not get to first base without some kind of personal account. Pressure groups, for example, know there is little point in complaining about benefit levels or housing policies unless they can produce at least one individual or family who will speak from 'personal experience' of poverty or homelessness.

As a form of political intervention the personal testimony can have an authority denied the theorist, statistician or demographer. (Personal testimony also has a special place in feminist politics, but I shall return to this later.) The personal testimony is given the status of a truth, unless the speaker can be disqualified effectively.

As second-wave feminist politics has moved increasingly towards the pressure-group model of lobbying, litigation and legislation-making, so it has gradually deployed the personal testimony in an instrumental way. I am using the term 'instrumental' here not as a criticism but as a way of distinguishing between personal testimony in consciousness-raising situations which are (ideally) safe, women-only and 'private', and personal testimonies used in highly public situations with a predetermined political goal in view. The distinction I wish to make is not simply one which sees the same account in two different fora; rather, that these become two very different accounts. As Valverde[4] has so succinctly pointed out, a story about sexual experiences in one context (a limited publication for women only) takes on a very different meaning when it appears in another (for instance, an established 'girlie' magazine). It is not just that the author may lose control of the meanings attributed to the statement (as this can never be guaranteed anyway), but the speech occupies a different symbolic space.

I want to suggest that the symbolic space, and hence the meaning, of the personal testimony (in general, but particularly concerning sexual matters) is overdetermined by an already established framework of meaning which comes into play as the narrative begins. The whole symbolic and actual framing of the narrative, usually given in the form of spoken or written evidence to a special committee, or indirectly through 'experts' speaking for those too distressed to speak for themselves, contributes to the way we can understand what is being said. Moreover, the simple repetitiveness of this strategy (one that has been used ever since the nineteenth-century purity and temperance campaigns combined with the development of lobby politics) ensures that we place accounts within a specific framework of meanings. The point is that we not only know we will be shocked and horrified, we also know that real villains will be unambiguously exposed, and that we will conclude something must be done. This is what I refer to as the 'regulatory imperative' of this form of rhetorical orchestration. The very framing of the issues and the obviousness of the harm render the value of intervention and regulation self-evident. To challenge this outcome is, of course, to side with the villains who rape, maim and exploit the innocent.

It is in this strategy that I see pro-censorship feminism embracing a very traditional form (if not content) of morality. Sharp dichotomies of good and evil are established: there is no nuance at all. Moreover, only the evil or wilfully misguided will stand in the way of putting matters right. This is precisely what MacKinnon does in her article 'On Collaboration'. She asks, for example:

> Why do women lawyers who identify as feminists buy and defend the pornographers' view of what a woman is for, what a woman's sexuality is? Why, when they look in the mirror, do they see the image of themselves the pornographers put there?[5]

Thus, in speaking against the legislation MacKinnon wishes to enact, women lawyers who call themselves feminists are portrayed as siding with the pornographers. This is the classic argument of 'Those who are not for me are against me', which contains the logic that since the 'I' of the statement occupies the moral high ground (being defender of the victimized) those who are opposed are *bad* people. This is an argument which depends on a heavily encoded set of moral messages so embedded in a Western Judaeo-Christian culture that we often fail to see its workings.

This form of argument, which might otherwise be transparent, is protected when used in conjunction with the personal testimony. For by opposing it in this context one is effectively placed in the position of speaking not against a relatively powerful woman like MacKinnon, but against less well-resourced women who have given testimony of abuse. Thus one appears to be denying their experience, or suggesting that it is of no consequence. As I shall try to argue later, this is a particular dilemma for feminists.

At this stage it might be useful to analyse a number of personal testimonies derived from different sources but following a virtually identical form:

> Formerly I had no complaints about my husband's conduct, but since the appearance of the sex films, he has changed. Now he is merely a 'bull performing to capacity', if you will, please, excuse the expression . . . And because I can no longer respond to him with what he desires, he calls me a frigid, uninterested old grandmother . . . I know with certitude that this change was caused in him by sex films because we were happily married for ten years before the films arrived. I hate to see him go to a sex film, for when he returns he falls upon me like a wild animal and I offer him too little.[6]

> Finally pornography took over and he stopped counselling. I continued on and on . . . He was drawn to pornography even though I offered him a loving

relationship and enjoyed sex with him before his involvement with pornography. Masturbation took over our sex life. I know for a fact that pornography destroyed our marriage.[7]

He called me on the telephone and he said that he had seen several short pornographic films and that he felt very horny . . . So he asked if he could come over specifically to have sex with me. I said yes, because at the time I felt obligated as a girl friend to satisfy him . . . This encounter differed from others previous, it was much quicker, it was somewhat rougher, and he was not aware of me as a person. I feel what I have to say here is important because I feel what he did, he went to this party, saw pornography, got an erection, got me to inflict his erection on. There is a direct causal relationship there.[8]

MS MACKINNON: Chairman White, might I be able to be permitted to read a letter which is written by Women Against Pornography . . .?

'Although our work has not curbed the power and influence of the pornography industry, it has made us acutely aware of the magnitude and severity of the harm done to girls and women by pornography. We have received calls and letters from women whose employers and co-workers have used pornography to harass and intimidate them. We have heard from wives whose husbands have pressured them to act out their favorite pornographic scenarios . . . Up to this point, however, there has been nothing we could do to help women victimized by pornography take action against those who victimize them. The proposed amendment to Title 7 would provide us with the means to help these women receive justice.'[9]

These four extracts come from three different sources. The first was a letter written to a doctor friend of Mary Whitehouse at the height of her campaign against pornography (and also against a much wider range of so-called permissive views on sexuality and the family). The letter is published in her book *Whatever Happened to Sex?* The second extract comes from the official transcript of proceedings of the US Attorney General's Commission on Pornography in 1985/6. The proceedings in this case were selected and edited by Phyllis Schlafly, author of *The Power of the Positive Woman* and other anti-feminist writings. The edited collection is entitled *Pornography's Victims*. The last two extracts come from the transcripts of the Public Hearings on the MacKinnon and Dworkin pornography ordinances in Minneapolis in December 1983 and were published by *Everywoman* magazine, under the title *Pornography and Sexual Violence: Evidence of the Links*, as part of a campaign to put new legislation against pornography on the political agenda in the UK.

My comments on these extracts are not of the usual sociological variety which might typically suggest that those who give evidence are never representative of a general population, or that further selections from an already self-selected group hardly constitutes a meaningful sample. While these would be quite useful comments, I am more interested in the fact that over a span of some ten years, from different sources and avenues of publication, the same story repeats itself. We have the same personal testimony harnessed to quite different political goals. It takes a specific narrative form with certain essential ingredients. A key ingredient is that without pornography these abuses would not happen, or that before the individual's discovery of pornography all was well. Pornography is presented as a drug to which men become addicted, so we have the slippery-slope element as well as the idea of people falling into the grip of something alien.

What becomes blurred in the first three more 'personal' accounts is whether what is found objectionable is the arousal of desire in men or the fact that their partners are ambivalent about, or quite appalled by, becoming the object of that arousal. This is an important distinction to make because accounts like these can produce a powerful, even visceral response, but whether this is to the idea of (male) sexual arousal or to the idea of using women (or other human beings) as means to an end is not always clear. The ensuing question is: why does our concern about the 'use' of women and others as means to an end seem to become a matter for alarm only in a sexual context?

Of course, there is an answer to this question from a radical feminist perspective: namely, that sexual oppression and exploitation are not only the source of all oppressions of women, but the means of disguising all sorts of other oppressions. But this is not what most personal testimonies say. These testimonies are much more likely to say that there is nothing wrong with (hetero)sex; the problem is unwanted (hetero)sex – a distinction of which MacKinnon is particularly scathing. Moreover, there is a strong theme in many of the testimonies given to the Attorney General's Commission and to the Public Hearings in Minneapolis: that there is a distinction to be made between natural and unnatural sexual practices. Pornography is seen to provoke unnatural sex. Once again, a distinction must be made between whether the horrified response occasioned by these accounts relates to hearing of 'unnatural' sexual practices, or whether it is because these practices are inflicted on unwilling partners.

I would suggest that the 'harm' element based on assertions of coercion operates not to produce the outraged response, but to make the account tellable. Thus, while for feminism in general the problem with pornography and certain forms of sexuality is that they may be directly coercive or related in a more complex way to a general coercion of women, in this wider political and public context I want to suggest that the 'harm' issue does quite different 'work' to the work it performs within feminist discourses. References to force, being drugged, being overpowered or simply being obliged, allow the speaker or her representative to tell the tale. If the tale were told without the harm dimension it would, of course, simply become a standard pornographic story in and of itself. What I am proposing is that ways of speaking about (hetero)sex are now thoroughly overdetermined, and that only two forms seem open: one is the pornographic tale (I did it and enjoyed it); the other is the anti-pornographer's tale (They did it to me and it was terrible). Feminism in the West (both first and second wave) has largely eschewed the former and employed the latter, which is unfortunately a narrative constructed on very different premises to those of feminism.

These accounts are therefore heard and read by an audience that *already* knows sex is harmful (even if ideas about who the real 'victims' are may vary). Thus the surprise is not in the rediscovery of what is already known; the visceral response comes from hearing about what is done. This is not simply a reiteration of the point that these accounts may be enjoyed as pornography is enjoyed, and therefore feminists should not be the vehicle for providing such accounts. My point is that in taking objections to pornography into the lobbying/evidence-giving mode, the pro-censorship feminists have stepped into a hermeneutic circle where certain meanings already dominate. The whole issue almost inevitably becomes one of (narrow, Judaeo-Christian, sexual) morality, not one of a politics which has transcended morality. There is therefore an undesirable slippage from one frame of reference into another which is quite antithetical to most of feminism's diverse aims.

The examples I have provided above may give the impression of too brief a history of the narrative mode I am discussing. Indeed, if I could point to only a decade or so of the deployment of such accounts regarding sexual matters and legal reforms, the power of such forms would be far less significant than I am claiming. However, it is possible to illustrate a much more firmly entrenched set of practices starting in the latter half of the nineteenth century. The 'confessionary' mode of talking about sex obviously predates this historical moment,[10] but the harnessing of the confession with the context of coercion to make the tale publicly palatable, and give it the force to generate legislation, was a specifically Victorian development. The melodramatic form, with its extremes of good and evil, of innocence sullied and lives ruined, was widely used and understood in Victorian writing. Journalists like W.T. Stead and publishers like Alfred Dyer deliberately used this mode in their vigilance campaigns on issues of the so-called White Slave trade and the age of consent.[11]

In 1881 Dyer reported to House of Lords Select Committee on the Protection of Women and Girls that he had spoken to many women who had been 'taken' or decoyed to Belgium and forced into brothels. This is part of the text of one account he relayed to the Committee. It was extracted from a letter by a young woman named as Jones:

> When I left London six months ago I was as innocent as a child, but it was soon taken from me and through compulsion I was obliged to take part in deceit and other things worse . . . [B]y God's help, I will prove to them that I have been sinned against not sinned. I cannot express my feelings on this slavery . . . once free and able to act, I will leave nothing undone to rescue girls that are unfortunately placed in these dens.[12]

The Select Committee heard many such accounts, and a large number of letters from young women were printed as part of the proceedings. They tell of promises of marriage from complete strangers, of charming men and helpful women who suddenly become cruel, of uncaring authorities, and so on.

These accounts can be compared to an account given a century later by Linda Marchiano, a key witness to the Minneapolis hearings in 1983:

> I feel I should introduce myself and tell you why I feel I am qualified to speak out against pornography. My name today is Linda Marchiano. Linda Lovelace was the name I bore during a two and a half year period of imprisonment. . . .

> It all began in 1971 . . . A girlfriend of mine came to visit me with a person by the name of Mr Charles Traynor. He came off as a considerate gentleman, asking us what we would

like to do [etc. . . .] Needless to say I was impressed, and
started to date him.

When I decided to head back north and informed Mr
Traynor of my intention, that was when I met the real Mr
Traynor and my two and a half years of imprisonment
began. He began a complete turnaround and beat me up
physically and began the mental abuse; from that day
forward my hell began.[13]

The important question about these testimonies is not, it
seems to me, whether they are 'true' or 'false'[14] but the way
in which they draw the reader into a set of apparently logical
connections leading to the seemingly inevitable consequence
that legislation must be introduced to end the abuse so
graphically detailed. It is virtually impossible to resist this
regulatory impulse without actually – or apparently – denying the harm of the experience recounted by the narrator. All
arguments based on grounds that new legislation will not
work as intended, or that it will catch a wider, 'innocent'
group in its sweep, or that it will be used by the wrong
people for the wrong purposes, are easily condemned as
collaborative prevarication.

MacKinnon's article 'On Collaboration'[15] is an example of
this. In it she elides some feminists' concern about using the
state apparatus against pornography with being *for* pornography. Anti-censorship becomes transposed as pro-porn.
The way in which the argument has been structured allows
of only two positions: anti-porn/pro-censorship and pro-
porn/anti-censorship. This binary dichotomy locates the
moral high ground with the pro-censorship lobby. In this
formulation good can easily be distinguished from evil.

Speaking like a woman
I have suggested above that there are particular difficulties
for feminists in responding to personal accounts and testimonies, and I now propose to add this dimension to my

argument. On the face of it one might imagine that feminists would 'see through' the device of using personal accounts to achieve a political goal. After all, we have rejected accounts suggesting that pornography helps individual men to avoid raping women, or that pornography saves marriages. Could it be that our response to the personal testimony is dictated by whether we agree with the perceived political goals it serves? While it would be sanctimonious to discount this suggestion completely, there is a deeper issue at stake.

Second-wave feminism in the UK developed a core principle through the practice of consciousness-raising which maintained that every woman's story was valid and should be acknowledged rather than silenced. This principle, which may have been honoured more in the breach than in its observance, has become even more elevated with the recognition that many women were indeed silenced by a largely white, middle-class movement. But now a further dimension has been added to the status of 'speaking' one's personal story: the influence of standpoint feminism.

Standpoint feminism appears to be the place where the politics of the women's movement(s) meshes with the construction of knowledge in more academic terms. Standpoint feminism has been most clearly articulated by Dorothy Smith, who is a proponent, and Sandra Harding, who is more critical.[16] Basically, this theoretical argument suggests that the standpoint of women provides the most accurate or truthful account of the workings of patriarchal society. However, standpoint feminism does not celebrate the vision of all women, only those who have collectivized and reinterpreted their experiences through processes of consciousness-raising or similar political activity. Hence standpoint feminism does not actually claim that all women have the correct political analysis of patriarchy, only those who have been politically transformed into feminists. Therefore an implicit hierarchy of knowledge is retained. I stress *implicit* because when standpoint feminism becomes rhetorical it fails to distinguish between women and feminists. Thus MacKinnon claims to speak from the standpoint of (all?) women, yet she retains the distinction between feminists and other women when she suggests that her opponents cannot be real feminists.

Now the problem with standpoint feminism in the debate on pornography is that it claims there is a *women's* position on porn which has been arrived at through the *feminist* process of consciousness-raising. Thus the feminist who speaks against this overly simplistic view commits two major sins. First, she speaks against the wishes of ordinary women; secondly, she fails as a feminist. The reluctance to commit these 'sins' becomes particularly problematic in the face of personal accounts in a public forum where personal testimonies become forms of evidence. It is even more problematic when women are giving statements on their experiences of incest, sexual abuse and sexual harassment, and are unproblematically linking these experiences to pornography. A rejection of this linkage becomes interpreted as a rejection of their experience.

The subsequent silencing of alternative analyses need not be interpreted as a deliberate strategy. It appears much more likely to be an outcome of a series of initially unconnected but gradually related events such as the rise of the New Right, the increasing concern over sexual violence, and the availability of a form of lobbying/argumentation that seems to pay dividends. Moreover, the difficulty for anti-censorship feminists in speaking against pro-censorship feminism, once personal testimonies have been deployed, has its roots in a much deeper problem within feminist approaches to the construction of knowledge and the relationship between knowledge, truth and experience.

Concluding remarks

Sexuality has always been a site of contested meaning for feminists, and we should hardly be surprised when differences erupt. But it seems to me that it is vital to be clear about what these differences are. The more forms of argument derived from strategies of moral panic and moral vigilance are used, or personal testimonies are deployed for instrumental reasons, the more we are forced to retreat into uncomprehending, opposing camps. Whilst I am deeply concerned about the faith being placed in a legal solution to pornography (let alone women's oppression generally[17]) what I have attempted to do in this essay is to draw attention to another development which I find equally worrying: the tendency to use pragmatic lobbying devices, most particularly in controversial areas for feminism. Another example would be in the field of reproductive technologies, where there are deep divisions between feminists, but the device of turning personal testimonies into political evidence is becoming manifest. Many forms of feminism may have used this sort of strategy in the past (for instance, asking prostitutes or lone mothers or battered women to speak to Select Committees) but if we are to continue to do this, especially in contested areas, we should perhaps become more acutely aware that the *content* of our message may be overlaid by meanings already encoded in the *form* we are using. In such circumstances we may find that we further empower precisely the wrong people, regardless of our intentions.

Jane Mills

Classroom conundrums
Sex education and censorship

In 1922 the birth-control campaigner Marie Stopes received the following letter:

> I am unmarried but the sex instinct is tremendously strong in me and your theory of the normal sex cycle in women is absolutely confirmed in my own case.
>
> I feel that desire is absolutely right and natural and the normal heritage of every healthy woman whether married or not.
>
> But I am not quite sure whether even under strong sexual desire it is ever *right* to induce excitation of the clitoris and the wonderful thrill which is the outcome of such an action? It is intensely difficult for an ardent woman to always refrain even when she deliberately diverts her thoughts into other channels. Do you think that an occasional indulgence viz two or three times a month is detrimental to health – or disloyal to the highest and best we know? It may interest you to know that I am 41 years of age and only realised the possibility of self satisfaction at 32.[1]

Marie Stopes's reply was one to which, in the more sophisticated 1990s, we might respond with a mixture of amusement and horror: 'I think for young people action such as you describe is very harmful, but for women over 30, if they understand it is dangerous, and control the use to not more than twice a month, it is *sometimes* beneficial.'[2]

We've come a long way ... or have we? Interviews with young people, teachers and sex educators show that we haven't. A feminist literature teacher at a girls' school in South London believes that silence on the subject of female pleasure can be just as harmful as a reactionary moral code:

> We can give them the basic facts about what goes where and how babies are conceived and even how babies aren't conceived. But there's a big silence when it comes to talking about why two people who don't want a baby might want sex. Why or, God forbid, how they might actually enjoy sex. I feel I have to skate over passages in Shakespeare or Keats which suggest sex might be fun or even beautiful. Mention the erotic? Forget it.

A recent British survey of young people found that over half the sixteen-year-olds were sexually experienced, with 41 per cent losing their virginity before they were sixteen; of these only 28 per cent used condoms and 89 per cent considered that they had no chance, or only a slight chance, of contracting HIV.[3] Facts and figures like these are constantly bandied about to support almost any argument in debates about sex education. The traditionalists, conflating ignorance with innocence, claim that sex education encourages young people to have sex 'before they're ready'; the progressives cite high levels of information and low teenage pregnancy rates in countries such as the Netherlands.

It is clear from this and many other surveys that a high proportion of young people in the UK are both sexually active and massively ill-informed. It is also clear that most young people receive their sex education from the media, from women's magazines, from pornography and from their peer group. According to one sex educator: 'There's no decent sex education in schools; they don't know much. We still get the myths like you can't get pregnant the first time ...'[4]

Society finds it convenient to treat sex in one of three

ways: as a problem (agony aunts), as a biological fact (experts in white coats) or as a guilty secret (the dirty joke, the prostitute). Sex educators, however, tend to concentrate on the protection angle – how not to get pregnant, how not to catch a sexually transmitted disease, how not to be sexually abused or raped. The female body is perceived as a site of passive vulnerability exposed to the danger of rampant male hypersexuality. What surveys never seem to explore and few sex educators dare to promote is the pleasure aspect of sex. As one teacher put it: 'I am very concerned that many children are taught about the dangers of AIDS but not about the role of sex in a natural life. Many seem to become terrified of sex. This cannot be good in a free society.'[5]

In short, sex education is in a mess, with sex educators not necessarily even aware of the constraints upon talking openly and freely about empowering women to pursue the possibilities for pleasure: 'Do we ever mention what the clitoris is for? You've got me thinking there. I doubt we do,' reports a fourth-form tutor at a girls' state secondary school.

In theory, schools take a large part of the responsibility for providing the young with sex education. It is partly fear that keeps young people from talking to their parents about sex – fear of being thought ignorant in a society that frequently equates ignorance with stupidity, or fear of being thought too knowledgeable when ignorance is also equated with innocence and knowledge with experience. A sixteen-year-old young woman I interviewed confirmed this: 'If I asked my mum about what it feels like to do it she'd either think I was doing it or that I was about to.'

Ignorance and, presumably, fear also play a part in parental reluctance to take the initiative in talking to their own children about sex. As one mother of a sixteen-year-old put it:

> I prefer her teacher to teach her about sex. It's kind of
> difficult to mention anything apart from the basic facts
> about periods and so on. Partly because, if I'm quite

honest, I don't really know about things like ovulation and hormones and all that. But also I don't think it's right for her to pry into my private sex life.

The 1986 Education Act requires schools to have a policy on sex education because, as the circular that accompanied it acknowledged: ' . . . some parents may not feel able to discuss sexual matters fully and freely with their children.'[6] The Act reinforces a generally felt ambivalence towards the subject and has created widespread confusion. No action has been taken to create an environment in which teachers can discuss the subject both freely and fully. On the one hand the circular states: 'Appropriate and responsible sex education is an important element in the work of schools in preparing pupils for adult life'; on the other, the Act places responsibility upon school governors to consider whether sex education should form any part whatsoever of the curriculum. The result has been anything but comprehensive or clear. A 1990 survey of 338 teachers in 180 schools revealed that over one-fifth had no policy at all. In a further 10 per cent there was a difference of opinion as to whether the school had a policy or not.[7]

The confusion does not end with the formulation of a sex education policy approved by school governors. Many teachers are unhappy with the compromise situation that the Education Act has introduced. As one woman sex educator put it: 'Parents on the whole want to leave it up to teachers and teachers are too scared of offending parents [who also sit on the governing body] to discuss sexuality.' A head teacher of a mixed comprehensive admitted: 'To be quite honest, I think my staff wish that our governors had decided that it should be banned.' More bluntly, a teacher of Personal and Social Education studies in a girls' secondary school told me:

It takes not so much courage as madness for a teacher to teach sex education these days. Yes, we've got a policy and the governors have approved it but after every lesson I just cross my fingers – there's bound to be at least one parent who would complain if they knew what was being discussed in class. Luckily most of the girls don't tell their parents.

Educators react to the pressures on them in a variety of ways. Some schools leave it to the science department, which tends to provide a basic 'facts of life' approach. Many pupils find this an unsatisfactory solution, as a nineteen-year-old from a mixed comprehensive reflected: 'I never got told nothing – well, nothing that was any use.' A fifteen-year-old mother never discovered how to deal with her sexual feelings: 'We were told all about how babies were born. We got the biology bit of it all. But what I needed to know was how not to have a baby – and keep my boyfriend.' Teachers are also aware that this is unsatisfactory. A science teacher at a mixed state secondary school explained her feelings:

I feel it is most unfair. I have to cover the core curriculum requirements in science and make sure my pupils reach certain standards as well as take on board the extra-curriculum teaching of sex education. In science I have to cover basic reproduction – but, as we all know, sex isn't just about reproduction. And nor should sex education be.

Not all sex educators are convinced of the role that governmental authority and legitimacy play in establishing state school provision of sex education. This doubt is stressed by Thomas Szasz:

The term sex education conceals more than it reveals. It conceals the specific social, educational, and economic policies used to implement sex education, the moral values secretly encouraged and discouraged; and last, but not least, the problems that derive inexorably from involving the school system – and hence the government –

in defining what constitutes education in human
sexuality.[8]

The easy way out for many schools is to ignore sexuality and
concentrate on the basic facts of life and/or issues of 'human
relationships'.

The influence of the women's movement of the late 1960s
and early 1970s did much to improve the teaching of sex
education in schools precisely because human relationships
were added to the agenda. No longer were children to be told
simply how rabbits reproduced and what menstruation was
all about. The facts of life were placed within a context of that
magic word 'relationships'. This was undeniably better than
the sort of sex education which preceded it, but some
feminist sex educators today believe that all this talk about
human relationships is, as one put it:

> . . . just another way of not talking about sexuality. It's
> been seized upon by those who wish to deny female
> sexuality or who have a vested interest in reinforcing
> conservative gender roles – it's all too easy for it to turn
> into a general 'how to please your man' sort of discussion.
> It means *not* talking about sexuality, especially not about
> female empowerment.

One of the constraints of the system imposed by the Education Act is that once the school governors have endorsed the
official policy, some teachers do not feel free to deviate from
it in lessons other than those specifically set up to deal with
the subject. 'How many religious instruction teachers dare to
even mention the Song of Songs?' asked a science teacher at a
mixed state secondary school. Desire, especially female
desire, is not on the government's agenda. Nor, it would
seem, is it on the agenda of many school governors.

In recent years sexual harassment has been included as a
part of sex education from primary school onwards. A

woman teacher at a mixed primary school admitted: 'I find myself concentrating on the "bad touches" and seldom mentioning the "good touches". I think I'm too embarrassed.' Whatever happened to notions of infantile sexuality? A male teacher at a primary school feels that the subject is too hot to handle, and that the anti-Freudianism of some feminists coincides with the views of those who support the repression of female sexuality: 'I'd really like some instruction on all this. But I feel if I dared even mention the idea of childhood sexuality my colleagues – especially, if I dare say so, my female colleagues – would think I was a paedophile.'

The problem persists into secondary schools; according to one sex educator: 'Esther Rantzen goes down well with parents and teachers because what she's really saying is that all we have to do is tell girls to say "No".' All too often women are presented as potential victims, men as uncontrollably supersexual: 'They [the teachers] scared the shit out of me. They went on and on about how randy men were all the time and how we women were so vulnerable,' said a nineteen-year-old young woman educated at a girls' school. This was confirmed by an eighteen-year-old from a mixed school: 'I asked my teacher how come if we could learn to say no, for some reason boys weren't able to say no. She just told me I wasn't taking the subject seriously so I shut up. I still wonder, actually.'

Perhaps because of the government's initial disastrous attempt to educate the nation about AIDS by using fear with an advertising campaign featuring icebergs and gravestones, and because of its decision a couple of years ago to pulp several thousand copies of a leaflet to which many sex educators had reacted positively, most teachers now realize that HIV/AIDS education has to be their responsibility. But here, too, confusion and self-censorship reign.

The majority of schools discuss HIV and AIDS at fourth- and fifth-form level: most pupils assert that this is too late. Teachers reveal themselves to be much happier when talking to their pupils about the scientific and moral aspects of the subject than when giving explicit or precise information about risks and prevention in relation to sexual activity. When asked whether their teaching about safer sex conveyed the understanding that there are many safe, non-penetrative sexual activities such as mutual masturbation and massage only 11.8 per cent reported that this was so; 30 per cent thought it to be so only 'to some extent' and 36.4 per cent thought it to be either not so or 'definitely not so'.[9] Talking about the process of viral transmission or about the moral responsibility for the use of the condom is easier, less embarrassing and less likely to incur parental outrage, than being explicit about sexual pleasure. Most young people think mutual masturbation means masturbating in front of each other, and a male teacher at a mixed secondary school expresses another concern: 'All this talk about condoms means one thing – vaginas are only there for penises to go into them.'

Governmental intervention on the subject of homosexuality has directly affected the teaching of sex education. As one female sex educator put it: 'It's difficult to define but clause 28 [Local Government Act 1988] and now clause 25 [Criminal Justice Bill 1991] have had a serious and very negative knock-on effect.' Supporters of these clauses and of sections 18 and 46 of the Education (No. 2) Act 1986 claimed that their purpose was to 'protect' children and young people from the 'cult of homosexuality'. The Department of Education and Science circular states unequivocally: 'There is no place in any school in any circumstances for teaching which advocates homosexual behaviour, which presents it as the "norm", or which encourages homosexual experimentation by pupils.' It is clear that the main effect has been to deny young people in maintained schools the right to know about sex and sexuality. According to a young woman in a sixth form at a mixed state school: 'One of the reasons we don't get taught anything about AIDS at my school until the fifth form is, I believe, because they're all too worried about mentioning the taboo word "homosexual".'

Despite the fact that the Department of the Environment guidelines accompanying the Local Government Act explained that 'Section 28 . . . will not prevent the objective discussion of homosexuality in the classroom, nor the counselling of pupils concerned about their sexuality', both teachers and pupils widely report a reluctance to raise the subject: self-censorship is safest. Asked how she dealt with homosexuality, a teacher of English at a girls' state school replied:

> We have a book-box of non-curriculum books which pupils can borrow. In it I've put *Annie on My Mind* and some Judy Blume novels which deal with lesbianism. I don't ever bring the subject up but feel I have to wait until they do.[10]

She also discussed one of the main problems confronting both teacher and pupil in all-girl schools:

> For some parents, one of the main reasons for sending their daughters to an all-girl school is to postpone the subject of sexuality. 'After they've passed their exams' seems to be the prevailing attitude. They believe it's a way of keeping their daughters unsexual. So if we teach sex education at an early stage of puberty or adolescence (which we do) some parents become most unhappy.

This particular teacher is committed to the equal-opportunities policy of her local authority in London and sees it as a help in forming her approach to sex education, in particular to female sexuality:

> We have to educate girls for choice, for choosing. They must be brought up to see themselves as a chooser with autonomy. This of course means that lesbianism ought to be treated as an option and sexuality ought to be taught with a 'choose what *you* like' approach.

She praised the way in which her local authority had forced teachers to investigate their own heterosexism: 'Until recently not even I [she is a lesbian] had really put this issue on my agenda.' On the subject of pleasure she expressed some reservations: 'I don't think any of us know how to deal with it.'

This teacher, like many others, has a high percentage of Muslim pupils. Multiculturalism is a feature of many teachers' lives, but not necessarily of their consciousness. A sixth-form tutor at a mixed school told me: 'To be honest I'd never read the Qur'an until I came across a leaflet from the BBC about their sex education programmes that I was showing. It gives details about which parts of the videos would offend Muslims. 'This booklet explains neutrally: 'Some parents and teachers will have objections to certain parts of this series for religious reasons. These notes detail which parts may be offensive to Muslims and Roman Catholics.'[11]

Problems arising from ignoring or failing to understand multiculturalism have been widely discussed in feminist publications and the mass media. The BBC booklet reveals the headache that fundamentalism, be it Muslim or Christian, creates for sex educators. Programme 1 talks of masturbation as a natural phenomenon, but the programme notes spell out that:

> The Qur'an forbids masturbation, and the Sunnah only allows it if a man is financially unable to marry or if masturbation prevents adultery . . . Catholicism holds that it is against the natural law . . . Surprisingly [for Muslims] wet dreams do not pose problems, save that girls should not know too much about a man's wet dream. Equally a boy should not have anything but the biological explanation behind a period.

Programme 3 is considered acceptable to Muslims: 'The love-making scene is set within a strong Islamic context – for the procreation of children in a loving married relationship. Woman's orgasm is encouraged in the Qur'an . . . as a husband is told to treat his wife in a kind, tender way.' Catholicism is covered too: 'Sexual intercourse is presented in a loving, married relationship and should therefore be acceptable. Some may find the nakedness of the man and woman in the bathroom inappropriate.'

Many teachers in multicultural schools find themselves pressured into structuring their sex education policy to conform to masculinist fundamentalist views. Misogyny goes unchallenged, as do traditionalist views of gender and class or caste. A twenty-one-year-old white woman told me how she had been taught: 'I never learned at school that one interpretation of the Qur'an suggests a woman can divorce her husband if he doesn't give her sexual pleasure.' A teacher at a girls' school in North London with a high Muslim intake revealed yet another problem:

It took me some time, I was so scared and ill-informed, to realize that not all Muslims are fundamentalists. It was some Muslim parents who hinted that I had a rather strict view of their religion when it came to sex education. On the other hand, I also had some pupils from very fundamentalist families. I guess I found it easier, safer, to pitch everything at the fundamentalist level.

The emphasis on placing sexual intercourse within the context of a 'loving married relationship' is something that baffles this sixteen-year-old at a mixed school: 'My parents aren't married or anything but it never really worried me until this teacher kept going on about husbands and wives having sex. She made me feel my mum was a prossie.' But teachers have little option, since the 1986 Education Act requires that sex education ' . . . is given in such a manner as to encourage those pupils to have due regard to moral considerations and the value of family life'.[12] It takes both imagination and courage for a teacher to challenge this ruling, as this sixth-form tutor has discovered:

I find it quite difficult to keep my own views out of the lessons. It's also quite daft. I've got so many kids whose parents have split up, others whose parents are lesbian couples. They know I live with a man and we're not married. And yet here I am supposedly having to extol the virtues of married family life. But I guess that's what's expected of me.

Suzie Hayman, author of several sex education books for teenagers, sums it up like this:

. . . teachers, in accordance with government guidelines, present sex as something that happens within the context of a morally responsible relationship, i.e. marriage. They're not allowed to address teenagers directly and talk about what you 'do' with someone you fancy. So sex education is sterile and remote – unconnected with what young people want to know.[13]

Pornography is yet another aspect of sex education that introduces an element of censorship into the working lives of teachers. Look at it from the perspective of a seventeen-year-old female pupil at a mixed comprehensive: 'It's weird. I know porno mags are supposed to be anti-women and all that. But looking at the pictures makes me feel quite . . . sort of . . . you know, randy sometimes. I suppose that makes me feel kind of bad.' It's no less difficult for her teacher.

God! I feel confused about this whole debate. I'm totally against pornography. It actually makes me feel sick when I see the boys in my class passing it round. I used to confiscate it. But now I try to use it as a point of discussion. I think the girls know how I feel but the boys probably think I'm just an uptight spinster. I wish there was something I could use in order to say to both the boys and girls 'women like sex too'.

Anti-pornography groups, MP Clare Short and her Page 3 campaign, and feminists like Andrea Dworkin, all use pornography as a metaphor for rape. But as the feminist writer Eileen Phillips points out: ' . . . anti-porn arguments [which] conflate power with violence and reduce sexism to sex, position the anti-porn movement as reactionary.'[14] Informing pupils about self-defence – both intellectual and physical – is an important part of sex education that many teachers take seriously, like this woman, a visiting sex educator: 'I use pornography deliberately in my lessons to tell both the girls and the boys that women aren't victims. We're not passive. We're not just toys for males to play with.' Another teacher suspects that the pornography debates which take place in the classroom all too often revolve around the issue of censorship because 'That's the easy way out. We all sit there looking at soft-core porn and get heated about female victims. We never get round to talking about the clitoris that is sort of staring us in the face.'

This issue is clearly complex, and one which divides both feminists and non-feminists. The science teacher already quoted said she could afford to be unequivocal about pornography: 'But then it's easy for me – there's nothing biological about it – it's to do with the realm of fantasy and I don't have to deal with that in a science class.' The Personal and Social Education teacher in a London girls' school found it more complicated: 'I do have to deal with fantasy. That's an important part of a young person's sex education. I don't want my pupils to feel guilty about their fantasies.' Another teacher bravely revealed that pornography was something she welcomed into the classroom:

> . . . because, to be honest, it's yet another way of avoiding talking about female pleasure. I can use pornography to concentrate on the exploitation of females. But the clitoris? It never gets a look-in. I somehow don't feel I can mention female pleasure to my pupils. How come I spend so much time stressing female pain? I never thought of it in this way before.

It ought to go without saying that sex educators have an incredibly difficult job. So, too, do young people growing up in a patriarchal society. Attempting to negotiate sexist assumptions and pressures is far from easy. Those who confuse ignorance with innocence have a responsibility to bear for much of the pain that is experienced by both females and males, not only in youth but also in adulthood. The letters received by agony aunts, the Marie Stopeses of today, bear witness to this ignorance and pain. As feminists, we must also bear some of the responsibility. It *is* easier to talk to our children, our pupils and our friends' children about female exploitation, about male domination, and about prevention of illness and the need for self-protection than about pleasure. And it's easier to talk about human relationships than about sexual pleasure and how to achieve it. Unwanted pregnancies, unwanted children, sexually transmitted diseases, sexual abuse and harassment, rape – all these can be prevented to an extent and young people, especially girls, have to be empowered to protect themselves. No teacher wants to see their pupils suffer, especially not from anything caused by ignorance. Given the pressures and government-sanctioned constraints, it is understandable why a teacher's priorities might give female sexual pleasure a low rating.

But to what extent is this emphasis upon protection the result of societal pressures and government policies which aim to maintain a silence about the positive aspects of female sexuality? To what extent are teachers aware of what they're doing? And, given these pressures, how does the sex educator establish a positive strategy of pleasures, freedoms and desires?

There are many interrelated factors which result in silence on the issue of female desire and pleasure among sex educators. The censoring of free and full information about female sexuality is clearly one of the outcomes of government legislation that has affected sex education in recent years. The absence of any comprehensive sex education training for the educators themselves must also be remedied. A young geography teacher at a mixed comprehensive laughed when asked about what she had learned at college:

> Training at college? You must be joking. We got probably only about two days in the whole three years. They took the view that unless you were doing Biology or PSE [Personal and Social Education] you didn't need to know anything. This is so unrealistic – there's probably no lesson when the subject of sex doesn't come up. What do they think is going on in my students' heads when I start teaching them about population increases?

Some schools take the matter sufficiently seriously to send their teachers on courses organized by the Family Planning Association, the National Association for Pastoral Care in Education, or their local Education Authority. But the recession, aided and abetted by the low priority which the government awards sex education, is beginning to hit hard; increasingly, such courses are seen as expensive luxuries. A sixth-form tutor expressed her frustration:

> I feel we're fighting a losing battle. We're so restricted by clause this and clause that. But worst of all are the cuts. With sex education treated as an optional extra and economic pressure on the school to attract pupils – they're more like clients these days – how they feel about themselves doesn't get taken seriously. You talk to me about empowering young women to realize their sexual potential and I want to just say 'give me a break'. But maybe we'll get there by covert means. It seems the only way we'll ever achieve it.

Covert. This means secret, disguised, covered. Is this what young women need, or deserve? Secrecy reinforces and perpetuates guilt and fear. Isn't this precisely what has disenfranchised women in the sexual political debate since the days of Marie Stopes and beyond? Isn't this what has prevented women from discovering their sexual potential? Censorship, whether direct or indirect, conscious or unconscious, imposed from above or from within the self, cannot lead to female sexual empowerment. The understandable need to protect girls and young women all too often provides sex educators with a welcome escape from discussing a very real issue: that of female desire and pleasure. There is a silence in our schools on this. It is a silence that has to be broken.

With thanks to: Janet Holland, Gill Lenderyou, Lucy Thane, Rachel Thomson, Ursula Owen, Marion Virgo, and all the young people and teachers who told me what it is like.

Harriett Gilbert

So long as it's not sex and violence

Andrea Dworkin's Mercy

This is the story. A poor young woman, alone in the world, refuses to compromise her ideals in exchange for a man's protection. As a result every man she meets feels free to humiliate, torture, mutilate or rape her. Even when one man rescues her from another it is almost always so that he, in turn, can abuse our heroine's virtue. Yet somehow, through a kind of magic inertia, she survives: an eternally renewable object of male sadistic pleasure.

Is this the synopsis of a pornographic novel? Of course, you might reply, if you happen to have read Sade's *Justine*,[1] of which it is a summary. It is also, however, a summary of Andrea Dworkin's *Mercy*:[2] a novel which cannot be pornography – can it? – since its author is one of the leading theorists and campaigners against the genre.

On its own, the above might appear to be a fatuous question. Few would seriously suggest that a story which has been removed from its narrator's voice, shorn of its imagery, slimmed to its bones, could be judged pornographic or otherwise. That would be like insisting that any depiction of a vagina, let us say, must invariably be pornographic regardless of its context. And yet it isn't just the story line of *Mercy* that echoes Sade's 'tortured and torturing' novel. There are other respects in which Dworkin's book is hard to distinguish from its predecessor: a work which, with its graphic depictions of 'the sexually explicit subordination of women', many would suppose to fulfil every one of Dworkin's own criteria for pornography.

Put aside for a moment the intriguing possibility that Dworkin is a double agent, is even now shaking with sodden-eyed mirth at her duplicity; for one thing, it isn't very likely. Instead, assume that *Mercy* was neither designed nor constructed as pornography – and this assumption will at once convey us to the troubled heart of the 'pornography debate'. How is pornography to be defined? By whom? And how, rather more importantly, is pornography to be understood?

I should say at once that I strongly suspect that the recent obsession with a definition – especially with a foolproof, clear-cut, legal definition – has not only distracted from but positively harmed understanding. Indeed, in the following discussion of *Mercy* I hope to explain why I find the whole business of defining 'pornography' ridiculous, and why we might even consider suspending our use of the word altogether, not least when we feel the temptation to use it in opposition to 'erotica'. The literature of sex – it is literature, here, with which I am largely concerned, as pictures raise rather different questions, especially when it comes to how they get made – the literature of sex is not so different from the literature of crime, religion, war, as people appear to believe. But – with the possible exception of religion – in no other case do people so fervently insist that there can be only two sorts: one that is morally virtuous, one that is morally evil.

The passion, of course, is because there are many who believe that this evil directly affects real lives. My own belief – which is no more grounded in rock-solid evidence than theirs – is that writing on its own simply doesn't have that kind of power. But in neither case does it seem very useful to behave as though matters were more straightforward, more easy to judge, than they are: to lump together the myriad voices, styles and forms of sexual writing, then swing down the scimitar of judgement and slice the lump in two.

Even if we confine ourselves to the ways in which feminists define pornography, we find that these are often contradictory or, at the very least, shaped by different priorities, altering from year to year. There are those, such as Susan Brownmiller,[3] who appear to use 'pornography' simply as the masculine form of 'erotica': the latter, the woman-made product, being 'good'; the former, man-made, product being 'bad'. For others, like Gloria Steinem,[4] it is any depiction of sex from which love has been extracted and replaced by power. For Annette Kuhn[5] it is primarily about the reduction of women to a 'sign', a visual object; while for Paula Webster[6] it is that which promotes 'traditional hetero-sexual intercourse'.

Not in all, but in many of the definitions – of which those listed are merely a sample – there does, however, tend to recur one persistent if sometimes blurred idea: that what distinguishes pornography from other representations of sex is its conjunction of physical pleasure with violence and women's 'subordination'.

To return, then, to Dworkin's *Mercy*. Andrea, its heroine-narrator, is absolutely clear that she gets no *pleasure* from all the humiliations, assaults and tortures to which she finds herself subjected as she tries to live freely and creatively in the moneyless, drink-fuelled, leftish, coke-dopey margins of New York society. But then, Sade makes it equally clear that torture and rape cause Justine distress, and – in casual conversation, at least – few people think to define his novel as less pornographic for that. Angela Carter, in *The Sadeian Woman*,[7] has suggested that Sade's depiction of women as 'sacrificial victims' makes him a *moral* pornographer, one who begins 'to penetrate to the heart of the contempt for women that distorts our culture'. She does not, however, deny that he is a pornographer. Besides, Dworkin's novel gives so many signals that it ought to be read as pornography that her heroine's protests might well be interpreted as a kind of flirtatious smokescreen. First, its preoccupation with sex and sexual violence is so overbearing that all other aspects of human experience – friendship, family, politics, work, to name but an arbitrary few – are either wiped out or transformed into sites of yet more sex and sexual violence. Indeed, as pornographic narratives do, this one opens by racing through half a dozen lines of rudimentary scene-setting – 'My name is Andrea . . . I was born down the street from Walt Whitman's house, on Mickle Street, in Camden, in 1946' – before settling down with a sigh of relief to its overriding theme: 'I wasn't raped until I was almost ten.'[8]

To be scrupulous, it should be said that a Prologue and Epilogue attempt to make it clear that *Mercy* should be read not for sexual excitement but as part of a feminist debate. Between them, however, these context-providers (which would in any case make little sense to anyone unfamiliar with internecine sisterhood) occupy six of the novel's 344 pages; while the Penguin edition of Georges Bataille's pornographic classic *Story of the Eye*[9] consists of just 59 pages of 'tale' and 51 pages of context, both psychological and literary, provided not only by the author himself but by Susan Sontag and Roland Barthes. The question is: does Penguin's packaging make Bataille's story less pornographic than it seemed in 1928 when it hit the streets stark naked? Or – to put it the other way round – is *Mercy* prevented from being pornographic by its author's polemical bookends?

Many would argue that it might be, in the way that a Robert Mapplethorpe penis, while seen as 'art' on a gallery wall, would, if encountered in a Soho bookshop by someone to whom his name meant nothing, be seen straight away as pornography. Similarly, in obscenity trials it is certainly common for the defence to point out that the text in the dock has high psychological, political or literary seriousness – 'artistic merit', as British law has it – and should therefore on no account be treated as though it were ordinary filth. This is not, however, the same as claiming that the book isn't pornographic. Rather, it is an assertion that pornography – or what some people *describe* as pornography; those who deploy the 'artistic' argument tend to be uneasy with that definition – can occasionally contribute to the sum of human understanding. But the vital point is that Dworkin herself dismisses such bourgeois, liberal ideas. For her, pornography both can be defined and, once she has defined it, must be outlawed.

Her most famous attempt at a legal definition, from which I have briefly quoted above, is the Minneapolis Ordinance, drawn up with the attorney Catharine MacKinnon in the early 1980s. This Ordinance describes pornography as 'the sexually explicit subordination of women, graphically depicted, whether in pictures or in words, that also includes one or more of the following . . .' The list of additional conditions includes: 'women are presented in postures of sexual submission' and 'women are presented in scenarios of degradation, injury, abasement, torture, shown as filthy or inferior, bleeding, bruised, or hurt in a context that makes these conditions sexual'.

All right. So could the following be described as a 'posture of sexual submission'?

> He holds my head still by my hair and he pushes his cock
> to the bottom of my throat, rams it in, past my throat,
> under it, deeper than the bottom, I feel this fracturing pain
> as if my neck shattered from inside and my muscles were
> being torn apart ragged and fast.[10]

And is this woman being presented in a scenario of degradation, injury, abasement and torture?

> He pulled me with one hand and punched me with the
> other, open hand, closed fist, closed fist, to my face, to my
> breasts, closed fists, both fists, I am on the kitchen floor
> and he is kneeling down so he can hit me, kneeling near
> me, over me, and he takes my head in his hands and he
> keeps banging my head against the floor. He punches my
> breasts. He burns my breasts with a lit cigarette.[11]

The only doubt, it seems to me, concerns the question of whether or not these conditions occur in a context which 'makes them sexual', by which I assume that Dworkin and MacKinnon mean 'makes, or attempts to make, them sexually arousing for the reader'. Not only are we back to the problem of context, but also to that of intention.

As I have said, those readers familiar with Dworkin's opinion of pornography may assume that she had no conscious intention of arousing sadistic or masochistic lust with her novel. What a casual reader of the book might assume – a man, let us say, who picks up *Mercy* with no prior knowledge of the author's reputation – is a question that might perhaps trouble the author; but, in any case, how much weight can we sensibly place on an author's intentions when assessing whether or not their work is pornographic? Quite apart from the fact that, for practical reasons, these will not always be discoverable, what people intend to do in their fiction is very rarely unambivalent. For instance, if *Mercy* is structured so that we identify with Andrea rather than her rapists, and so that we are invited to be shocked by rather than enjoy her suffering, it is also the case that the novel's descriptions of sexual abuse and violence are designed to be far more engaging and disturbing than those, for example, in *Justine*. At least, I believe they are designed like that; what I can say with more certainty is that that is how I received them. If I was not erotically aroused by them (but then, would my conscious mind admit it if I were?), there are certain images in Dworkin's novel that have clutched my imagination more strongly than anything I've read by Sade.

There, the abuses suffered by the heroine are mostly dismissed in a couple of perfunctory lines: 'Fired with mad lust, he struck with all his might. No part of the poor girl escaped his ferocity.' . . . 'In a second orgy they wreaked their every whim on her.' Moreover, these 'sex scenes' are scattered like sequins (albeit with carefree fingers) over what is otherwise a sometimes witty and sometimes tedious polemic. *Mercy*, on the other hand, is an unbroken incantation of horrors, described and redescribed until they colonize the mind. Even when the author shifts position to discuss women's creativity, the rhythm, tone, vocabulary, imagery and message remain the same:

> I have buckets of blood, nurses give it to me, raped nurses; and I cover everything, the slave clothes, the bikinis, the nighties, the garter belts, and the things they tie you down

221

with and the things they stick up you and the things they hurt you with, nipple clips and piercing things; I drench them in blood; I make them blood-soaked, as is a woman's life; I think over time I will engage in a new art, painting their world blood red as they have painted mine; simple self-expression, with a political leaning but neither right nor left per se, the anti-rape series it will be called, with real life as the canvas.[12]

It could well be argued that Dworkin's novel is more – or at least *as* – likely as Sade's to persuade the reader that violence, power and pain are the whole of sexuality (and not just male sexuality; we are offered no female alternative) and even to create the feeling that this is in some way horribly exciting. And to point out, as Dworkin quite truthfully could, that her novel ends not with a pitiful heroine struck dead by lightning (like Sade's) but with Andrea striding out into the night in order 'to smash a man's face in' in no way invalidates the argument. The 'smashing' may be presented as revenge, not sex; but inevitably, because of the way the novel conflates sex with violence throughout, it carries within it a great deal of sexual meaning. No, more than that: it really does appear to be *soliciting* a sexual response. This is Andrea's description of the men whose face she most enjoys smashing: 'I like them with fine shoulders, wide, real men, I like them six feet or more, I like them vicious, I pick them big and mean.'

Similarly, although on one level *Mercy* does, as I have said, repeat that *being* hurt is ugly, frightening, not remotely erotic, the rhapsodic quality of the prose consistently undermines the sense, suffusing the heroine's suffering with a glow of ecstatic martyrdom. And God – albeit the Jewish God – is never far absent from the novel. If His angel doesn't actually thrust a burning spear into Andrea's stomach, He Himself will occasionally ride on the back of one of the men who is raping her. Given the recognized quasi-erotic nature of this kind of imagery, could Dworkin not be said, at the very least, to be playing games with pornography?

The point of all this is not to denounce a novel which, in

some ways, I respect. And of course I don't seriously wish to establish that *Mercy* is 'pornographic', since I don't believe that the word serves any useful purpose. But I do want to show that it could be done, especially by a lawyer appealing to an already sympathetic magistrate or jury, because I don't think it can be emphasized enough how dangerous it is, as well as absurd, to act as though a simple definition were possible. *If a novel denouncing men's violence towards women can be defined, by the author's own criteria, as pornography, then surely the insistence on a legal definition must be dropped.*

Of course, one novelty of Dworkin's and MacKinnon's suggestion for abolishing pornography was that they drafted their legislation in terms of civil rights: in other words, they proposed that, instead of the state bringing criminal 'obscenity' charges, the maker or seller of a pornographic work should be liable to be sued by any woman who could show that the work had harmed her. It might therefore be argued that a novel such as *Mercy* would never be taken to court because its depiction of rape as ugly, unerotic, barbaric means that reading it would never be the cause of a man assaulting a woman. If you believe that no book causes a man to violate a woman, then this is not hard to accept. But if, as so many people appear to, you believe that a book can be the immediate impetus for acts of sexual violence, then I fail to see why *Mercy* should be exempt. Its author must know as well as anyone that descriptions of torture, whatever their intention, are found sexually arousing by many and, by some, are read for precisely that reason.

And given that readers' sexual responses – as distinct from their sexual conduct – are at least as ambivalent, complex and out of control as authors' intentions, how can a writer presume to know if what she or he has written is 'arousing', or, if it is, to whom and under what circumstances? Even more, through what kind of power does any third party presume to assess if this or that description has a context which 'makes it sexual'? The truth is that this 'pornography', for which so many people are hunting, lives not in the *product* but beyond it, in the active relationship between product and reader. Paedophiles sometimes masturbate while looking through catalogues of children's clothes, or watching the choirboys singing in 'Songs of Praise'.

Having said all this, I should add that the striking thing about Dworkin's novel is how, unlike the Mothercare brochures, it carefully echoes so many classic pornographic conventions: especially those of such 'literary' explorations of sex and violence as *Justine*, *Story of the Eye* and Pauline Réage's *Story of O*.[13] Any reader who knows those works can scarcely avoid the hot breath of their whisper seeping between Dworkin's lines.

God or His terrible absence, for example, are as closely entwined with violent sex in the works of Sade, Bataille and Réage as they are in Dworkin's novel. And then, as I have said, there is the heroine's (in Bataille's case, hero's) isolation: a separation from 'everyday' society which – whether chosen, enforced or both – invariably serves to transport both characters and readers across a dark frontier. In the country of Dworkin's novel, it's true, there is a shortage of decadent English lords and of castles so large and remote that no one can hear the screaming in their dungeons. It is, however, an Englishman 'with a distinguished accent' – characteristics with no very obvious relevance to the plot – who performs the ultimate outrage against the heroine's body and trust; while an earlier rapist lures her, if not precisely to a castle, then to what must surely be the Manhattan equivalent: a vast, lonely house with 'creaky' steps, 'maybe a hundred of them', at the top of which waits a bedroom-cum-torture-chamber. Even the tenement block in which Andrea finds some temporary refuge has much in common with the château to which O is taken in the Réage novel: although both heroines have their own rooms, in neither case is this any protection against the sexual demands of whatever rapist happens to be passing.

The differences, it should quickly be said, are as marked as the similarities. When, for example, Dworkin writes about Andrea's constant exposure to rape, the emphasis is on how insecure this makes her: 'You can be sleeping inside with everything locked and they get in and do it to you no matter how bad it hurts.' In Réage's novel, the tone, the vocabulary, the implications are altogether other, with helplessness presented as childlike security. Shortly after O's arrival at the château to which her lover has driven her, she is courteously instructed in the house rules: 'Your hands', she is told, 'are not your own, neither are your breasts, nor, above all, is any one of the orifices of your body, which we are at liberty to explore and into which we may, whenever we so please, introduce ourselves . . .' To which O's reaction is to kneel at her lover's feet and 'joyously' fellate him.

Indeed, of the 'pornographic' novels that I've mentioned, each is distinct from the others. To take just the Sade and the Réage, for reasons that I shall explain below: while *Justine* (1791) is basically a philosophical quarrel with Enlightenment trust in reason, science and people's potential once freed from religious superstition – and its heroine's sufferings, at least in part, are an illustration of the wrongness of those who insist that nature, human or otherwise, would, if left to its own devices, be 'virtuous' – the 1954 *Story of O* moves through its deadpan, stately paces to evolve into a nightmarish exploration of wilful self-annihilation. Whether or not it was written by a woman (Pauline Réage is a pseudonym, but of whom it has not yet been established), many women readers both find it erotic and are profoundly troubled by its climax: the heroine, naked except for a leash and the golden-brown feathery headdress of an owl, reduced to nothing, to zero, to the 'O' of the novel's title.

My reason for referring to these novels in particular is that in *Mercy* Dworkin also refers to Sade and to Réage, describing the latter as 'a demagogue and a utopian, a kind of Stalinist of female equality, she wants us all equal on the bottom of anything that's mean enough to be on top'. In other words, it seems pretty obvious that the overlaps between Dworkin's novel and two of the West's most famous works of 'pornography' is no coincidence. And, for at least two reasons, I find this interesting.

First, Dworkin must obviously have read and been in one

way or another impressed by books which, under her proposed legislation, would probably disappear from the shops: either because of a civil action taken against them specifically or because of a generalized caution among publishers and booksellers. While I am certain that Sade, Réage and Bataille are fairly low down on the list of those whose work the anti-pornography campaigners would like to see abolished – partly because no written product is likely to have involved the abuse of a real, living woman in its manufacture – it is none the less the case that without the safety-net clause of 'artistic merit', they would as surely be shovelled underground as prints of Linda Lovelace's *Deep Throat*.

Should anyone care? Not those who believe that 'the sexually explicit subordination of women, graphically depicted' is precisely responsible for men's abuse, both sexual and otherwise, of women. For them to distinguish one such graphic depiction from another would be absurd. But it might, nevertheless, be hard for them not to do so, if only in secret, for surely *everybody* must distinguish between the ways in which sex and sexual subordination are represented. At one extreme, even the most libertarian anti-censorship campaigner is unlikely to believe that women or children (or, for that matter, men) should be forced by fists, knives or economic need to participate in pornographic videos, movies or still photographs. In most countries even the law believes, however carelessly, that this is wrong. On the other hand, many of those who campaign against pornography are likely to approve of representations that others of their number would think 'subordinate' women. As Lisa Duggan, Nan Hunter and Carole S. Vance have pointed out in *Feminism and Censorship*,[14] while some anti-pornography campaigners might exclude from their condemnation depictions of consensual lesbian sex, for others those might be precisely the sort of image they were hoping to ban. If it isn't entirely true that 'What turns me on is erotica; what turns you on is pornographic', it does appear that issues of sex and violence, of power and subordination, are not quite as simple as would-be legislators continue to pretend.

Dworkin, for instance, might quarrel with Sade and with Réage, but she takes what they have to say seriously enough to engage in a passionate debate with them – a debate with what their books have to say, not with their right to say it – and, moreover, accepts at least part of their formal and imaginative language. Surely she cannot be saying that it is all right for *her* to travel this country, but too dangerous for lesser, less sophisticated people? This is certainly a common delusion among anti-pornography campaigners, whether they assess sophistication by sex, education or class.

The publication of *Mercy* in Britain by a non-academic, non-feminist imprint would seem, however, to indicate that Dworkin was not especially concerned about limiting the book's readership. So the question remains: why has she played with the fires of rape, predatory men, woman-as-victim, descriptions of torture – all within what could easily be perceived as a sexually arousing context – when she has spent so much energy trying to shield us from just these things? One answer returns us to ambivalence: the ambivalence towards sex and violence displayed by so many writers and readers, the ambivalence which makes such nonsense of simple, yes/no attempts at legislation. For even in Dworkin's theoretical writing, what is striking is her imaginative engagement with men and their violence. I'm sure that she hates the latter entirely; however, instead of avoiding it, or thinking up ways in which it might be minimized, controlled, removed, what she does is to describe it over and over again in all its worst horrors, drumming up a country where nobody is left but slaves and masters, Jews and Nazis, political prisoners and the torturers slick with their blood.

That Dworkin should be fascinated by violent sexuality is neither peculiar, of course, nor reprehensible; merely paradoxical. She lives in the same world as the rest of us: one in which the orgasm is the only remaining, readily accepted, extracorporeal experience; one in which death and sexual desire are the only remaining mysteries. Although, with both, we are doing what we can to bring them under our control – freezing our corpses while scientists sweat to discover a cure for whatever we died of; categorizing our sexual desires and checking them out with our analyst – we remain as awestruck before them as people before God when religion still mattered. And, as people used to do with God and other such mysteries as illness and luck, we tend to conflate them with one another: death with sex; sex with death; the identical twin annihilators of our fragile sense of ourselves.

In *The Sadeian Woman*[15] Carter quotes Michel Foucault:

Sadism is not a name finally given to a practice as old as Eros; it is a massive cultural fact which appeared precisely at the end of the eighteenth century, and which constitutes one of the greatest conversions of Western imagination: unreason transformed into delirium of the heart, madness of desire, the insane dialogue of love and death in the limitless presumption of appetite.

Certainly, fictions in which 'love and death' have a dialogue – or, to be more exact, in which they howl their confusion of identity – appear to have burst from the French Revolution and Sade like a need, not a fashion. After all, real deaths were occurring: of the monarchy; of God; of our faith in reason. We were left alone with our bodies and, after two hundred years, they still frighten us. Is it any wonder that we write about them and read about them with panicky 'delirium', deploy their representations as a stage for our greatest furies and terrors?

We? Or only the male kind of 'we'? Aren't those bodies that frighten women not their own but men's, especially when used as violent depictions of sex encourage them to be? Isn't 'pornography', in fact, the cause of women's fear, not its exorcism?

Neither I nor anybody else yet knows. But if we consider that women's revolution against the power of the father, the family, the whole 'patriarchal state' both echoes and multiplies the exhilaration and terror of 1789, then is it not possible that women's need for a literature in which sex and violence, love and death, can wrestle with one another is as great as – perhaps even greater than – men's? This is not to deny that we also have a need for sexual literatures of pleasure, fun, satire, self-confirmation, information, masturbation; it is simply to ask that the doors of violence, power and 'subordination' not be padlocked and zealously, jealously guarded.

For there is one thing of which I feel sure and of which, in a paradoxical way, thinking about both *Mercy* and Dworkin's efforts to outlaw 'pornography' has made me even surer: because we have laughably little idea about what anyone, male or female, is actually doing when writing or reading about sexuality and violence, we are in no position, either moral or practical, even to *attempt* to stop them.

Part 4

To each their own
Differing pornographies

Linda Williams

Pornographies on/scene

or Diff'rent strokes for diff'rent folks

Pornographies on/scene

The last decade of American culture is likely to be remembered for its unprecedented confession of sexual secrets. Telling all, showing all, seeing all has become a national preoccupation. Pornography – however defined – has emerged from the relative privacy of the gentlemen-only 'secret museum' [1] into the glaring light of day. And it has been pushed, often precipitously, by the forces who most want to prohibit it. Indeed, the many accusations of obscenity and pornography – whether in anti-pornography books, in slide shows and films, in the Meese Commission's travelling public confessionals and later *Final Report* (1986) or in Senator Jesse Helms's finger-pointing at National Endowment for the Arts-funded artists – can qualify as obscenity and pornography just as easily as the objects of their condemnation. Even the impotent slogan 'Just say no' – whether to sex or to drugs – necessitates some 'hard-core' knowledge about just what kind of drugs and what kind of sex to 'say no' to.

The impression exists that the problem posed in our contemporary age of proliferating sexual representations is one of an extreme explicitness of representation – the question of where acceptable speech, expression and practice end and gratuitous filth, 'pure' smut, an irredeemable 'hard core', begins.[2] However, not only has such line-drawing become increasingly difficult as sexual identity has become more politicized and as 'speaking sex' has become as necessary to gay and lesbian activists as to Jesse Helms, its strategic value for a feminist or minority sexual politics now seems almost nil. Explicit sexual representations have quite determinedly moved from a place off/scene (ob/scene) to a new prominence on/scene.[3] With this move, sexual politics has changed. Feminists are beginning to recognize that the perverse sexuality of the 'other' can be crucial to the empowerment of women as sexual agents.

To cite only a few recent examples of how 'perverse' sexualities have become present on/scene: X-rated moving-image pornography has moved from sleazy men-only porno houses to the middle-class bedrooms of heterosexual couples, where women have freely criticized pornographic sexual fantasies from which they were once excluded as viewers; new lesbian and bisexual pornographies (discussed below) have become surprisingly popular and important to the assertion of different (non-heterosexual) sexualities; banned from MTV as too explicitly sexual, Madonna's soft-core pornographic music video *Justify Your Love* moved to the much more respectable 'Nightline', where many more viewers witnessed her special brand of female-authored soft-core sexual fantasy; and, finally, in a performance that inserted a speculum into her vagina, ex-porn star Annie Sprinkle recently moved from live sex shows and porno films to the Cleveland Performance Art Festival by offering an ironic demystification of pornography's typically objectified female body.[4]

What all these examples of sexual pleasures – once deemed ob/scene, now insistently placed on/scene – have in common is their diversity, the fact that the sexual fantasies of 'perverse others' now take their place as authoritative subjectivities, as provoking sexual agents seeking different pleasures from those presented in mainstream representations as the norm. In what follows I wish to examine, within the field of commercially available moving-image pornography, the important transgressive role of these perversions in undoing the rigid hierarchies that underlie sexual difference. My – perhaps quixotic – goal is to defend diverse pornographies through an analysis of their perversions.

Previous defences of pornography have, for obvious reasons, glossed over the role of perversion in pornographic fantasy. Perversion is understandably difficult to defend. This is especially important in an area of film and video analysis where the analytic terms of perversion have been both crucial (normal) and ambivalently condemnatory. It was not so long ago, some of us may remember, that the fundamental pleasures of film viewing were described and condemned under the rubric of a perverse sadistic-voyeuristic-fetishizing 'male gaze'.[5]

Under the banner of the critique of a perverse masculine visual pleasure, feminist film critics once condemned the 'norm' of masculine heterosexual desire as manifested in narrative cinema. Pornography was usually assumed to be the extreme, and grossly explicit, instance of this perverse, voyeuristic, fetishizing pleasure. While it was enormously important for feminists to critique pornography's phallocentric nature as well as its sadistic excesses, the demonizing effects of this condemnation, as well as the oversimplified understanding of the role of perversions as exclusively pathological and harmful to others, has left us with a problematic heritage: the sexual politics of normal and perverse. In the name of what norms do feminists condemn the perversions of dominant masculine heterosexual desires evidenced in art, mass culture and a much-maligned pornography? Where is the enablement of female sexual agency in this condemnation of masculine dominance? Should we even speak in such binary terms of a female (versus a male) sexual agency?

If feminism succeeded in critiquing masculine phallic sexuality, it did so at the price of demonizing it as a perverse 'other' whose eternal victims were women. It is now possible to see how this feminist critique has fed into a larger critique of deviancy now being used by the right to mount new arguments – not only against pornography but also against gays, lesbians and sadomasochists in NEA funding of art deemed obscene. Feminism has rightly set itself up as a critique of sexual desires that seem oppressive to women, but it has not always been sensitive to the complex ways power and pleasure operate in sexuality.

If, therefore, unlike either Jesse Helms or Andrea Dworkin, we do not want to participate in a politics of demonizing the pervert – whether that pervert is defined as heterosexual or homosexual, or as voyeur, sadomasochist or fetishist – then we need to gain some degree of clarity about these difficult issues. I therefore propose to probe the role of perversion and transgression in the proliferating genres of pornography, dominant and non-dominant, that are currently available on the scene. For the simple dichotomy of the perverse (because sexual?) male and the normal (because less sexual?) female has failed: fantasies that make appeal to transgressive pleasures may indeed be perverse, but as fantasies and representations that offer pleasure they are not necessarily pathological. In an era of diverse sexual identities – of proud gays, lesbians, bisexuals and sadomasochists – and of a pervasive commodity fetishism and a society of the spectacle whose visual pleasures depend upon a certain normative fetishism and voyeurism, the very terms 'norm' and 'perverse' cannot be assumed to attach permanently to features that are *a priori* 'good' or 'bad' for women.

Rethinking perversion

In attempting to rehabilitate the term 'perversion' for feminist analysis, I follow Gayle Rubin's advice that it is analytically essential to separate the categories of gender and sexuality, once too simply conflated, in order more accurately to reflect their separate social existence.[6] Rubin argues that feminist conceptual tools developed to analyse gender-based hierarchies work when these hierarchies overlap with erotic stratifications, but when issues become less those of gender and more those of sexuality, feminist analysis based only on gender can become misleading and irrelevant:

> Although it pains many lesbians to think about it, the fact is that lesbians have shared many of the sociological features and suffered from many of the same social penalties as have

gay men, sadomasochists, transvestites, and prostitutes.
(p. 308)

She argues, therefore, for the need for the feminist critique of
gender hierarchy to be incorporated into a radical theory of
sex. But where is this radical theory of sex? It is certainly not
fully developed. But let me sketch two important compo-
nents of it.

Teresa de Lauretis has argued[7] that 'normality' is a term
that increasingly needs to be placed between quotation
marks: 'It was Freud who first put the quotation marks
around the "normal" in matters sexual . . . And he did it by
daring to pursue his exceptional insight – whether genius,
vision or fantasy – into what many see as a revolutionary
theory of sexuality' (p. 7). De Lauretis points out, in a precise
reading of the concept of negative and positive perversion in
Freud, what I wish to emphasize in a more general way with
respect to pornography: that his theory of sexuality is inherently a theory of perversion. The concept of 'normal' in Freud
is more a kind of projection of social norms than an actual
state of being, and the gap between pathology and non-
pathology is bridged, as de Lauretis puts it, on the one side
between neuroses and normality and, on the other side,
between normality and perversion (p. 9).

The classical Freudian model of desire begins with the
premiss that sexual desire is founded in the encounter with
sexual difference. This difference is classically portrayed as
the masculine subject's encounter with the difference of
woman: her famous 'lack' of a penis and the erection of a
phallus in its place. In this account desire is engendered by
the encounter with sexual difference. Desire is attributed to
the father and assumed by the son through the Oedipal
complex, which renders him neurotic but 'properly' male-
identified and desirous of women.

In psychoanalytic theory desire is a 'problem' for women
because of their 'different' relationship to the phallus. As
Parveen Adams has noted, in order to assume their 'proper'
masculine and feminine subjectivities, both the boy and the

girl must submit to 'castration' – code word for the knowledge of difference and the split in subjectivity. The girl's
biological sex – the fact that she does not have a penis – is
said to obstruct her 'normal' entry into desire by blocking
her assumption of the phallus. But what if the entry to desire
occurs not just through the neurotic's assumption of the
phallus in the Oedipus complex, but also in the pervert's
relocation of the phallus in places where it does not belong?
For the phallus functions in the perversions as well. And
here its function, as Adams notes, can be transgressive of all
that is proper about the phallic order and its hegemony of
masculine, heterosexual desire.[8] If the phallus is not attributed to the father, if it is attributed elsewhere – to the
mother, for example – then we are in the domain of the
perversions.

Now if the perversions are, in fact, more 'normal' to the
functioning of desire than the normative account of them has
led many to believe – if in fact, as Freud writes, the 'sexual
instinct and the sexual object are merely soldered together',[9]
if instincts are independent of their objects, then, as de
Lauretis argues, it may be possible to 'build a theory of
sexuality along the negative trace of the perversions' – her
example is fetishism (p. 20).

If such a theory is possible – de Lauretis acknowledges that
it may not be applicable to everyone, but that the normal
theory of sexuality is not either – it would certainly aid in the
analysis of a female desire found either lacking or excessive
with respect to a phallic male norm; it would also aid in the
analysis of those pornographies deemed perverse. For pornography, like sexuality, *is* often polymorphically perverse.
There is no avoiding the appeal to the Freudian psychoanalytic model in an effort to understand these perversions. I am
aware that this model can be frustrating to feminists in its
location of desire with the phallic function, but it is indis-
pensable in the analysis of a genre that is so literally and
metaphorically phallic.

The other influential model of sexuality and the perversions is offered by Michel Foucault, who sees sexuality as

inseparable from perversions which are constructed, 'implanted', in discourse and specific to historical eras.[10] Foucault's general notion of an escalating incitement to the confession of sexual secrets in the modern age is useful for understanding the proliferation of all sorts of discourses of sexuality in the modern age, including that of moving-image pornography. Rather than attempt to reconcile the inconsistencies of these two sexual theorists, I propose that we take from each the idea that perversion is, as Jonathan Dollimore has recently put it, intrinsic to desire and a 'crucial category for cultural analysis'.[11] Dollimore argues that unless we are willing to see reproduction as the common goal of all sexual drives, we have to admit that we are all perverts. How are we positioned as perverts by contemporary pornographies? And how shall we apply these notions of an inherent (to Freud) or a constructed (to Foucault) perversion of sexuality to our thinking about pornography? Let us turn to the field of contemporary hardcore film and video for an answer.

'Diff'rent strokes'

In my book on hard-core pornography[12] I argue that the dominant form of feature-length heterosexual pornography that emerged in the United States in the early 1970s was especially marked by new discourses of sexuality that constructed sex as a central problem of human identity and happiness. The formula I found useful for describing some of the most popular pornographic films of the seventies – those films which, in the wake of the 1973 Supreme Court *Miller vs. California*, arrived forcefully 'on/scene' in the USA – was that in them sex was constructed as a problem to which more, better or different sex was the solution. The new, legal, feature-length film pornography that emerged out of the complexities of the 'sexual revolution' (and into the even greater complexities of a feminist revolution) were unlike previous forms of hard-core film pornography: sexual pleasure was both crucial *and* problematic; some perversions and not others were seriously explored as solutions to these problems.

In *Deep Throat* (Gerard Damiano, 1972), for example, sexual pleasure is a problem to the female protagonist. 'Normal sex' (implicitly defined by this film as heterosexual intercourse) does not provide the solution. What the pornography industry calls a 'meat shot' – visual evidence of heterosexual penetration – occurs frequently but, unlike earlier stag films, it does not constitute the film's climax or its idea of ultimate and satisfying sexual acts. A new solution is sought in sexually adventurous 'swingin'', for example, experimentation with what a character in the film calls 'Diff'rent Strokes for Diff'rent Folks'.

This banal line, borrowed from a contemporary popular song, deserves consideration, for it is the slogan by which a new pornographic ethic of sexual diversity, a proliferation of perversions, was inaugurated in a new, post-Kinsey, post-Masters and Johnson (but pre-Shere Hite) awareness of diverse sexual pleasures. *Deep Throat*'s 'solutions' to the problem of female pleasure are, of course, quite fanciful. But I maintain that the importance of this film and its many imitators was the simple posing of the problem of sex and the solution of 'diff'rent strokes' – the recourse, in this particular case, to the substitute perversion of fellatio followed by 'money shots' (explained below) for heterosexual intercourse – that was crucial to the history of 'hard-core' pornography.

In other words, the 'diff'rent strokes' elicited by the pornographic genre's quest to see more, to know more, of the pleasure of the other turn out to be at odds with its attempts to subsume this pleasure within the terms of the reigning, but always fragile, 'normal' masculine heterosexual economy of desire. That this 'normal' economy of desire *is* fragile, that it does not even – or perhaps especially – in its perversions succeed in confidently showing the pleasures it seeks to show, is worth emphasizing. For what is most misleading in the feminist and moral-majoritist critique of pornography is the belief that an absolutely perverse masculine sadism, voyeurism and fetishism solve the problems of knowledge and pleasure they address. Any close study of the texts of film and video pornography, including even the puerile and aesthetically uninspiring but culturally significant *Deep Throat*, reveals quite the opposite: (1) a constant crisis in the attempt to portray sexual pleasure in a hard-core 'frenzy of the visible', the very real difficulty of seeing the truth of pleasure; (2) a further crisis in the field of the sexual altogether as previous minorities in the field – women, gays, lesbians, sadomasochists, bisexuals – seek to express their desires and sexual agency through different representations of pleasure.

In this first crisis – the crisis of the visibility of pleasure in a genre committed to showing the spectacle of 'it' – pornography seeks, through the deployment of what Foucault calls the 'scientia sexualis',[13] to confess the irrefutable, self-evident truths of sex. One goal of film and visual pornography thus coincides precisely with the intensifying goal of modern Western society's quest for the knowledge of pleasure, and thus one pole of hard-core heterosexual pornography is perhaps best characterized as a regime of the visual knowledge of pleasure. This aspect of the genre is characterized by a *cinéma vérité* devotion to the revelation-confession of real bodies caught in the act of sexual pleasure – in, for example, the 'meat shot'. Here, in confirming close-up, is irrefutable, visible evidence of penetration, really taking place, with no possible faking. Here, also, is a primary heterosexual reproductive 'norm' of sexuality.

On the other hand, however, some of the truths of sexual pleasure are not always self-evident and visible. The female body, for example, whose secrets of pleasure are especially solicited by the dominant mainstream of heterosexual pornography originally created for men only, tends, in the regime of the visible, to keep some of its secrets. Thus the other, contradictory side of heterosexual moving-image pornography is its quality of sexual fantasy, role play and performance, none of which is a self-evidently visible, unfakeable truth, nor necessarily genital. This pole of pornography is therefore characterized by fetishism and a perverse swerving away from direct genital aims on to a wide range of substitutions.

At different times in its history and in different categories of pornography, these two contradictory forces have been in different balance. For example, I have characterized the moment of the emergence of feature-length legal pornography – the sort introduced to general American audiences by films like *Deep Throat* – as one in which 'sex', in keeping with other discourses of sexuality of the early seventies, was constructed as a problem in need of increasingly energetic solutions. These solutions of more, better or different sexual acts encouraged the smorgasbord approach to hard core. Throughout the seventies the smorgasbord included the following range of numbers – I am quoting here from a list of possible sexual numbers suggested by *The Filmmaker's Guide to Pornography*: masturbation; 'lesbian' or 'girl–girl'; *ménage à trois*, cunnilingus, fellatio, sadie-max (single numbers with sadomasochistic elements), and orgy. Often all these numbers would be included in a single film.[14]

But amid this wealth of possible numbers there was usually one shot of a sexual act that tried to be the climactic 'it' of ultimate pleasure: this is what the industry calls the 'money shot', male ejaculation of the penis. While the money shot was usually positioned as the climax of most heterosexual pornography, it was a paradoxical confession of the 'ultimate truth' of sexual pleasure. For while it afforded a perfect vision and knowledge of one genital organ's pleasure, the climax and achievement of a final sexual aim, this aim quite literally missed its mark: the genitals of its object. In fact, the genital 'object' of masculine desire and pleasure is often missing altogether as a visual representation in the frame.

As if to make up for this lack, the money shot would throw in a special rhetorical flourish, with slow motion, optical printing or elaborate montages which would attempt to substitute for what the film could not show: the visible, involuntary convulsions that would be proof of the woman's pleasure. External ejaculation, while ideally visible and affording incontrovertible evidence of at least the male's pleasure, thus 'perverts' 'normal' genital aims. It is a substitute for the invisible female orgasm that this stage of the heterosexual pornographic genre especially solicits. This shot, while undoubtedly explicit and to some certainly obscene, is perhaps most importantly described as contradictory in much the same way that a fetish is contradictory. Like the fetish, it attempts to disavow difference – in this case that the female orgasm is any different from the male's – offering up the spectacle of ejaculation as a substitute for what is not there: the invisible female orgasm. The genre's solution of substituting the male orgasm for the female is thus, by definition, perverse in the literal sense of swerved away from an original aim.

Now it is all too easy to condemn, ridicule or demonize these perverse substitutions. What I have tried to suggest in my book and would like to develop further here, however, is that a *perverse dynamic* operates in all forms of sexual fantasy; that it is inevitable both within heterosexual pornography and outside it, in the non-dominant, non-mainstream forms of gay, lesbian, sadomasochistic and bisexual moving-image pornographies.

I borrow the term 'perverse dynamic' from Jonathan Dollimore, who argues that although perversion is regulated by a binary opposition between the natural and the unnatural, it is nevertheless inextricably rooted in the natural: as in de Lauretis's argument that perversion is intrinsic to sexuality, Dollimore argues that perversion originates internally to the very norm it threatens. The perverse dynamic is thus paradoxically both alien to and inherent within the normal.[15] This idea of perversion is important to the agency and empowerment of those non-dominant, minority sexualities frequently condemned as perverse and evident in gay, lesbian, sadomasochistic and bisexual pornography. It is therefore with an awareness of a non-pathological *perverse dynamic* already at work within the heterosexual category of pornography considered the most normal and dominant that we can begin to chart the other commercially available pornographies existing alongside this heterosexual mainstream.

'Other' pornographies

These pornographies are: homosexual (originally mostly gay male, now also lesbian), sadomasochistic and bisexual. While these categories are not absolutely inclusive – I exclude the many new forms of 'amateur' pornography and the occasional, but not systematic, appeal to racial or other body-types – they constitute the broad areas of profession-ally made hard-core film and video on the market in the USA today. Of course heterosexual films and videos are almost never marketed *as* heterosexual, since heterosexual, as the presumed norm, needs no mark. It is usually up to the other categories to differentiate themselves from this norm, as they sometimes do with images on box covers or key words in titles (*Hot Male Mechanics*, *Oversize Load* connote gay: *Suburban Dykes* directly speaks its targeted audience; *The Punishment of Anne* and *China de Sade* suggest sadomasochis-tic themes; and the ubiquitous word 'Bi' indicates bisexual videos). These different categories of pornography are some-times integrated into rental outlets that specialize in adult, X-rated materials, sometimes available only in special venues (gay and lesbian rental and sales outlets).

Homosexual pornography, characterized most basically by same-sex object-choice, can be considered, initially, in opposition to the heterosexual 'norm' of opposite-sex object-choice. Let us begin with the most prolific form of homo-sexual porn – that aimed primarily at the gay male audience. This pornography is almost as prolific and as long-lived as its straight counterpart. In many ways the two forms are much alike: both are devoted to revealing visible evidence of phallic power and potency, and both do so with frequent money shots.

Richard Dyer, in a ground-breaking article on gay male pornography, criticized this form of film and video pornog-raphy for its similarities to the heterosexual mainstream, especially in its use of money shots and what he character-ized as the emphasis on penetrator's over penetrated in anal sex. Dyer argued that the form was still too enmeshed in a masculinist, goal-orientated model that was too much like heterosexual pornography.[16] Good gay porn, he argued, needed to differ from the mainstream more than in mere object-choice. While the question of what constitutes 'good' pornography is notoriously difficult to answer, the fact that gay porn constitutes its different pleasures in relation to those of heterosexual porn is significant. Part of the pleasure of gay male porn would seem to reside in its play of both similarity and difference from this 'norm'.

More recently, David Pendleton[17] has challenged some of Dyer's observations, describing the structure of gay porn as rhapsodic and combinatory – a series of sexual acts which, in contrast to the relatively purposeful, problem-solving nature of heterosexual pornography, are paratactic, lacking hierarchy and ultimate goals – except, that is, for the goals of visible orgasm. This critic also challenges Dyer's notion that gay porn is 'too phallic' and interested only in thrusting and the thruster, citing the fact that top and bottom often trade places during anal sex.

The question may be less a matter of who is right – though my own observations bear out Pendleton's description over Dyer's – than of interpreting the role of the phallus – that crucial symbol of sexual difference and desire – in the context of debates about how gay porn differentiates itself from heterosexual porn. That the phallus *is* important in this pornography is not at all surprising. It remains in gay sexual representations – and, as we shall see, in lesbian representations as well – a compelling symbol of power and potency. What does need further examination is how this phallus signifies within different intrageneric contexts of desire and pleasure.

Let us now turn to a third long-standing category of pornography, one related to the heterosexual and the homosexual categories yet marketed with an eye towards yet another 'perversion'. This group of films and videos is what I shall call the sadomasochistic or s/m category. While s/m, or 'sadie-max', *numbers* occur with some frequency in the smorgasbord of heterosexual pornography, the sadomasochistic category is marked by scenarios devoted entirely to a thematics of domination and submission.

Sadomasochistic pornography differs from heterosexual pornography most notably in its tendency to linger over intermediate relations to the sexual object, rather than proceeding directly towards 'ultimate' end goals. Scenes of prolonged torture – for example, in the whips, chains and needles deployed in *The Punishment of Anne* (Radley Metzger, 1979) – are typical. While Anne, the tortured woman, appears at first to be the victim of her male and female dominators, things are rarely as they seem. What seems to be pure victimization of the woman is actually a complex play of power and pleasure. We mistake the very nature of this category if we assume that, like heterosexual pornography, it is all about the active power and pleasure of phallic domination.

But what *is* it about?[18] Psychoanalytic theories of sadism and masochism have been useful in explaining these pleasures up to a point, but they have mostly been used to describe regrettable syndromes in which pathological individuals are trapped rather than identificatory positions which are chosen for the pleasures they provide. Since I do not wish to repeat here the long debates about whether sexual identities are born or made – which usually conclude that they are both born *and* made – I will simply note that pornographic texts, though often aimed specifically at certain markets of pre-established sexual identities, are also, with their proliferation in mass culture, increasingly open to any interested voyeur with a VCR. And voyeurism, as feminist film theorists know quite well, is a remarkably normalized perversion in our contemporary image culture. This safe voyeurism of the film and video viewer who will never be caught looking by the objects of his or her gaze is available to many individuals who can vicariously engage in and experience at a distance sexual predilections and tastes without necessarily acting them out.

These mass-market fantasies are, moreover, not discrete and separate forms existing only for – and consumed only by – those whose sexual aims and objects are depicted in them. In other words, there is no guarantee that only practising sadomasochists watch s/m or only gays watch gay porn. And there is good reason to believe, as I shall argue later, in a rather lively interaction between these forms and their 'preferred' viewers, sometimes resulting in the creation of new forms.

With this in mind, let us ask about the pleasure of sadomasochistic pornography. First, the sadomasochistic fantasies of these films and videos differ from the hetero-sexual and homosexual pornographies examined above in their lack of emphasis on genitals. While traditional hetero- and homosexual pornographies can be defined in terms of same- or different-sex object-choice and a genital organi-zation of ultimate pleasures, sadomasochistic pornography is more diffuse. The 'object' of desire can be described only as the whole scenario of dominance and submission which psychoanalytic theorists have tended to interpret as a dis-avowal of genital sexuality. According to these theories, the masochist wishes to disavow genital sexuality because his desire is to re-merge with the powerful oral mother of the pregenital phase.[19]

Contrary to the sadist, who seeks to repudiate and differ-entiate himself from the mother through a kind of overiden-tification with the phallic power of the father, the masochist regresses to an earlier infantile sexuality. In effect, what the masochist does is suspend or put off orgasmic gratification and condition it with a pain that disavows genital pleasure. Submission to pain is the price paid for possessing a genital sexuality that is at odds with infantile desires. The masochist puts on a theatrical show of passive suffering staged as the disavowal of what is nevertheless obvious: his sexual pleasure.

Psychoanalytic theory has usually presumed the domi-nated partner of the sadomasochistic contract to be male and the dominator to be female. While this is often true in classic cases of clinical masochism, it is not always true in contem-porary sadomasochistic pornography, which portrays domi-nators and victims of both sexes. And it is certainly not true in the popular imagination of pornography, which has so dramatically polarized discussion around male sadists and female victims coerced into the masochist's position. I have tried, in a chapter on sadomasochistic pornography in *Hard Core*, to analyse the socially and psychically different status of the female victim of the sadomasochistic scenario. I argue there that the female victim of this scenario cannot be viewed as equally transgressive of Oedipal law as is the male masochist, who is sometimes heroicized for his transgressive challenge to this law. Since the woman is not as dependent on that law for her (hetero)sexual identity and since female victimization is, unfortunately, already so 'normal' in our current psychosocial arrangements, the dominated woman of the sadomasochistic scenario has often seemed the very emblem of a system of sexual fantasy geared entirely to masculine pleasures.

While there is every reason to object to the sexual subordination of women, there is also good reason to be suspicious of aligning this too-rigid binary of gender difference with other binaries of good/bad, passive/active, normal/perverse. It is therefore precisely here, in thinking about the non-pathological pleasures of sexuality that cut across this basic binary of male/female sexual difference, that we might benefit from Gayle Rubin's advice that feminism's critique of gender hierarchy needs to be incorporated into a radical theory of sex. It is no accident, for example, that the origin of the feminist 'sex wars', of which the bitter debates about pornography have been an offshoot, began with what B. Ruby Rich has called the 'return of the repressed' of a certain 'bad girl' sexuality in the form of lesbian sadomasochism.[20] The feminist lesbian sadomasochist has arguably been the key provoking agent of these wars, unsettling all the comfortable received opinions about sexual power, pleasure and perversion. There is thus a need for a complication of the feminist binary of sexual difference with other binaries of difference that are not grounded only in gender but in sexuality as well.

Sadomasochistic pornography, like the fantasy of sadomasochism analysed by Freud in his famous 'A Child is Being

Beaten', is of interest for its revelations of the processes of identification at work in fantasy. In 'Fantasy and the Origins of Sexuality',[21] psychoanalysts Jean Laplanche and Jean-Bertrand Pontalis argue that fantasy is not so much a narrative that enacts the quest for an object of desire as a setting for desire in which desubjectified subjectivities oscillate between positions of self and other, occupying no fixed place in the scenario. I have already characterized pornography in general as composed of the tension between a goal-orientated quest to reveal the hidden secrets of 'sex' in a 'frenzy of the visible' (the goal-orientated compulsion to show 'it' so common to the heterosexual *and* the gay male hard core) and a contradictory appeal to fantasy, role play and performance which is neither necessarily visible nor genital. Sadomasochistic pornography typifies this more fantasy-based pole, marked by the prolongation rather than the attainment (of objects) of desire.

To understand the pleasure of sadomasochistic fantasy, we need to disengage it from the stereotype – true, certainly, of a great deal of heterosexual pornography of the seventies – of a sadistic, goal-orientated, purely masculine desire, and see it through the grid of many more polymorphic perversities. Psychoanalyst Parveen Adams, in a reworking of Freud's 'A Child is Being Beaten' from the perspective of both masculine and feminine sexual identity as well as hetero- or homosexual object-choice,[22] shows, for example, how identification with any of the three roles posited by this scenario – the beater, the beaten, or the onlooker – is not dependent upon a fixed masculine or feminine identity, nor upon the sexual object-choice that presumably follows from this gender identity. Adams argues instead that it is in the very nature of fantasy to permit multiple identifications with the full gamut of positions within the imagined scene.

Citing a well-known fantasy of Freud's Dora, Adams argues that if Dora identifies with her father in this fantasy, that does not mean she also takes up a masculine position in it . . . that she, in effect, chooses only female objects. The reason Freud went wrong, Adams argues, in this case and with masochism in general, is that he too rigidly assumed that identification – the process by which a subject says 'I *am like* him or her' – was linked to, and produced by, object-choice – the process by which a subject says 'I *like* him or her'.

Adams thus argues that the point of the fantasy is not whom Dora loves (the male or the female object) but rather that her bisexual identification with the various roles in the scenario is not limited by a male or female object-choice. What this means for the feminist concerned about pornographies in which women seem to be encouraged to 'lose' themselves in an abandonment to pain (or pre-Oedipal merger, as the case may be) is quite simply that identification does not work this simply or this singly. Consider Claire, the apparent dominatrix who derives pleasure from punishing Anne in *The Punishment of Anne*. As the female dominatrix of the submissive Anne, we could identify her as a lesbian. Yet this would be to presume – as Adams suggested was not so in Dora's case – that sexual identity follows from the gender of object-choice, which is not always true in sadomasochistic fantasies produced by women, or in this film. Although it does not escape the binaries of sexual difference at work in all sexuality, and although it quite often maintains at least a pretence of 'normal' heterosexual object-choice, one important feature of sadomasochistic pornography – in contrast to both heterosexual and homosexual pornography – is thus that it is much less concerned with the biological sex of its sexual objects.[23]

Because genital sexuality is, for the most part, de-emphasized in s/m porn, scenarios of dominance and submission played out between same-sex partners do not powerfully connote a specifically gay or lesbian desire, but neither do they connote heterosexual desire. In contrast to both heterosexual and homosexual pornographies, sexual identities and sexual pleasures are presented in this type of pornography as more a function of performance than of biology. It is this performance of perverse desires which do not follow the expected routes of sexual identity (hetero or homo) or gender (male or female) that keeps both viewer and protagonists guessing about desires and pleasures that take surprising twists and turns.

Claire's calculated control of Anne's torture at first seems a lesbian passion to dominate another woman. Later, as she begins initiating the heterosexual male Jean into the realm of these pleasures, she seems simply a voyeur of Jean and Anne's relationship. Yet certain lapses of control suggest that something else is at work in Claire's desire – that she can occupy the vulnerable position as well. In the end we learn that Claire's ultimate goal is to teach Jean how she wishes him to dominate her in the future. She succeeds in this goal, and occupies this position at the end of the film. But who has really been dominated? The education of one person in the sexual fantasy of another through complex role-playing rather than fixed sexual identities, cued often to works of art – in this case a set of black-and-white photographs Claire shows Jean – is arguably the most distinctive feature of sadomasochistic fantasy. While the film ends with the spectacle of female domination by a male dominator, the pleasures of this domination are quite actively of Claire's own making.

The remarkable, but 'politically incorrect', popularity of sadomasochistic fantasy among many contemporary women does not mean that feminism has retreated and the masculine sadists have won. Indeed, it could mean that the compulsion for women to be strong necessitates an erotically transgressive release in being dominated. Or, conversely, it could also offer a way for more traditional, dominated women whose desires have not been recognized as legitimate or important to explore sexual agency in the 'devious' and indirect ways familiar to women.

Before moving to the next category of 'other' pornography, let me comment so far on the relations obtaining between the three categories mapped so far, and on what may now be perceived as the missing link of lesbian pornography needed to complete the discussion of the general category of homosexual pornography. I have saved the discussion of this subcategory until now because, as a new type of pornography that has emerged on the market only in the last few years, it needs to be situated in relation to – and in a sense as a comment on – previously existing forms: conventional heterosexual pornography 'for' men; the newer heterosexual pornography that is also 'for' women; gay male pornography; and sadomasochistic pornography which is not otherwise marked as gay or lesbian. In particular it needs to be situated within the discussion of female agency in the domain of sexual representations. For my point about all these categories, not only the new ones, is not their autonomy and absolute difference from previous forms of the genre, but the sense in which intrageneric forms of pornography (like all popular genres) 'talk' to one another about what it is like in pornotopia.

The new lesbian pornography, for example, is not simply the counterpart to gay male pornography but has a very different relationship to the phallus that we have seen to loom so large in all forms of pornography, even in the sadomasochistic disavowal of it. Indeed, this category appears to have borrowed a great deal from the role-playing of sadomasochistic pornography while still retaining the goal-orientated, problem-solving couple orientation of certain kinds of heterosexual couples' pornography.

In addition, lesbian pornography has the rather special problem of differentiating itself from the lesbian numbers that were already staples of heterosexual pornographies aimed primarily at male audiences. In this dominant form of pornography it is rigorously taboo for a male to take another male as his object of desire, but almost a requirement of the 'diff'rent strokes' ethic of post-1970s heterosexual pornography for women to do so. Masculine heterosexual identity has long been threatened by the perverse swerving away from 'proper' to 'improper' object-choice in male-to-male numbers, but has not similarly been threatened by what the industry calls girl–girl numbers.

In heterosexual pornography these girl–girl numbers, though included under the 'diff'rent strokes' ethic, were often constructed as not quite satisfying in themselves. Such numbers would then be spied upon or interrupted by an always welcome male intruder. For example, in a sequence of the popular heterosexual (yuppie) porn marketed primarily to couples, *Every Woman Has a Fantasy* (1984), the 'lesbian' number is performed and shot for the obvious visual pleasure of a man who first watches and then joins in. In this film, as in many others, the pleasure of the lesbian encounter is contained and consumed by masculine, heterosexual frames.

Nevertheless, there was never any guarantee that girl–girl numbers originally constructed for the heterosexual pleasure of masculine viewers could not be appropriated to different ends by different viewers, or performed with inspiration by atypically enthusiastic performers.[24] For example, not only might a lesbian viewer who happened upon a pornography that was not marketed to her enjoy these numbers despite their heterosexual frame, but as couples' pornography began to work harder to appeal to women viewers in the 1980s[25] lesbian numbers began to be treated with a new respect – not necessarily a representation of 'authentic' lesbian desire, but at least no longer functioning simply as a warm-up for the male intruder. Sometimes, as in the videos by Femme Productions, it could even function as an 'ultimate' sexual act, fulfilling in itself but usually still existing within a range of other, heterosexual numbers.[26] In this context the lesbian number conveyed the idea not of an exclusively same-sex object-choice but of an oscillating bisexuality viewed, until very recently in all pornographies, as unique to women.

In the new lesbian pornography 'for' lesbians that has been appearing on the market since the mid 1980s, the lesbian number functions neither as 'warm-up' to heterosexual sex nor as an exotic variation on more normal relations. However, the quest for knowledge of an other does not dissipate just because the other is the same sex – nor, perhaps surprisingly, does the significance of the phallus as signifier of difference and desire. Rather, what tends to occur in this new lesbian pornography are wide varieties of sexual numbers devoted to playing out roles of butch/femme which were once entirely suppressed in the girl–girl numbers of heterosexual pornography.

For example, in *Suburban Dykes* (Debi Sundahl, 1990) a mildly differentiated butch/femme couple worry about 'lesbian bed death' – a loss of desire occurring in lesbian couples of their acquaintance. Like mainstream heterosexual pornography – and unlike gay porn, which tends to be more haptic and combinatory – sex is presented as a problem to which more different, better sex is the solution. A voyeuristic glimpse of another lesbian couple's passionate lovemaking in a garage encourages the couple to become more adventurous – to try phone sex. They make a call. At the end of the line a certain 'Mistress Marlene' guides them through a masturbatory fantasy that includes the description of a dildo. Surprised at their pleasure in this fantasy, they next invite a 'big bad butch' with a bag of paraphernalia to take charge of their pleasure. In a scene that includes instruction on safe-sex techniques, the leather-clad 'big bad butch' authoritatively shows the butch partner how to use a dildo. The properly instructed butch partner then takes on the 'big bad butch' herself, and a *ménage à trois* ensues.

Quite self-consciously, *Suburban Dykes* embraces butch/femme role-playing and certain mild forms of s/m that had been kept off-scene both in previous lesbian feminist celebrations of woman-to-woman sexuality[27] and in the girl–girl numbers of heterosexual porn. Such role play, especially that of the butch, was once attributed to a 'perverse' desire to impersonate a male that was deemed insufficiently feminist with respect to a 'normal' lesbian sexuality idealized as non-hierarchical. Yet perhaps because it transgresses these norms, perhaps because it has been taboo among 'politically correct' lesbians, this differentiation and the accompanying roles of dominance and submission have emerged as a powerful source of eroticism in lesbian pornography. In this video, feminist goals announced in the form of written text at the beginning state: 'As women and as homosexuals lesbians deserve to have available to them quality sexual entertainment materials. These materials reflect the feminist right for control over our bodies, thereby promoting female sexual autonomy.' Where an earlier lesbianism eschewed both penis and phallus, as well as the image of butch and femme, on the premiss that it represented a perverse feminine appropriation of masculine power and potency, in the new lesbian pornography this perversion is embraced; the dildo is a fetish if ever there was one, but for what does it stand?

The difficulty in answering rests in the fact that a simple binary of the male and female gender does not accurately characterize what is going on when the lesbian sadomasochist puts on the dildo. When this woman puts on the dildo her fantasy does not seem to be that she *is* a man. Psychoanalytic theory, so devoted to its case histories of male fetishists and masochists, has too often presumed this to be the case and has therefore not done much to illuminate female desires, perverse or otherwise.[28] Nevertheless, psychoanalytic theories of the formation of the 'normally' gendered and sexually desiring subject can help us to formulate why 'perversions' such as the lesbian with the dildo have been perceived as erotically empowering.

As noted earlier, desire is a problem for the normal woman because her biological difference from the man gives her a different relationship to the phallus. According to Freud, the girl's incomplete resolution of the Oedipus complex leaves her with three options, each of which offers her an unsatisfying relationship to the paternal phallus: to remain within the Oedipus complex, unresolved about sexuality, not acceding to desire, perhaps envying the penis (one mode of the 'masculinity complex'); to exit the complex and accede to desire by identifying with the father (another mode of the masculinity complex: the fantasy that she really *is* a man and does possess the penis, and must thus masquerade in order to 'pass' as a woman); finally, to perceive that a baby would be a good substitute for the phallus she cannot have (femininity complex).[29]

Such, at least, is the grim story told by psychoanalytic theory of the differently gendered subject's relationship to the paternal phallus. But Adams goes on to tell the story of the female sadomasochist and the female fetishist's different relationship to this phallus. She notes that in the 'normal' neuroses the phallus shores up the familial and social order, while in the perversions it is the occasion of transgression. Where the 'normal' neurotic recognizes that the father is the possessor of the phallus and identifies accordingly, the pervert, as we have already seen in the case of the masochist, disavows this paternal phallus. While the phallus continues to function as the signifier of desire, there is a sense in which the pervert recognizes, as Adams puts it, that no one has the phallus: 'It is in the perversions that we see the possibility that the form desire takes will be freed from the penile representation of the phallus and freed into a mobility of representations' (p. 258).

We see this mobility of representations when the lesbian sadomasochist sports the dildo. By possessing a mock penis, this woman accedes to desire without entrapping herself in the masculinity complex of a fantasy masculine identity. For the point about this dildo is not only that she puts it on but also that she takes it off. The dildo is an option, not a necessary fantasy; it offers a welcome manipulation and perverse, but not pathological, play with an inevitable symbol of 'normal' desire. The point of this play with the phallus to the lesbian viewer – and, perhaps, to any other viewer who wishes 'in' on the play – is neither that the dildo is a penis *manquée* nor that it is believed in as substitute for the 'real thing', but rather the proof that there is no 'real thing' based in biology. In addition, as a detachable organ manipulated by the 'butch/top' this phallic symbol is proudly asserted as better able to give pleasure than the 'real thing'.

It is ironic, of course, that such a blatant phallic symbol should be the tool of the subversion of the phallus by aiding the assertion of woman's sexual sufficiency. But we are in the realm of the erotic organization of the visible, where impossible attempts to show the elusive and impossible 'it' abound. What is significant about *this* 'it', however, is just how (literally) detached from biological gender it is.

Context is, of course, crucial. As performance theorist Kate Davy, building upon work by Sue Ellen Case, has argued, attributes which in dominant culture are associated with strict gender roles are not sex–class-specific in butch–femme iconography because they have different meanings in this same-sex culture.[30] In a genre so dependent upon the engagement of fantasy, it may be a mistake, then, to assume that these subcultures are fixed enclaves of non-heterosexuality or non-male homosexuality, lest we reify the shifting and multiple identities and roles that pornographic texts, like other discourses of sexuality, are themselves constructing. Rather than preconstructed dominant sexual identities to which each discrete category of pornography speaks, we might more usefully think – especially in these newly emerging forms – of the various constructions and performances of different sexual and gender positions. We might also think of these positions as operating both in and across these different categories.[31]

This certainly seems to be the case in the final category of pornography I wish to map. I have saved this fourth category of pornography until last because, as the most recent form of commercial pornography to emerge on the market, it can best be understood as 'talking' to all the others. It may even make the most sense as a transgressive and perverse response to these other pornographies.

Bisexual film and video pornography tends to be recognizable by the word 'bi' – or sometimes the word 'switch' – in the title. This category has been growing since the mid 1980s: *Bi-Coastal* (1985), *Bisexual Fantasies* (1986); *Bi-Night*; *Bi-Dacious*; *Bi-Mistake* (1989); *Karen's Bi-Line* (1989) are a few typical titles. In these videos women engage in sex with men *and* women (not unusual in mainstream heterosexual pornography); men engage in sex acts with men *and* women (very unusual in mainstream). However, this often quite symmetrical switching of objects does not mean that bisexual pornography aims at a market of viewers identified only as bisexual. This would be commercially too restricted. The more paradoxical phenomenon of the 'bi' category – and the quality that has earned it the disdain of both hetero- and homosexual critics of the genre – seems, rather, to be its remarkable lack of fixed appeal, its ability to occupy hetero, homo, sadomasochistic and bi positions all at once without, however, being any one of them exclusively.

These videos most often begin with heterosexual presumptions of prescribed sexuality that appropriate objects of desire are of opposite sexes. But then, in the heat of pursuing this 'original' desire, 'diff'rent strokes' just seem to happen, usually without the intention or will of either stroker or stroked. Once these new, taboo pleasures are experienced, a kind of what-the-hell attitude prevails.

For example, heterosexual taboos against male-to-male sex might be broken via sadomasochistic injunction by the command of a dominating woman whose desire is to watch the men together. In one vignette from *Bisexual Fantasies* (Don Christian, 1986) a woman PE teacher catches two high-school boys peeping into the girls' shower room. The teacher punishes them by forcing them to strip and proceeds to stare at them in pleasure, then to direct their oral, then anal, activities, then to join in. The inscription of a female voyeur whose pleasure derives from watching and articulating her pleasure in watching men engaged in sexual acts with one another is an obvious reversal of heterosexual pornography's male voyeur and girl–girl number.

In other bisexual videos the world of rigid gender categories dissolves into a pornotopia of polymorphous perversity. For example, in *Bi-Mistake* (Shelton Howard Productions, 1989) a horny man goes to the 'No Expectations Dating Service'. Through a mix-up, the date he is fixed up with, Sandy (five foot eight, very oral), turns out to be a guy. Without any attendant implications for his sexual orientation, he makes the adjustment. The 'diff'rent strokes' ethic is articulated by the woman owner of 'No Expectations': 'Over here we have your garden-variety heterosexual; over there we have your homosexuals and over here we have your Tri-sexuals – they'll try anything once.'

No expectations, trying anything, 'diff'rent strokes' that do not originate from the fixed identities of 'diff'rent folks' – these are the new lessons for viewers of the new bisexual pornography. Bisexual videos make appeal to gay, straight and bisexual fantasy; everybody does it with everybody else, every which way; diversity is all. It is striking, for example, how often the ultimate and culminating number of these videos is a threesome rather than a twosome. The frequent introduction of a third party (either a man with two women or one woman and two men) into the binary system of sexual difference unsettles the usual masculine/feminine oppositions of heterosexual porn as well as the butch/femme opposition of homosexual lesbian porn. As in the punning notion of 'tri-sexuals', the introduction of a third party articulates pleasures that are not ascribed to strict oppositional differences.

Perhaps the most dramatic illustration of this desire to escape the sexual binary occurs in what might be called the subcategory of the 'bi- and beyond' videos. In *Bi- and Beyond: The Ultimate Union* (1986) the slim narrative begins with two women deep in discussion over what constitutes 'ultimate' pleasure, yet the word 'ultimate' here connotes neither a final aim of the subject's desire nor a climactic end. Rather, in this and other 'bi- and beyond' videos, 'the ultimate fantasy' exceeds and subverts both the heterosexual fantasy of the union of opposites and the homosexual fantasy of the union of same.

The video begins with a quotation from Ovid: 'Neither man nor woman yet both in a single body'. In the discussion of 'ultimate' pleasure, one woman says to another: 'I need to understand what a man feels.' Unthinkable in traditional masculine heterosexual forms of pornography, where the desire for and knowledge of the other originated from a masculine subject position and journeyed to knowledge about the always unknowable pleasure of women, this curiosity posed from the position of the feminine about the masculine is explored with a different twist: in terms of the fantasy of the hermaphrodite presumed to know both.

Here, the quest to know the other leads initially to a lesbian number. Like most 'first numbers' in pornography, it proves less than satisfying. In dialogue now with a man friend, the first woman 'confesses' her lesbian adventure and the news that 'it wasn't quite enough' to experience what a man feels. The man helpfully suggests that it might have been 'more complete' had he been there. While this scenario might seem to be setting up a conventional heterosexual threesome, the logic works differently in the bisexual category. The couple wake a male friend from a deep sleep. As in all 'bi' porn, he is as easily interested in him as in her, and his sleepy awakening seems symbolic of the not fully conscious slide into polymorphous perversity that is typical of the 'bi' category. The *ménage à trois* that ensues is marked, however, by an added level of interest in similar body parts – those parts of the male and female anatomy that are alike and might therefore have similar feelings.

For example, the initial male and female couple delight in exploring the buttocks of the awakened male. Later the first male delights in the similar buttocks of the male and female bottoms lined up in a row. A later scene emphasizes all three bottoms. The exploration of similar erogenous zones of the male and female body by a third party – male or female – represents a distinct aspect of the 'diff'rent strokes' of this category. But it is in the 'beyond' part of *this* bisexual fantasy that the quest to know ultimate pleasure is most completely explored – not by feeling what the other feels, but by encountering another body which combines being like one's own with being like the other.

In a museum the first woman runs into a mysterious woman who had fled an earlier sexual encounter. They are attracted to each other, but when the first woman pulls up the dress of the second she discovers a penis. 'You're a guy!' she exclaims. 'No, I'm both,' he/she replies. As in the discovery of the bisexual switch, there is no shock, only pleasure; as the video's theme song puts it, 'It's the best of both worlds.'

The woman investigates the hermaphrodite's body and discovers that she/he has penis, breasts, vagina, clitoris – indeed, everything but testicles, though even these are claimed to be hidden inside. A joyous and uncategorizable sexual number ensues, exploring a whole new range of 'diff'rent strokes' made possible by coupling with this multi-purpose body. In the next scene the woman takes the hermaphrodite as a gift to her male friend. The ensuing threesome emphasizes the orifices not explored in the previous number: namely, the vagina of the hermaphrodite and the anus of the male penetrated by the she/man. The video concludes, somewhat predictably, with a ritual orgy of bisexual, heterosexual and hermaphroditic couplings accompanied by pseudo-Ovidian rites.

How are we to describe, in our limited language of sexual dimorphism, the couplings depicted above? Where is male, where is female; where is active, where is passive? And in the subsequent subcategory, when the inevitable coupling of hermaphrodite with hermaphrodite occurs – as it does in *Bi-and Beyond III: The Hermaphrodites* – how shall we describe the pleasures of this sexual performance? The only thing that seems clear is that we cannot describe it in such binary terms. The hermaphrodite is welcome in (though not essential to) this bisexual category, as he/she is not in 'normal' life – nor, for that matter, in heterosexual, homosexual or sadomasochistic pornographies – because she/he embodies a knowledge of the other from both sides; he/she knows how both a man and a woman feel pleasure; she/he also symbolizes the continuum and variety of the basic binary oppositions of sexuality. He/she embodies a third sex, the tri-sexual who represents a pornotopian escape from the rigid binarism that actually prevails outside pornotopia among most gender-indeterminate beings who must quickly be assigned to one 'sex' or another.

In a famous passage in *The History of Sexuality*, Foucault writes that it is 'the agency of sex that we must break away from if we aim . . . to counter the grips of power with the claims of bodies, pleasures, and knowledge, in their multiplicity and their possibilities of resistance'.[32] If we assume that by the agency of sex Foucault means the basic binary of male and female, it is tempting to see, in the bisexual category of pornotopia, something akin to the realization of the celebration of 'bodies and pleasures' free from these binaries.

But it may be somewhat utopian to embrace this 'bodies and pleasures' conclusion too eagerly. For although these videos are restless and resist the fixed position of sexual difference and orientation, they offer no absolute escape from the binaries of sexual difference. It might be more appropriate, then, simply to note the increasing complexity and power of the perverse dynamic at work in all of these 'other' pornographies I have been mapping.

What we can say, however, is that bisexual pornography, even more than sadomasochistic pornography, is less fixed in either object-choice or aim than any of the other categories with which it is in dynamic relation. Thus, while there is no static and eternal binary of natural and unnatural, normal and perverse, while there is no 'metaphysical fixity' – of sexual identity, object or aim – that can be glimpsed in the field of pornographic moving-image representations, there *is* a perverse dynamic – an order and relation of perversions and norms – mapped here, imperfectly, in the tensions of these four categories – heterosexual, homosexual, s/m, and bisexual – which determine what can and cannot be brought 'on/scene' in any one category.

Conclusion

What conclusions can be drawn from this comparative analysis of the contemporary pornographic field? Perhaps the first is that while there is no escape from the power and dominance of the masculine heterosexual norm, it is precisely in the proliferation of different pornographies – of 'diff'rent strokes for diff'rent folks' – that opposition to the dominant representations of pleasure can emerge. It is thus in the profusion rather than the censoring of pornographies that one important resistance can be found to what many feminists have objected to in the dominance of the heterosexual masculine pornographic imagination. For it is because moving-image pornography became legal in the USA that the once off-scene voices of women, gays, lesbians, sadomasochists and bisexuals have been heard opposing and negating the heterosexual, males-only pornography that once dominated. Because heterosexual women wanted better sexual fantasies and engaged in a critique of the dominant heterosexual pornography, Femme Productions began to make heterosexual pornography for women, with clean sheets, handsome men and no money shots.[33] Because gays, lesbians, bisexuals and sadomasochists – all sexual identities or sexual practices defined as perverse with respect to a heterosexual norm, but all identities and practices which exist in dynamic relation to one another as well – were critical of the old straight-men-only pornography, some of the pornographies I have described above arose.

A second conclusion must be to note what pornographies did not arise in this new proliferation of perversions: there is no commercial market for kiddie porn. If an occasional underage performer is discovered, it is a source of great scandal and embarrassment to the industry. And, despite all the hype, there is no snuff; nor does rape figure prominently in the narratives of recent pornography.[34] Since pornography is about pleasure and aims to produce sexual pleasure in its viewers, it is actually one of the few types of contemporary film narrative not to punish its female protagonists for seeking pleasure. Compare, for example, almost any recent porn video to the 'legitimate' Hollywood genres in which women are regularly punished for seeking pleasure: for example, *Fatal Attraction* (Adrian Lyne, 1986), or the 'slasher' horror films.

A third conclusion is that while it is instructive to categorize these different pornographies as I have done, it would be a mistake to assume that each category makes its appeal only to particular fixed gender and/or sexual orientations. Indeed, the most striking feature of recent film and video pornographies is the extent to which specific and unitary sexual or gender address – masculine, feminine, gay, lesbian, sadomasochistic, bi – have begun to blur.

For better and for worse, pornography has emerged from the privacy of the males-only 'secret museums'. In coming 'on/scene' so forcefully, pornography has revealed a truth that its would-be censors would prefer not to face: that 'perverse' pornographies can no longer be confined to the wings of our sexual stage; that perversions of all sorts are intrinsic to sexuality and to sexual representations. The history of pornography, if it is ever written, will be a long and complex dynamic between shifting norms and perversions whose relations are not fixed. Certainly the history of visual media in this century reveals a steady normalization of the perversion of voyeurism. The norms of sexual (and visual) pleasure have always been in flux, but in contemporary film and video pornography – in what I would like to call the on/scenity of one increasingly important discourse of sexuality – we can observe remarkable instances of flux.

Moving-image pornography is diverse and perverse, but there is no monolithic pathology that can be demonized as obscene pornography, and there is no fixed opposition between norm and perversion. All attempts to represent the ultimate pleasure of sex have recourse to some kind of perverse dynamic. Rather than condemning the sexual pleasures of perverse others – the many 'diff'rent strokes' of many 'diff'rent folks' – we do better to rethink the very meaning of the terms 'obscenity' and 'perversion'. I have already suggested the term on/scenity as an appropriate replacement for ob/scenity. Such a term at least suggests that these representations can no longer be conveniently placed beyond all understanding. Obscenity is already onscenity; we are all perverts in our desires.

This essay has proved harder to write than any I have ever attempted. I fear, moreover, that this is only a preliminary sketch of much more substantial work that needs to be done in this area. In the year I have been writing – and often unwriting – it I have benefited from the comments of many friends and colleagues who have taken the time and effort to help clarify my thinking about these 'other pornographies'. I would like to thank especially Judith Gardiner for some particularly penetrating insights about sexual agency. I am also indebted to: Rhona Berenstein, Susie

Bright, Nick Browne, Ted Bunner, Kate Davy, Paul Fitzgerald, Chuck Kleinhans, Chris Straayer, Sharon Ullman and Peter Wollen.

Loretta Loach

Bad girls
Women who use pornography

The subject of pornography weaves persistently in and out of thoughts and conversations about sex, politics and feminism. But for all the talk, reading and listening, I have never managed to come away with a satisfactory belief about it. I don't mean an opinion or analysis, but something more. It seemed as if one could only either accept the topic neutrally, or reject it with ferocity and indignation. Either way, I was confronted with a dead end. For me there was always a missing element which I only later identified as that realm of *experience* which fell between these two implacably opposed positions. It is the women who consume pornography, and in increasing numbers, who might, I thought, offer me a way into that kind of experience – one which would inevitably result in some discomfort.

'Every question,' says Julia Kristeva, 'no matter how intellectual in content, reflects suffering.'[1] I didn't feel anything quite so sublime when I questioned the small number of women who had kindly agreed to talk to me about their enjoyment of pornography. But I did suffer a shuddering, a disorientation of some kind: a realization that I myself, at some deep level, am as perverse as they – not in a pejorative sense, but in the way that human nature can be perverse while at the same time being many other things besides. This simple discovery shook the tenuous ground upon which I had structured a belief in feminism. I have only the women I interviewed to blame – and to thank – for that.

*   *   *

Josephine Ventnor lives among the quiet gardens and pathways of a council estate in Oxfordshire. It's a modern, open estate where house upon house sit together in a regiment of drives, crofts and avenues.

In this settlement, days are taken up with the customary rhythms of home life: washing, ironing, mowing the lawn. Every Sunday Josephine uproots herself from this comfortable landscape to attend church and receive communion. Her religion is a strong personal feeling which she describes as 'not unlike sex in many ways', her passion being excited more by ritual than by piety. Ritual plays quite a part in Josephine's life, but for all my metropolitan knowingness nothing had quite prepared me for the part it played in her sexuality.

So many things about Josephine stood in contrast to what I heard: conventional Christianity, a secure, happy marriage, and – dare I say it? – motherhood. Sexually, though, there were also many things about Josephine which were quite straitlaced. She doesn't like oral sex, certainly never anal sex, and she's never been into doing it in strange places. There's nothing exaggerated about her femininity either, yet her sexual satisfaction is almost entirely conditional on her own ritual humiliation: 'There's a battle going on inside me; a lot of the time I'm very independent and very strong-willed. I have a very equal relationship with Bill [her husband] in everything except for that moment in sex when he takes over and becomes boss, it's quite safe.'

Sex only ever happens if Josephine wants it, and it has to happen in the particular way that she wants it. As with any practised masochist, chosen passivity coexists with a convenient self-assertion; it's this which enables boundaries to be drawn between pleasure and precariousness.

Twenty years ago, when she married Bill, it took a long time to persuade him to take part in her desires: 'He didn't like it, he didn't want anything to do with it, so I plonked all these magazines in front of him and said this is what I'm into and he's had to come to terms with it; it has been a long period of discovery together.' The magazines were pornographic – not the girlie kind which relies on the body and nothing else: a voluptuous Tara or a sullied Madonna, breasts straining off every page. Josephine's taste is for lustful exchange, not easy to come by in Britain.

Apart from Ireland, Britain has the most extensive censorship laws in Europe. Hard-core pornography is illegal here, yet in many respects it has a more sophisticated sexual language than its soft-core counterpart. Because it deals more explicitly in sex and sexual happenings, it offers more potentially to women than the unsprung imagery of *Mayfair* or *Penthouse*.

The term 'hard core' is curious. For the uninitiated like myself, it conjures up images of horrendous acts with animals or children, or violent and unspeakable goings-on among adults. In fact, 90 per cent of the total volume of hard-core business is 'mainstream'[2] – that is, variations on the stable and popular narratives involving lonely housewives visited by the central-heating engineer and the window-cleaner who sees them both and ejaculates all over the window. Or there is the husband who comes home to find his wife in bed with the maid – invariably he joins them, proving that no sex is quite complete without a man. In other words, couples, sometimes more, have sex in different ways, different positions and different places.

Colour Climax, a popular Danish magazine and a favourite of one of the women I spoke to, usually has a story line and photographs involving a group of people who end up having sex together. The locations vary: English stately homes, castles in Spain – one issue had two Mexican men making love to a Swedish blonde in the mountains. 'It's like going to a restaurant,' one woman said about her taste in porn. 'You want something a little bit more unusual than you'd cook yourself.'

The women I spoke to enjoy and seek out pornography. They are the hidden participants in the porn controversy, the transgressors, the bad girls who refuse to be repressed by politics. They form part of a growing number of women who inhabit the marketplace for porn. A clear estimate of just how many they are is not yet known, but they appear in surveys:

30 per cent of consumers in Australia are women, a third in Copenhagen, 40 per cent in the States. The American magazine *Redbook* concluded from its survey of 26,000 women that nearly half watched pornographic films regularly, and a recent study from the Institute of Clinical Sexology in Rome found that 85 per cent of the women interviewed fashioned their sexual fantasies around stories they gleaned from pornography.[3]

Porn has its own history, just like any other medium, and it is a history which is inseparable from the contemporary shifts in sexuality. As a way of speaking about sex, more sex, different sex and better sex, porn inevitably encounters women's pleasure as well as men's. Recently, the British soft-core magazine *Forum* published a discussion between women about sexuality. The editor, Elizabeth Caldwell, told me: 'Men will undoubtedly read this – they want to know what women talk about behind closed doors, they want to know what women like, and our message to our readers is always that whatever you do, think about the other person; if they don't want to do something, if they don't want to try something out, then that must be respected.'

Forum's popularity with women (it claims to have a female readership of about 40 per cent) has a lot to do with the absence of girlie photographs. One reader I contacted told me that *Forum* worked well for her because of this: 'It stimulates the imagination.' Another found the illustrations, usually of unspecified gender, artful and erotic; a refreshing change from the 'sleazy stuff where everything is exaggerated – the girls are sticking their tongue out or she's holding herself open looking thoroughly bored as though she's saying, "Here it is, you load of old wankers" – that turns me right off.'

Clearly some pornographic genres – the majority, in fact – are based on the power of the phallus (in every sense of the word), a focus reinforced by soft-core magazines. *Forum*, on the other hand, caters for female pleasure too: 'For the past four years the entire editorial staff have been women,' says the editor. 'That doesn't mean what's being put across is from a woman's point of view, but it isn't quite a man's either. We feel we've got to keep people up to date with everybody's sexuality, whether they're man, woman, straight or gay, because there's so much intolerance around. Just by concentrating on heterosexual men, as some magazines do, you miss out, you get a very narrow view, and that's how myths get reinforced.'

It is overwhelmingly men who buy *Forum*, but research confirms that women read it: 'We found that couples often read it out loud to one another in bed; it's very sexy.' Couples' pornography seems to have had some effect on the medium in general. Research by another contributor to this volume, Linda Williams, showed that material aimed at couples offers a 'softer, cleaner, nicer version of the stock numbers. The improved qualities include higher production values, better lighting, fewer pimples on bottoms, better-looking male performers who now take off their shoes and socks and female performers who leave on shoes and expensive-looking lingerie.' In the couples-market context, women's pleasure is taken more seriously and the story line embraces the quest of helping women to achieve it. According to Williams, 'This pornographic speech by women hasn't developed out of any altruistic spirit of democratic inclusion but rather strictly as a matter of capitalist expansion.'[4]

So pornography has its uses: it may reinforce traditional sexuality, but it apparently overturns it too. Each of the women I spoke to believed that porn had enabled her to detect layers of repressed sexuality as well as confirm existing desires. In other words, it gave them power; pornography wasn't in itself a means of gratification, but it was a necessary help towards it. By releasing themselves from what they described as taboos, they have become sexually erudite about things which for many still remain hidden as a set of disturbed, inchoate emotions.

Their comments suggested a common-sense view of sex, but at the same time they are wise to its complexities. They see romance as part of the game but they resent its greater legitimacy, its idealization of men's power and protective-ness: 'A lot of women are stuck in a romantic thing,' one woman told me. 'This might sound as if it's better than what I'm into, but I feel as though I know myself better. I know the difference between a love relationship and a lust relationship and when I'm just playing at something. I know when I'm being sadistic or masochistic, all of which are present in a person but they can often be just used emotionally – I mean, men and women torment each other dreadfully, there can be so much unconscious abuse.'

'I suppose I've got a cruel streak,' another confessed, with chilling honesty. 'I used to be mean to my boyfriends sometimes, then I'd think, "Why am I being so vile to this chap? He hasn't done anything to deserve it." I realized that if I could get a kick out of hitting someone with a whip that would be okay and I didn't have to feel guilty because after all the person would be enjoying it.'

Each of these women had in common the enjoyment of punishment and sexual surrender. Some liked to give it, others liked to receive it, one or two even liked to do both. Josephine, who began this story, likes to be spanked and dominated by her husband. He is not a very convincing sadist – he looked rather embarrassed when he opened the door to me and shook my hand. It's obvious that he cannot quite understand his wife's propensities, that at first he found them disturbing, then provocative, but now they're an accepted part of her, just like everything else. *Painful Promotion* and *Bondage Nightmare*, two porn favourites of Josephine's, coexist happily in her life with the diligent work she does for the parish newsletter.

However, despite the subject's recent and fashionable exposure in our culture, the market for heterosexual sadomasochism remains small, accounting for about 10 per cent of total sales. Rodox Trading, one of the biggest Scandinavian porn businesses, sells a magazine called *Sex Bizarre*. It contains serious s/m stuff but its circulation is about 25,000, well below the 40,000 figure which puts a hard-core magazine into the bestselling category and even further below the

227,980 sales of something like the soft-core *Club International*.

According to the recent and comprehensive survey of research on pornography commissioned by the Home Office, there is more evidence to suggest that violence is rare rather than extensive, as its many detractors claim. One North American study cited found that out of three hundred titles roughly 7 per cent involved s/m with women being submissive and 9 per cent involved the man in that role.

In one sense these women see anti-porn feminists as terrorizing their sexuality. They voiced concern about anti-porn feminists' claims, and they wanted to resist the definition this feminism makes of them: it suggests implicitly that women who use or enjoy pornography are dupes, oppressed and unwilling victims of male sexuality. Such views are regarded by the women I spoke to as inappropriate, as hopelessly misplaced as the views of their parents articulated several generations earlier.

There is agreement that sex is about power, but not always men's power in relation to women. In the women's sexual life, power isn't experienced only as force or domination, though it can be; it produces pleasure, knowledge and control too. It is this ambiguity which is so unsettling to the politics of feminism.

I confess I was disturbed by aspects of my interaction with these women. It wasn't that I thought them unusual, grandiose or degenerate. On the contrary, they seemed to me quite ordinary, though perhaps braver and more adventurous than most. But there was something about how far they were prepared to go which left me with the disquieting feeling that there weren't any boundaries left. I suppose I'm talking about moral boundaries – not that I considered the women immoral; on the contrary, it was that I felt too moral, I felt that their approach to what they did, their way of thinking and feeling about it, challenged me, made me excited and fearful at the same time.

It then occurred to me that the conflicts within feminism about sexuality aren't so much about a difference in politics as a difference in how far we are each prepared to confront and accept the 'dark side' of various human endeavours. Tensions arise because our response to the sexual pleasures of others is inescapably moral; certain forms of pleasure appear to us as opposed or indifferent to the principle of better relationships.

The arguments about pornography seem to be underpinned by these unacknowleged ethical concerns, especially as it is 'dirty' or 'naughty' sex heightened by illegality. Is it a positive, liberating and enlivening force thwarted and repressed by culture, or is it a primitive force needing to be controlled and humanized by feminism? Such questions underlie the ambivalence women have about their own sexual power and freedom. If pleasure cannot be evaluated by love and egalitarianism, then how can we judge it? How can it be positive or productive towards the progress of humanity as a whole? What appears to be particularly disturbing to some feminists is that female sexuality, at least for some women, has now become much more associated with aggressive, tough, sometimes even violent behaviour; it is the unacceptable face of female power – unacceptable not only to many men (witness their hostility to Madonna, for example) but to a great number of women too.

For many feminists power is something negative, omething men have in relation to women, seen as cultural a temporary disturbance in what is otherwise reassuringiy clear – the 'true' relations of equality between the sexes. Once these distorted power relations are removed, the aim, politically, is to establish a point of balance and reconciliation. But what if no such point exists? What if, as Nietzsche said, 'When the oppressed want justice it's just a pretext for saying they want power themselves'? If this is the case, if we accept that women can be 'into' power in the same way that some men are, it appears as if we're saying that there is something inherently oppressive in all forms of human society, and what happens to the hopes of feminism then?

Our present political landscape is furnished with such anxieties. They're not so much about the formalities of feminism, its theory or ideology, but about the feelings we invest in ideas and how they come to have such a hold over us. These feelings exert palpable pressures upon our beliefs; they impede; they make us quick to condemn on the one hand or collapse without hope on the other. Above all, they make us forget history and our place within it – we have no awareness, as Kate Soper argues, 'of how parochial it is to present the loss of hope or progress as a universally available mode of adjustment to the ugliness of our times'.[5]

The continuing discrepancy between ideals and conduct indicates the complexity of our nature. Criticism or judgement of specific power relations is no less correct for this. But judgement can mean different things; it should aim at understanding. Yet those who campaign against pornography consistently fail to offer this to the likes of the women I spoke to. Is it because, if they looked and listened, they might not be able to distinguish between the good girls and the bad?

Gillian Rodgerson

Lesbian erotic explorations

In August 1988 the American lesbian writer Joan Nestle visited London in connection with the publication of her book *A Restricted Country* by Sheba Feminist Publishers. As she gave readings from her work and was interviewed by the gay and feminist press, Nestle lit a spark in the city's lesbian community. Pornography and erotica, butch and femme, the place of sadomasochism in our sexual repertoires – these had all been discussed before, but during Nestle's visit, battle lines were drawn.

A Restricted Country exemplifies what many anti-censorship feminists mean when they talk about a new kind of erotica or a lesbian-feminist pornography. In Nestle's personal, sexy stories women have orgasms and they have emotions; their sexual lives are chronicled as part of their political and social lives. They make no apologies for being lesbians but, perhaps more importantly, they make no apologies for being fat, for being over thirty, for liking to be vulnerable or powerless when they are having sex, or for liking their lovers to feel that way.

In the United States, *A Restricted Country* has been part of an explosion of explicitly sexual material produced by and for lesbians. Publications have included *Coming To Power* (1982), a collection of short stories about lesbian s/m sex and other work by Pat Califia, the magazines *Bad Attitude* (started in Boston by Cindy Patton and Amy Hoffman) and *On Our Backs* (launched in San Francisco by Debi Sundahl and Susie Bright, who worked in the women's sex toy shop Good

Vibrations. Later came the lesbian videos of Blush Productions and others.

Our antiquated, protectionist Customs laws give British lesbians only limited access to American sex material. We must risk smuggling it in in our suitcases after trips abroad, begging friends to do the same, or take a chance on mail order being seized by Customs authorities. If it's seized we risk public embarrassment, fines, destruction of valuable property, and at worst prison. Only one woman, lesbian grandmother Jenny White, has publicly challenged HM Customs for seizing sex videos imported through the post. Ms White lost her case but won a moral victory when the magistrate refused to award costs to Customs against her. Unfortunately, however, her copies of *Hungry Hearts*, *Clips* and *Aerobisex Girls*, ordered from Good Vibrations, were destroyed, at a cost to Ms White of £80.

In spite of all this, and in spite of repressive obscenity laws, which judge lesbian sexuality as being in itself offensive and degrading, and in spite of a growing attitude of censoriousness within the lesbian-feminist community itself, there has been a small but significant explosion of lesbian sex material in Britain. I spoke to Della Grace, an American photographer now living in Britain, whose first book, *Love Bites*, has recently been published by GMP, to Michelle McKenzie and Araba Mercer of Sheba, producers of the lesbian erotica collections *Serious Pleasure* and *More Serious Pleasure*, and to Sophie Moorcock and Lulu, the editors of the British lesbian sex magazine *Quim*. These women voiced similar reasons for wanting to produce lesbian erotica, and described similar reactions to it from the lesbian community. Lesbian pornography is different from the glossy material produced for heterosexual men, and it's not just that there's no room left for the man. I asked the women I spoke with what they thought made good porn.

Sophie and Lulu told me that the personal element in the writing is what makes *Quim* so special. They took a hardback notebook round to some of their favourite lesbian pubs and asked people to use the book to respond to a series of questions for various sections of *Quim*. 'People put in their own fantasies: whether they've been able to create them or whether they're in their heads, what comes through is the passion of it being personal.'

The call for submissions to *Serious Pleasure* elicited more formal manuscripts. These suggested that even this relatively new genre was becoming standardized into common types of stories such as teacher fantasies on leather club tales. The Sheba women say they try to address the problems of formulaic writing in workshop discussions.

In the better stories there are realistically developed characters. Whether you can identify with them or not, there's something about them that isn't just cardboard, and there's a real situation, a believable context, and then the sex scenes complement the rest, whereas porn is only about getting to the point of having sex.

More Serious Pleasure, a second collection published in November 1990, built on the lessons learned with the first book. One criticism of *Serious Pleasure* was that everyone, in the end, had an orgasm. *More Serious Pleasure* is about how sex and love and relationships work together or don't work together, sometimes one and not the other. There are also more stories by older writers.

There is often debate among lesbian feminists about whether our sexually explicit material should be called 'erotica' or 'porn' or both. Photographer Della Grace says of these terms: 'I have problems with both of them. I don't consider myself a lesbian pornographer. I could be if I wanted to be. But I think pornography is a very subjective term that's very charged politically and I don't set out to take erotica and I don't set out to do pornography. I'm happy if someone gets an erotic buzz. To me pornography is skin magazines. It's like cocks and cunts. I don't have any problems with it, I've used it but it also has a feeling of shame to it, and that's why I don't like to call my work pornography.

'It's something I might have a wank to and then immediately close and forget about. I don't want my photographs to feel like that.'

Both *Quim* and *Love Bites* feature photographs of lesbians in a variety of situations, sexual and non-sexual. Della, Sophie and Lulu all felt it was crucial to portray lesbians' lives in their larger context, so that we are not reduced to just sexual beings, but without that dimension being discounted. The first issue of *Quim* was purely about sex; the second also featured club and music reviews.

Love Bites shows women, in sexual poses, but it also contains shots of demonstrations and happy evenings in bars. This affirmation of lesbian sexual and public lives was important to all the women I interviewed and they hoped it would be clear to their readers, and help them feel positive about their sexual choices. They all stressed that their work was produced from a feminist perspective, and all expressed sadness and anger about reactions from that part of the feminist community which seeks to censor sexual images of women on the grounds that they are always exploitative and violent, regardless of how they are produced.

Della Grace wants her audience to include 'women who feel quite shut out by the women's movement, by the lesbian movement . . . but we're being told that we're not feminist, that we're colluding with the enemy, and I want them to know that that's not the case with everyone. I want them to look at the pictures and see that sex isn't necessarily a shameful dirty secret.'

When the first issue of *Quim* came out it caused an uproar in some British feminist circles, prompting personal abuse and accusations of encouraging rape. Despite a solid feminist reputation, Sheba was also the target of attacks by the pro-censorship lobby. Critics of *Serious Pleasure* cited the American writer Audre Lorde, whose book of essays, *A Burst of Light* was published by Sheba in 1989, as an example of the kind of work the company should stick with. Lorde's book contains an essay against sadomasochism. Sheba's editors are convinced that, through pro-censorship attacks, they have lost the support of many erstwhile readers. Hostile reviews alone have convinced some feminists that the collective was purveying pornography and impugning feminist moral integrity. They now see part of the fight as being about who can define or own the term 'feminism': 'Because of *Serious Pleasure* we are now referred to as Sheba "Feminist" Publishers, in inverted commas.'

At the heart of these divisions is women's status as 'eternal victims', suggests Michelle McKenzie. She rejects the view 'that we've always been victims and we always will be victims – victims of abuse and of patriarchal power. Do we always have to define ourselves in that way? Do we always have to come at things in a reactive way as opposed to a productive, creative way? Do we always have to be reacting to how men define women, how men define porn or men define sex? Or rather how heterosexual men and women do.'

Lynda Nead

The female nude
Pornography, art, and sexuality

> To my mind art exists in the realm of contemplation, and
> is bound by some sort of imaginative transposition. The
> moment art becomes an incentive to action it loses its true
> character. This is my objection to painting with a
> communist programme, and it would also apply to
> pornography.
>
> (Kenneth Clark, testimony to the Longford committee
> on pornography)

The evidence given by Kenneth Clark, one of the world's
leading art historians, to Lord Longford's committee on
pornography in Britain in 1972 is just one fragment of a vast
body of discourses that has been produced on the subject of
pornography over the last few decades.[1] The Longford committee was a privately sponsored investigation that claimed
to represent public opinion. Its report, published in the form
of a mass-market paperback and launched in a blaze of
publicity, fuelled the pornography debate in Britain in the
1970s. From the seventies onwards, feminists, moral crusaders, governments, and various other pressure groups
have presented their views on the issue, with the result that
pornography has become one of the most fiercely and publicly contested areas within contemporary cultural production.[2]

Perhaps one of the most disabling limitations of much of
this public debate has been the attempt to look at pornography as a discrete realm of representation, cut off and clearly

distinct from other forms of cultural production. This perspective is frequently attended by the view that the pornographic resides *in* the image, that it is a question of content rather than form, of production rather than consumption. Even when pornography is defined in terms of its circulation, as a matter of audience expectations, markets, and institutions, it is still separated off as though it exists in isolation and can be understood outside of its points of contact with the wider domain of cultural representation.

To suggest that pornography needs to be examined in relation to other forms of cultural production, however, is not to move towards the position that claims that *all* of patriarchal culture is therefore pornographic. It is simply to argue that we need to specify the ways in which pornography is defined and held in place. We need to get behind the common-sense notions of pornography in order to uncover the processes by which the term has been defined and the historical changes in its meaning. At any particular moment there is no one unified category of the pornographic but rather a struggle between several competing definitions of decency and indecency. As John Ellis has written,

> These definitions will work within a context defined by several forces, the current form of the pornography industry and its particular attempts at legitimisation; the particular forms of the laws relating to obscenity and censorship; and the general mobilisation of various moral and philosophical positions and themes that characterise a particular social moment.[3]

Ellis's comments begin to move the debate towards a model of the discursive formation of pornography; a formation that includes its operations as an industry, its forms of distribution and consumption, its visual codings, and its very status as the illicit.

One of the most significant ways in which pornography is historically defined is in relation to other forms of cultural production; we know the pornographic in terms of its difference, in terms of what it is not. The most commonplace opposition to pornography is art. If art is a reflection of the highest social values, then pornography is a symptom of a rotten society; if art stands for lasting, universal values, then pornography represents disposability, trash. Art is a sign of cleanliness and licit morality, whereas pornography symbolizes filth and the illicit. In this cultural system, aesthetic values readily communicate sexual and moral values. This is the basis of Kenneth Clark's testimony, in which art and pornography are defined in terms of their effects on the spectator. Art is pacifying and contemplative, whereas communist painting and pornography incite the viewer to action and therefore cannot belong to the realm of high artistic culture.[4]

Although conventionally art and pornography are set up in this oppositional relationship, they can be seen instead as two terms within a greater signifying system that is continually being redefined and includes other categories, such as obscenity, the erotic, and the sensual. All these terms occupy particular sexual and cultural spaces; none of them can be understood in isolation, since each depends on the other for its meaning. From this position we can begin to examine the changing historical relationships between the terms and the ways in which the boundaries between these categories have been and continue to be policed in order to maintain the aesthetic and the pornographic as a necessary ideological polarity in patriarchal society.

The female nude: Policing the boundaries

It is often at the very edge of social categories that the work of definition takes place most energetically and meaning is anchored most forcefully. For art history, the female nude is both at the centre and at the margins of high culture. It is at the centre because within art-historical discourse paintings of the nude are seen as the visual culmination of Renaissance idealism and humanism. This authority is nevertheless always under threat, for the nude also stands at the edge of the art category, where it risks losing its respectability and spilling out and over into the pornographic. It is the vagueness and instability of such cultural definitions that make these marginal areas so open and precarious. Since pornography may be defined as any representation that achieves a certain degree of sexual explicitness, art has to be protected from being engulfed by pornography in order to maintain its position as the opposition to pornography. In other words, through a process of mutual definition, the two categories keep each other and the whole system in place. Categories such as the erotic and the sensual play an important role as middle terms in the system – defining what can or cannot be seen, differentiating allowable and illicit representations of the female body, and categorizing respectable and non-respectable forms of cultural consumption.

Within the history of art, the female nude is not simply one subject among others, one form among many, it is *the* subject, *the* form. It is a paradigm of Western high culture with its network of contingent values: civilization, edification, and aesthetic pleasure. The female nude is also a sign of those other, more hidden properties of patriarchal culture – that is, possession, power, and subordination. The female nude works both as a sexual and as a cultural category, but this is not simply a matter of content or some intrinsic meaning. The signification of the female nude cannot be separated from the historical discourses of culture – that is, the representation of the nude by critics and art historians. These texts do not simply analyse an already constituted area of cultural knowledge; rather, they actively define cultural knowledge. The nude is always organized into a particular cultural industry and thus circulates new definitions of class, gender, and morality. Moreover, representations of the female nude created by male artists not only testify to patriarchal understandings of female sexuality and femininity, they also endorse certain definitions of male sexuality and masculinity.

In Britain in the 1970s, the discourse of critics and art historians was implicated in a radical redefinition of sexuality. In the art world, there were renewed efforts to pin down the female nude in high art so as to free it from debasing associations with the sexual. These efforts were countered by other attempts to implicate the images of high culture in the pornographic. In the 1980s context created by AIDS, political conservatism and religious revivalism, the debate regarding sexuality and representation that took place in the 1970s has taken on a renewed significance. The boundaries between art and pornography continue to shift and to raise complex issues for feminist cultural and sexual politics.

The decade of the sixties in Britain was characterized by a series of legislative reforms in the sphere of moral and sexual conduct. Stuart Hall has described the general tendency of British national legislation in the 1960s as the shift towards 'increased regulation coupled with selective privatisation through contract or consent'.[5]

The Sexual Offences Act of 1967 changed the laws on male homosexuality, decriminalizing private sexual relations between adult males. In the same year, the Abortion Act extended the grounds for a lawful termination of pregnancy, and the Family Planning Act introduced wider provision of contraceptives by local authorities. Other legislation made divorce more accessible (1969) and introduced the defence of literary merit into trials charging publications with obscenity (1959 and 1964). At the same time, modification of cinema and theatre censorship allowed more explicit portrayals of sexuality in film and on the stage. This series of legislative reforms represents a shift in the style of moral regulation. Although collectively the British legislation shifted towards the general direction of a more relaxed, permissive moral code, the reforms of the sixties should be recognized as a revision of an older conservative moralism and an attempt to create a liberal form of morality at a moment when the main political and economic tendencies were also in the direction of a more libertarian form of capitalism.

Beginning in the late 1960s, the notion of permissiveness began to take on a particular symbolic importance. With signs of a breakdown in the old order, a growing sense of social crisis gave way, by the early 1970s, to a generalized moral panic – a moral backlash against the permissive legislation of the 1960s. On the left, the women's movement and the emerging gay liberation movement challenged the extent of the liberalism of the reforms, while on the right there was a revival of moral traditionalism, led, with evangelical fervour, by individuals such as Malcolm Muggeridge, Mary Whitehouse, and Lord Longford. According to this new authoritarian morality, the sixties legislation had been the final nail in the coffin of traditional values and Christian principles. The faction's leaders called for a return to family values and retrenchment behind the institutions of law and order.[6] The focus for this moral panic was the issue of pornography. Obscene and blasphemous material was seen to be the source of social and moral decay, undermining the family and corrupting both the public and the private spheres. As Jeffrey Weeks has commented, pornography became for the moral crusaders of the 1970s what prostitution had been for the social puritans of the 1880s – a symbol of decay and social breakdown.[7]

The new moralism of the 1970s focused on the image and the word. In the early 1970s there was a cluster of prosecutions for obscenity: the National Viewers' and Listeners' Association organized a popular campaign against immorality in broadcasting, and in 1972 Lord Longford published his report on pornography. The Longford report concluded that exposure to pornography adversely affected social behaviour and morality. The state, it seemed, could not be relied on to maintain sexual standards, and the report cited the Danish and American situations as examples of the state either failing to cohere and reflect public attitudes or adopting a radically libertarian position.[8] The most important point to be made about all these tactics is that moral regulation in the 1970s took the form of the regulation of *representations* of sexuality as opposed to regulation of sexual behaviour. Indeed, representation was at the centre of discourses on sexuality during the period.

In the context of this public debate, cultural classification became particularly significant, and the differentiation of terms such as the erotic and the obscene took on a heightened importance. The aesthetic had to be distinguished from the titillating; art had to be sealed off from pornography.

Historically, high culture has provided a space for a viable form of sexual representation: that which is aestheticized, contained, and allowed. In the 1970s, this site had to be reinforced and shored up. The differences between paintings of the female nude and 'pin-ups', glamour photography, soft- and hard-core porn had to be redefined. During this period the British Library catalogued the 1976 edition of Kenneth Clark's high-art survey, *The Nude*, in the general stacks, but relegated Arthur Goldsmith's *The Nude in Photography* and Michael Busselle's *Nude and Glamour Photography* to the special locked cases.[9] The special cases are reserved for books that are prone to theft or damage and include commercial or titillating representations of sex – in other words, books that are regarded as an incitement to action rather than contemplative reading. In the 1970s, photographs of the female nude were clearly seen to fall within these guidelines; but the images included in Clark's text escaped the contaminating associations of pornography and could be consulted without fearful consequences to either the book or the reader. In this way the classifications of the British Library map on to the conventional opposition of high and low culture, of fine art versus mass media.

Within traditional aesthetics, the painting has a peculiar status. Valued as an authentic and unique object, the singular product of a special act of creativity, the painting is, as Victor Burgin writes, 'part holy relic, part gilt-edged security'.[10] In contrast, the material and cultural value of the photograph is reduced by its reproducibility, and the photograph carries none of the connotations of human agency and cultural dignity. Unlike the connoisseur of high art, the consumer of photographic art does not possess a unique object, and within the polarity of high and low art, the photograph is devalued as the product of mass technology, popular and vulgar.

Thus, paintings of the female nude such as those illustrated in Clark's book were set apart physically as well as symbolically from photographic images of the female nude. With obscenity as the focus of sexual regulation, high art had to be maintained as an edifying, moral, and privileged form of cultural consumption. Emphasis was placed on the nude as an ideal form that embodies perfection, universality, and unity. These conventions were in opposition to the codes and functions of pornography – fragmentation, particularity, titillation. Above all else, paintings of the female nude had to be closed off from any associations with commercialism or sexual arousal. Refusing the connotation of commodity, the discourse of high art retreated into a vocabulary of contemplation and aesthetic response. As Kenneth Clark explained to the Longford committee:

> In a picture like Correggio's *Danaë* the sexual feelings have been transformed, and although we undoubtedly enjoy it all the more because of its sensuality, we are still in the realm of contemplation. The pornographic wall-paintings in Pompeii are documentaries and have nothing to do with art. There are one or two doubtful cases – a small picture of copulation by Géricault and a Rodin bronze of the same subject. Although each of these is a true work of art, I personally feel that the subject comes between me and complete aesthetic enjoyment. It is like too strong a flavour added to a dish. There remains the extraordinary example of Rembrandt's etching of a couple on a bed, where I do not find the subject at all disturbing because it is seen entirely in human terms and is not intended to promote action. But it is, I believe, unique, and only Rembrandt could have done it.[11]

In the end, Clark comes up with an extremely personal and idiosyncratic set of distinctions. Indeed, it is the very obscurity of his criteria that is most striking. His definition rests on a precarious differentiation between a *sensuality* that can be incorporated within aesthetic contemplation and a *sexuality* that disrupts this response and becomes an incitement to behaviour. Sensuality thus performs an essential role, signifying a form of sexual representation that remains within the permissible limits of art.

But other art historians during the 1970s did not seek to keep high art as a discrete, desexualized category. In fact, they deliberately sought to break open and redefine the category's boundaries and to address directly the representation of the sexual within paintings of the female nude. Far from being a separate plane of activity, art, they claimed, participates in the social definition of male and female sexuality. Three of these texts, all of which were produced outside the mainstream of art history, reveal the competing definitions that were thrown up by the issue of cultural representation and sexuality during this period.

John Berger's *Ways of Seeing*, first published in 1972, established a fundamental distinction between female nakedness and nudity. Whereas the nude is always subjected to pictorial conventions, 'To be naked', he writes, 'is to be oneself.'[12] In this framework, Berger juxtaposes European oil paintings with photographs from soft-porn magazines, identifying the same range of poses, gestures, and looks in both media. The particularity of the medium and cultural form is not important. What matters is the repertoire of conventions that *all* nudes are believed to deploy, irrespective of historical or cultural specificity. But according to Berger, there are a few valuable exceptions to the voyeurism that is constructed through the European high-art tradition:

They are no longer nudes – they break the norms of the art-form; they are paintings of loved women, more or less naked. Among the hundreds of thousands of nudes which make up the tradition there are perhaps a hundred of these exceptions. In each case the painter's personal vision of the particular woman he is painting is so strong that it makes no allowance for the spectator . . . The spectator can witness their relationship – but he can do no more; he is forced to recognise himself as the outsider he is. He cannot deceive himself into believing that she is naked for him. He cannot turn her into a nude.[13]

Berger's evocation of the hundred or so exceptions to the tradition of the female nude in European art assumes that the relationship between the male artist and the female model, a heterosexual relationship, is inherently natural and good. Power, for Berger, is constituted as public. Private relationships lie outside the domain of power; love transforms the *nude* into a *naked woman* and prevents the male spectator, the outsider, from turning the female figure into a voyeuristic spectacle. This interpretation, of course, is entirely based on a naive, humanist faith in the honesty and equality of private heterosexual relationships. It also assumes a familiarity with artistic biography; the spectator needs to know the nature of the relationship between a particular artist and his model in order to make this reading of the picture. Significantly, both Berger and Lord Clark, in his statement to the Longford committee, invoke paintings by Rembrandt as unique representations of sex. Great artists, apparently, produce exceptional images regardless of subject matter, and cultural value is thus a safe index of moral worth.

Linda Nochlin's feminist essay 'Eroticism and Female Imagery in Nineteenth-Century Art', also published in 1972, represents one voice from the women's movement, which during this period addressed the construction of patriarchy in high culture.[14] Nochlin shares Berger's analysis of the female nude as a patriarchal image for male consumption, but she goes much further, rejecting the idea of the personal erotic imagery of individual male artists in favour of a social basis for the sexual definitions established in images of the female nude. She also points to the absence of any public imagery for women's desires and calls for an available language to express women's erotic needs. This call for female erotica was part of a much wider demand by members of the women's movement during the early 1970s. Unfortunately, Nochlin's argument was recast by the publisher's dust jacket once again to present female erotica from a male perspective: 'The book is superbly illustrated and combines the pleasures of a rich catalogue of esoteric erotica, with the satisfaction of a penetrating and original study.'

Another effort to redefine sexuality and sexual pleasure in relation to the visual arts can be seen in Peter Webb's *The Erotic Arts*, first published in 1975. The book is a paradigm of the sexual libertarianism that emerged in the late 1960s and continued into the 1970s, particularly within certain sections of the gay liberation movement. For Webb, sexual freedom was synonymous with social freedom, and sexual liberation was the first step towards social revolution. Webb challenged directly the anti-pornography lobby and obscenity trials of the early 1970s, which set up liberation in opposition to the authoritarian morality of censorship. However, he was also keen to isolate a category of erotic art from that of pornography:

> Pornography is related to obscenity rather than erotica and this is a vital distinction. Although some people may find a pornographic picture erotic, most people associate eroticism with love, rather than sex alone, and love has little or no part to play in pornography . . . Eroticism, therefore, has none of the pejorative associations of pornography; it concerns something vital to us, the passion of love. Erotic art is art on a sexual theme related specifically to emotions rather than merely actions, and sexual depictions which are justifiable on aesthetic grounds.[15]

Webb assumes an essentialist model of human sexuality, conceiving of it as a driving, instinctive force that must find expression through either legitimate or illegitimate channels. In his attempt to distinguish erotic art and pornography, he relies on a familiar set of oppositions: love versus sex, aesthetic value versus bad art, and feeling or emotion versus action. Again, as with the arguments of Clark and Berger, there is a juggling of aesthetic and moral criteria in order to justify one category of representation and invalidate another.[16]

The female nude and sexual metaphor

In the three examples considered above, the authors directly address the issue of sexual definition in cultural representation, but they do so from different political and moral standpoints. In the mainstream of art history, however, the approach is more indirect: sex has to be implicit rather than explicit in order to keep the art/contemplation coupling intact and to maintain the conventional polarity of art and pornography. Within traditional aesthetics, the language of connoisseurship has developed as an expression of aesthetic judgement, taste, and value. The way language is mobilized in discussions of paintings of the female nude allows us to assess the role of sexual metaphor in recent art criticism.

As cultural commodities, oil paintings have been relished by critics and art historians, and the practice of applying paint to canvas has been charged with sexual connotations. Light caresses form, shapes become voluptuous, colour is sensuous, and the paint itself is luxuriously physical. This representation of artistic production supports the dominant stereotype of the male artist as productive, active, controlling, a man whose sexuality is channelled through his brush, who finds expression and satisfaction through the act of painting.[17] The artist transmutes matter into form. The canvas is the empty but receptive surface, empty of meaning – naked – until it is inscribed and given meaning by him. Surface texture is thus charged with significance; the marks on the canvas are essential traces of human agency, evidence of art, and also signs of sexual virility, a kind of masculine identity.

These phallic and sexual metaphors take on an astonishing resonance when the painting is of a female nude. The artist transmutes matter into the form of the female body – the nude, ideal, perfect, the object of contemplation and delectation. Within the discourse of art history, sex is written into descriptions of paint, surface, and form. The category of art does not permit a sexuality that is an obvious or provocative element, but such sexuality *can* be articulated in the discussion of a particular painting's handling and style. The sexual, then, is distanced from the subject represented on the canvas and is defined instead through the metaphorical language of connoisseurship. Lawrence Gowing, for example, describes a small female figure in a Matisse interior as 'abandon[ing] herself to the colour'.[18] In *Nude Painting*, Michael Jacobs refers to Titian's *Nymph and Shepherd*, in which 'the dynamics of flesh and blood are revealed in their rawest state, all distracting movement, colour and meaning are stripped away by the rigorous harshness of the artist's late style'.[19] And Malcolm Cormack describes a Veronese in which 'the whole is a riot of the senses where the sensuous mode of expression emphasises the theme'.[20]

However, the issue of the representation of the female nude is not simply a question of the male artist or viewer imposing order on and controlling the canvas or the female body. There is another relationship at stake. The mythology of artistic genius proposes a model of masculinity and male sexuality that is free-ranging, unbounded, needing to be contained within forms.[21] Woman and femininity provide that cultural frame; woman controls and regulates the impetuous and individualistic brush. In a review of an exhibition of Impressionist drawings at the Ashmolean in Oxford, the art critic William Feaver considered the representation of the female nude. 'A Renoir drawing "Nude Woman Seen from the Back", in red chalk with touches of white, illustrates more clearly than any painting the Impressionist concept of untrammelled instinct: Renoir's caress, Monet's spontaneity. But drawing was the basis. Without it Renoir would have been incoherent.'[22] Just what is invoked by 'the Impressionist concept of untrammelled instinct'? What are we to make of 'Renoir's caress' and 'Monet's spontaneity'? Artists and lovers, paintings and sex are collapsed into each other. Masculinity is defined as the site of unregulated instinct, potentially anarchic and incoherent. But the discipline of drawing and the form of the female nude – high culture and femininity – give order to this incoherence; together they civilize and tame the wild expressiveness of male sexuality.

Thus, pictures of the female nude are not *about* female sexuality in any simplistic way; they also testify to a particular cultural definition of male sexuality and are part of a wider debate around representation and cultural value. The female nude is both a cultural and a sexual category; it is part of a cultural industry whose languages and institutions propose specific definitions of gender and sexuality and particular forms of knowledge and pleasure.

The relationship between art and pornography as illustrated by the British discourse explored here begins to reveal the ways in which cultural and aesthetic designations are mapped on to the moral and sexual values of Western patriarchal culture generally. To date, the popular debate about pornography in both Britain and America has focused on a limited and rather too familiar set of issues. At the centre is the issue of legal censorship. Debate about censorship has become polarized between those who advocate state intervention to ban pornographic material and those who invoke the right of individual freedom of choice, particularly as it is reflected by the private consumption of pornography as opposed to its public display. Supporters of state intervention argue that at issue is the safety of women, that pornographic representations incite violence against women. Yet social investigation, empirical research, statistics, and personal testimony have been used both to endorse and to refute the links between pornography and acts of sexual violence.[23] Besides the ambiguities concerning these investigations and their conclusions, some of the social effects of pornography, such as women's fear, embarrassment and anger, cannot be measured and accounted for in any straightforward way.

The parallels between the poles of this debate and the poles of the pornography/art debate are striking. Both debates focus on the impetus to action as a criterion for classification of images of the female body. Art critics argue over the merits of sensual or erotic images, and those who would either regulate or deregulate pornography argue over the implications of a patriarchal representation of female and male sexuality. These parallels suggest that the relationship between representation and reality, image and action, is not going to be resolved by tugging empirical data backwards and forwards between positions. Rather, the meanings of eroticism and obscenity, sensuality and sexuality, art and pornography, change over time, their boundaries shaped by the forms and institutions of culture and society. Thus, censorship is only a provisional strategy by which to 'contain' patriarchal culture; it is a categorization that reflects pornography's present definition as outside the norm, as deviant, hidden culture. Only by continuing to examine the complexity with which such categorizations as pornography and art map out broad cultural notions of the licit and the illicit and societal notions of male and female sexuality will we come to a more subtle understanding of the implications of images of the female body.

Marybeth Hamilton

'A little bit spicy, but not too raw'
Mae West, pornography and popular culture

> Bystander: You're a fine gal, Lady Lou, a fine woman.
> Mae West: One of the finest women that ever walked the streets.

Mae West. The name brings fond images immediately to mind: the swaying hourglass figure, the appraising gaze, the ironically murmured invitation to 'come up and see me'.

Mae West has lingered in popular memory because she was no ordinary sex symbol. In her starring screen début as Lady Lou, the good-natured courtesan of *She Done Him Wrong* (1933), West introduced audiences to an enigmatic persona that she herself came to call 'the Mae West character': a *femme fatale* gifted with a touch of irony, a hint of self-mockery, a suggestion that she was not simply conveying sexuality but parodying it too.

Mae West is remembered today as a saucy but harmless and rather trivial performer; her relevance to the pornography debate may seem tangential at best. Yet before she developed 'the Mae West character', West herself was deemed a pornographer. She earned that label in a 1926 Broadway play, parading a raunchy working-class sexual identity that middle-class critics found explosive and threatening.

Born to immigrant parents in Brooklyn in 1893, drawn to the stage by the age of seven and sexually active by the age of twelve, West grew up as (in turn-of-the-century parlance) a 'tough girl': a sexually adventurous, rebellious young woman who flaunted an aggressive erotic style. At the turn of the century, tough girls dominated the urban working-class landscape, performing in its raunchy commercial amusements and mingling in its flamboyant underworld street life.

At the turn of the century, tough girls were outcasts. To a middle class that valorized female gentility their sexual flamboyance made them indistinguishable from prostitutes. By the 1910s and 1920s, however, that middle-class consensus was beginning to crumble. The chief agents in that disruption were a new generation of young middle-class women who seemed to be taking tough girls as models, adopting their short skirts, silk stockings and garish cosmetics and participating in their raucous urban nightlife.

Mae West capitalized on that controversial development. In April 1926, after ten years in obscurity in burlesque and vaudeville, she burst upon the notice of the New York City public with a self-scripted play that marketed the tough girl to Broadway's middle-class audience. West's creation, *SEX*, was reviled by critics but drew massive and heavily female crowds. Such patronage horrified powerful moral traditionalists: within months West was arrested on charges of public obscenity and served ten days in New York's Women's Penitentiary.

Judging by what she produced in *SEX*, most contemporary observers deemed Mae West a pornographer. Our familiarity with West as the self-mocking temptress may make such a perception seem inconceivable. Yet the Mae West of 1926 was a different performer from the one she would become only two years later, when she assembled a more domesticated sexual identity. And as her story reminds us, 'pornography' is often a convenient label with which to stigmatize a deviant female sexual style.

SEX starred Mae West as Margy Lamont, a tough, bitter, imperious prostitute who runs the roughest brothel in Montreal. The play follows Margy from Montreal to Trinidad to the suburbs of New York, as she banters suggestively with her sponging pimp and entices the lust of her male customers, all in pursuit of money, adventure and sex.

It is almost impossible to exaggerate the amount of condemnation that critics heaped upon SEX. These were not simply negative reviews, dismissing the play in terms of theatrical technique: SEX's critics all but abandoned that vocabulary to vent their utter revulsion at what they had seen onstage. One typical example came in the New York Daily Mirror, under the headline 'SEX An Offensive Play. Monstrosity Plucked From Garbage Can, Destined To Sewer'. The reviewer continued:

> This production is not for the police. It comes rather in the province of our Health Department. It is a sore spot in the midst of our fair city that needs disinfecting.

The Daily Mirror was a tabloid, and thus used hyperbole as a matter of course. Yet in making their case against SEX, even the more restrained papers employed a vocabulary of infection, disease and filth. The script, wrote the New Yorker, was composed of 'street sweepings'; the play, argued another critic, left the viewer afflicted with 'that "dark brown" taste which results from proximity to anything indescribably filthy'. The reviewer for the New York Herald Tribune was somewhat more subdued, but he too came to essentially the same point. SEX, he wrote, was:

> an ostensible reflection of the underworld as it is
> supposed to exist in Montreal and Trinidad. A world of
> ruthless, evil-minded, foul-mouthed crooks, harlots,
> procurers and other degenerate members of that particular
> zone of society. Never in a long experience of theater-
> going have we met with a set of characters so depraved . . .
> All the barriers of conventional word and act that the last
> few seasons of the theater have shown us were swept
> away and we were shown not sex but lust – stark, naked
> lust.

Breaking all 'barriers of conventional word and act', *SEX* was condemned as bald, crass pornography. That vitriolic reaction may be hard to take seriously – and, certainly, Mae West herself always dismissed it. To judge by West's own accounts of her past, her critics were simply naive Victorians, unaccustomed to plays about sexual desire and fearing sex itself as dangerous and degrading.

The truth, however, is more complex than West paints it. Mae West did not introduce sex to Broadway. While the nineteenth-century legitimate stage had indeed specialized in sentimental productions tailored to genteel Victorian audiences, in the 1920s Broadway became a major outpost of the middle-class sexual revolution. Its most avid patrons were young middle-class women in vehement revolt against 'outdated' prudery, and Broadway producers rushed to comply with their tastes. *SEX* followed a long string of 'sex plays' whose subjects often included prostitution: for example, *The Shanghai Gesture*, the story of China's most successful madam, and *Lulu Belle*, the tale of a mean, unrepentant mulatto hooker who seduces black and white lovers from Harlem to Paris.

With those facts in mind, we must interpret critics' response to *SEX* in a different light from that suggested by Mae West. Broadway critics in the 1920s were themselves a product of this generational change: they were accustomed to sexually expressive plays; in many cases they praised them; and they prided themselves on their bemused tolerance for even inept producers' infatuation with sex. Their response to bad sex plays was typically ridicule, not condemnation; moreover, they were always capable of responding to these productions *as theatre* – of analysing them in the terms of dramatic criticism, with attention to structure, technique and execution.

But *SEX*, clearly, was different. With *SEX*, critics' carefully wrought tone of urbanity disintegrated, replaced by one that sputtered with talk of disease, infection and filth. Reviewers did not simply hate West's play – they were incapable of responding to it in the terms of their trade, incapable of reviewing it as theatre.

Indeed, that it was not theatre was precisely the point. Remember the distinction the *Herald Tribune* reviewer had drawn – that West's play presented 'not sex but lust – stark, naked lust'. Critics implied that *SEX* was no theatrical representation of a brothel, but uncomfortably resembled a real one – that it was not merely about sex, but somehow a literal presentation of it, a 'sore' that fell into the province of the Health Department or vice squad. They deemed it pornographic, in other words, not because it dealt with sex but because it presented sex in a 'stark, naked' manner – a manner bereft of Broadway polish, bearing an uncomfortable appearance of realism.

Unfortunately, the label 'realism' in itself gets us nowhere at all. As a quick glance at West's tale of a globetrotting prostitute reveals, there was little that was obviously lifelike about it. We must ask instead in what qualities that seeming realism resided and why it should have carried such unsettling power – even for a sexually liberated post-Victorian audience.

In part, *SEX* unsettled critics because it broke with conventions of middle-class performance. *Variety*, deeming it a 'nasty red-light district show', was more accurate than Mae West ever admitted. The play did not really have much of a plot. It gained what coherence it had not by any development of character or situation but by a series of comic sketches – rapid-fire exchanges between Margy Lamont and her pimp, her fellow prostitutes and her male customers, exchanges laden with leering double entendres and punctuated with unmistakably graphic motions. In one of *SEX*'s most notorious scenes, a customer named Lieutenant Gregg looms over Margy while explaining what it is that he has waited three months to give her:

Gregg: Oh, I've got something for you, wait until you see this, wait until you see this.
Margy: Well, come on and let's see it.
Gregg: You'll get it, you'll get it. I don't mind telling you I had an awful time saving it for you. Why, all the women were fighting for it.

Margy: It better be good.
Gregg: It's good alright. It's the best you could get, but
you've got to be very careful not to bend it.

In speaking the final line, Lieutenant Gregg accompanies it by what one critic described as 'a Rabelaisian gesture to indicate a certain anatomical virtuosity'. After completing this 'Rabelaisian gesture', Gregg reaches into his pocket and pulls out Margy's gift – an ostrich feather.

This style of humour, marked by rapid-fire comic banter, transparently sexual double meanings and graphic physical movements, characterized one type of theatre above all: the burlesque show. Nearly all the critics who condemned SEX made precisely that comparison – and a damning one it was. In the 1920s burlesque had no rival as the outcast of the popular theatre – in so far as it was regarded as theatre at all.

A *mélange* of suggestive songs, dances and comedy sketches, burlesque had taken root in the urban United States in the late nineteenth century, a fixture of working-class, male-orientated entertainment districts along with concert saloons and variety theatres. But unlike variety – which, under the flashier name of vaudeville, was able to tone down its performers, move to central shopping and theatre districts and broaden its appeal to a middle-class public – burlesque never managed to 'class itself up'. By the twentieth century, if anything, burlesque's status had sunk: it drew an audience that middle-class observers regarded as the most dissolute and degraded of the male working class.

Yet what really branded burlesque as a theatrical outcast were its apparent real-life links to the sexual underworld. Broadway plays may have represented the underworld; burlesque appeared to be genuinely an underworld product. Located outside the Times Square mainstream in lower-class areas associated with drugs and prostitution, burlesque flaunted its purportedly authentic glimpse into the culture of metropolitan vice. It spotlighted raunchy female performers who seemed to be lifted straight from the neighbouring streets – and who indeed were occasionally nabbed for

criminal solicitation. Observers in the 1920s deemed burlesque not theatre, but pornography: squalid entertainment
that drew no clear line between the stage and the street,
between sexy performance and sexual act, between the
theatre and the disorderly house.

With *SEX* Mae West brought burlesque humour to Broadway. In itself it hardly merited calling out the vice squad. But
while its jokes exacerbated its offensive appearance of 'realism', the most explosive factor was Mae West herself. West
paraded elements of lower-class female sexual experience
that profoundly unsettled even the most liberal critics. In
their eyes her performance was 'raw', 'crude', 'unvarnished'
– no conventional theatrical representation of a prostitute,
but something uncomfortably close to the real thing.

West gave this unsettling depiction in part by her plain-
spoken definition of prostitution as an economic, and specifically working-class, activity. Margy Lamont was clearly,
unmistakably, a working prostitute. She took money for sex,
and West's play made no attempt to gloss over that fact. To
the contrary – much of its 'repellent' humour turned on just
that circumstance, dwelling on it with a kind of gleeful relish.
Take, for example, the following moment, when Margy
responds to a rival prostitute's accusation that she has stolen
one of her customers, Sailor Dan from Kansas:

Margy (*flipping through her customer book*):
Sailor Dan from Kansas, Sailor Dan from Kansas – oh
Sailor Dan from Kansas. Yeh Sailor Dan from Kansas, flat
feet, asthma, check came back, O, baby, I'll make you a
present of that bird, he's yours.

Jokes like this made glaringly clear the basic reality of
prostitution: a meeting of bodies and an exchange of cash,
and often (as the bounced cheque reminds us) very little cash
at that. It was a jarring truth, at least in a theatrical context.
For while prostitutes had long been depicted on the legitimate stage, that depiction had assumed a romanticized form
that had obscured the reality of what they did – its place at

the bottom of the economic order and its nature as paid labour.

Margy, in contrast, was explicitly a sexual commodity, an ill-paid sex worker who traded her body on the streets. West made that fact unmistakable. As she embodied her, Margy was palpably from the lower orders: she spoke in working-class slang and she voiced a violent hatred of 'decent folk' – of the supposedly 'respectable' who sin on the side. Margy is bitterly conscious of her membership in an oppressed class, and the grimness and harshness of her manner are reflected in the world she inhabits. Her Montreal red-light district is mean and unglamorous, rife with class antagonisms – the kind of place a middle-class person would feel distinctly uncomfortable upon entering. As one critic noted, 'It may be said of [Mae West] and *SEX* that they do not make sin attractive. The hell they picture is uninviting, a horrible place whose principal lady-viper has a tough hiss, an awkward strut and an overplump figure.'

That last statement suggests the most crucial element in West's 'unsettling' portrait of Margy Lamont. That she high-lighted prostitution as a class-based activity was bad enough; even more incendiary, however, was her vivid enactment of lower-class sexuality. West flaunted an animal delight in physical sensation that was alien to even liberated middle-class experience, an untrammelled pleasure in her body that many observers found foreign and threatening.

West conveyed that explosive eroticism through her distinctive physical style, developed during her years in the 'cheap theatres' and refined according to burlesque conventions. She walked with a controlled, deliberate slouch, her full hips swaying in a languid rhythm. She delivered her lines in nasal yet resonant tones that spilled from the corner of her mouth, lending every word an insinuating sexual toughness.

To anyone who has ever seen Mae West onscreen, all that might sound familiar, but in *SEX* there was a crucial difference: there was not the least hint of an ironic joke. There was no amiable self-mockery in *SEX*, no suggestion, either in the script or in West's performance, that she was parodying a sexy woman as well as playing one. Remembering this is crucial to understanding the startling impact of West's physical presence. As contemporary reaction makes clear, when her sexual style was unmediated by self-mockery, it evoked a lower-class presence with unnerving force.

To understand how it did so, one has to look at the broader context of female sexual style on the Broadway stage. Broadway did not shy away from sexuality in the 1920s, but its representation of female sexuality reflected the fashions and styles of a middle-class public. And while that public was seemingly united in its revolt against Victorian 'prudishness', much of it was not nearly as comfortable with women's sexuality as it often liked to pretend.

Middle-class fashion in the 1920s seemed to flaunt its liberation from traditional constraints: it put the female body on display, with short skirts and silk stockings that contrasted sharply with the neck-to-toe gowns of the genteel Victorian lady.

Yet this seeming validation of female sexuality had its limits, as other elements of middle-class high fashion suggest: bound breasts, a straight silhouette and a slender, boyish body, evoking aloof sophistication or sporty independence rather than overt eroticism.

Middle-class entertainment, like middle-class fashion, reflected this unease. The Ziegfeld Girls from Flo Ziegfeld's 'Follies' took the stage with their breasts bared, but they did so with an aloof, near-motionless elegance – a style that gave them a detached, aristocratic allure. The Broadway hit *Lulu Belle*, in contrast, did put its prostitute heroine emphatically in motion. But as portrayed by actress Leonore Ulrich she was a stylishly slim, buoyant, kinetically charged woman whose sexiness emerged flapper-style, through jazzy physical exuberance.

What Mae West displayed in *SEX* was indeed, as critics charged, raw and unvarnished by comparison: eroticism conveyed through an insolent nasal hiss, an awkward, deliberate slouch, and the graphic undulations of her thickset body. (One police officer reported that West 'moved her hips and buttocks in such a way as to suggest an act of sexual intercourse'.) The heaviness of that body, clad in short and flimsy modern attire, was particularly crucial. In the 1920s, when a boyish silhouette defined respectable sexuality, a thickset body like West's brought seamy and distinctly lower-class associations to mind: above all, burlesque actresses, who were widely equated with prostitutes and whose overblown figures reputedly signalled an aggressive embrace of sensual passion.

Like a burlesque chorus girl, Mae West as Margy Lamont manipulated her full figure to convey a full range of sexual appetite, freely indulged and unabashedly savoured. So convincing was she, and so unsettling, that most critics could not see it as a performance. While none accused West of being herself a prostitute, a few implied that she received actual sexual pleasure onstage – in their minds the most offensive 'realism' of all. As one disgusted reviewer assessed West's performance: '[She] cavorts her own sex about the stage in one of the most reviling exhibits allowed public display. She undresses before the public, and appears to enjoy doing so.'

It was that unfettered enjoyment of physical sensation that helped to brand Mae West a pornographer. Her play transgressed powerful, if unspoken, boundaries: it flouted Broadway's conventions of theatre and its conventions of sexual display. It drew on the rawest elements of working-class culture: its 'men-only' theatre; its class resentments; its sexual styles. In so doing it paraded elements of sexual experience that even a liberated middle-class sexuality suppressed.

This was not an intentionally political act – West was, from all accounts, colossally uninterested in politics; rather, it was performed with an eye fixed squarely on the Broadway box office. The sensational success of *The Shanghai Gesture* and *Lulu Belle* had revealed an eager middle-class market for racy tales of the sexual underworld. *SEX* was a product of that cultural moment: shrewd exploitation by a would-be celebrity working with an unsubtle sense of theatrical trends; a conviction that, if audiences flocked to the ersatz realism of *Lulu*

Belle, they would come in droves to the real thing. As West allegedly told one of *SEX*'s backers when he expressed hesitation about the play's rawness, Broadway audiences *wanted* 'dirt' – and, she added emphatically, 'I'll give it to them!'

In feeding 'dirt' to the Broadway public, West initially succeeded beyond anyone's expectations. *SEX* became what we would term a 'cult' hit, drawing a young, affected, self-consciously 'jaded' crowd – *Variety* called its members the 'Broadway weisenheimers' – who were bemused by the novelty of real 'dirt' on Broadway. Young women, in particular, stormed the box office. (According to one police officer, they outnumbered men in the audience by three to one.) Yet their numbers ultimately proved limited. *Variety*'s records indicate that attendance had begun to flag by early 1927, before the police raid in February sent it skyrocketing once more.

With *SEX* West earned cult stardom and city-wide notoriety, but she misjudged what she needed for long-term success. From a middle-class perspective *SEX was* 'raw', 'unvarnished': a cheaply staged play by a working-class actress that made an openly lurid appeal. For Broadway's middle-class public it was the theatrical equivalent of a slumming excursion; and while that indisputably recommended it to some, the majority, less adventurous, were definitely scared off – just as they would have balked at venturing into the back alleys of Harlem to seek out rough blues alongside a black clientele.

As an aspiring mass-market performer in the turbulent twenties, Mae West had to appeal to a broad, varied public – to a range of moral tastes and temperaments, from the wildly adventurous to the timidly staid. Rather than intensifying those divisions, West had to bridge them. She needed a revamped sexual style: one that retained its appeal to the 'Broadway weisenheimers' but was acceptable to the more traditional too.

She accomplished this in 1928 with her self-scripted comedy *Diamond Lil*. The story of an 1890s Bowery madam who bewitches the preacher who sets out to reform her, *Lil* proved an immediate triumph, drawing West's first truly broad-based audience, the timid no less than the adventurous. Its appeal proved no less stupendous on film. Her starring screen début, *She Done Him Wrong*, brought *Diamond Lil* virtually unchanged to the screen. It captivated the American film public – the top box-office hit of 1933, and the most successful film since *The Birth of a Nation*.

In *Diamond Lil* West assembled what would eventually become her trademark persona – a shrewd creation that would allow her to market working-class sexuality to a divided middle-class public. To a greater degree than even she herself realized, she fundamentally altered her performance style. She mediated both her links to underworld theatre and her presentation of lower-class sexuality, and the results made possible a broad-based success.

On the surface *Diamond Lil* followed *SEX*'s lead: it presented itself as a slumming excursion, a tale of underworld sex and violence. Set in New York's prime red-light district, the Bowery, at the depths of its notoriety at the turn of the century, it centred its tale on a tough, alluring Bowery prostitute and her triumph over her middle-class foes. In three acts it showcased a range of underworld vice of the sort that was endemic to the 1890s Bowery: petty theft; drug-peddling; male and female prostitution.

Its content in many ways mirrored that of *SEX*, but what helped make *Diamond Lil* more broadly appealing was the style with which it brought that content to life. While in *SEX* West had wriggled her way through a seemingly authentic piece of lower-class theatre – a cheap production marked by the anatomical humour and raunchy bumping and grinding that were the hallmarks of burlesque performance – in *Diamond Lil* she abandoned those hallmarks. The signposts of lower-class performance disappeared, replaced by a theatrical context with a decidedly more comfortable appeal.

In place of the leering sensationalism of *Sex*, *Lil* cultivated a chuckle of bemused nostalgia. It was definitely a sanitized slumming excursion, a fond look back at a romanticized and caricatured past. Abandoning *SEX*'s anatomical wisecracks, it drew gentle humour from supporting characters lifted straight from early-twentieth-century popular culture: endearing 'Bowery thugs' of the sort whose mangled English and dim wisecracks had animated newspaper short stories in the 1910s. Costumes, sets and musical interludes dispelled lower-class authenticity too: they presented the period setting as a picturesque 'Gay Nineties', a time of quaint sexual innocence – as *She Done Him Wrong* would put it, 'when there were handlebars on lip and wheel – and legs were confidential!'

Yet while this reformed theatrical context contributed to *Lil*'s broad-based appeal, the critical factor was Mae West herself. In *Diamond Lil* she created a new kind of character, and enacted her in a subtly new spirit. She revamped her presentation of underworld sexuality – particularly those elements that had given it the power to shock.

Unlike Margy Lamont, Diamond Lil is strictly detached from the world of cash exchange: though she lives in a brothel and has a 'past', she does not work at sex for a living. While Margy's customers pay her for services rendered, giving her cheques (and bad ones at that), Lil's lovers ply her with diamonds in the hope of retaining her interest. Lil, unlike Margy, is in a position of power: she is rich, with a choice of lovers and wealth that represents not payment but 'gifts'. As a consequence, she is classless: part of the Bowery underworld and yet, dripping with diamonds, somehow exalted above it.

As such, Lil is a far more assimilable figure than Margy Lamont could ever have been – and, in a theatrical context, a far more familiar one. Since the late nineteenth century, beginning with Alexandre Dumas's *La Dame aux Camélias*, prostitution had been represented onstage in much this same manner, embodied in the beautiful, desirable, enigmatic woman – the 'courtesan' – whose luxurious lifestyle and power of choice gave her the appearance of classlessness. As art historian T.J. Clark has noted, the mythical courtesan provided a means of representing prostitution comfortably:

in her beauty, her wealth, her power of choice, she obscured her real-life counterpart's status as a sexual commodity who sold her body on the street.

Lil was no sexual commodity, and that fact carried enormous importance. In Diamond Lil the audience had a figure they could recognize with comfort, a character who paraded an abstract sexuality free from uncomfortable social realities that might scare the more timid away.

By detaching sex from underclass economics, West defused some of its power to disturb – and she accelerated that process by altering her enactment of her physical mannerisms. West swivelled her way through *Diamond Lil* with the same gestures that had animated *SEX*'s Margy Lamont: the sullen nasal delivery, the appraising gaze, the undulating hips and torso. Developed in the world of the lower-class 'tough girl' and crafted according to burlesque conventions, those gestures had long been Westian staples, as one newspaper critic was able to see:

> Miss West seems to belong to the single characterization class of actress with trademarks quite as definite as the fluttering of Pauline Lord's hands or the horizontal elevation of Charlotte Greenwood's legs. As Diamond Lil she oozes her way through a rowdy melodrama with the familiar undulation of hips, the porcine manner of gaze and the red plush thickness of accent that kept *SEX* running at Daly's 63rd Street Theater for about a year.

The gestures were identical, but the response was different. *SEX*'s critics had reviled West's performance for its raw and 'unvarnished' sexuality; *Diamond Lil*, in contrast, sent them into raptures – and precisely because of those same physical mannerisms. 'She plays with a controlled, slow-paced undulation that extends from her head to her hips,' wrote critic John Mason Brown in *Theater Arts Monthly*, 'and with a low-toned, casual toughness that seems to spill from only one corner of her mouth.' 'She is a plump, almost Circassian blonde whose ample figure overflows her girdles in graceful cascades,' wrote Percy Hammond. 'She walks with a cunning strut and she talks in a quiet monotone, never disturbing her humorous lips with the noises of elocution.' The *New Yorker*'s Charles Brackett evocatively admired West's entrance in Act 1, 'pushing hip after hip with defiant languor', and his colleague Thyra Samter Winslow agreed: 'She is slow, rhythmic, insinuating. She moves with almost feline intensity, a curious sort of wiggle, inside her corsets of the nineties.' But it was the *New Republic*'s Stark Young who most effectively described what his fellow critics found so remarkable:

> Nobody, seeing her play, can fail to wonder at that audacity of leisure, motion which becomes almost an intensity of movement by its continuity, but is almost stillness because it is so slow. The whole body – not a beautiful one – is supple, flowing, coolly insinuating, the voice and enunciation only more so . . . [The] whole result of her presence and her acting is something less usual . . . and more abstract, impressive, ironical and teasing in its unreality, and unforgettable.

This was a remarkable shift in opinion for Young: he had walked out after the first act of *SEX*, finding West's performance 'ugly' and 'crude'. Yet it was a shift in opinion that most critics shared. No longer disdained for their repellent 'realism', West's physical mannerisms were suddenly heralded as the hallmarks of a uniquely 'abstract', enigmatic style.

Mae West made that new perception possible by delivering her mannerisms in a new spirit. While as Margy Lamont she had played her role straight, wriggling and writhing with a bald, crass intensity, in *Diamond Lil* she wrapped her sexual style in a veil of irony and detachment. She strutted and swaggered and undulated with an enigmatic air of ironic bemusement, aware of her sexuality but vastly entertained by it.

The dialogue itself encouraged this: as the script reveals, Lil exhibits that attitude within moments of her entrance, fresh from a photographic studio and bearing pictures of herself that she has had taken for her admirers. As she distributes them around the saloon, she comments on each with a bemused detachment, a mix of self-love and self-mockery that suggests that her sexiness is a good-natured pose, that she is keenly aware of and entertained by the impression she makes.

With *Diamond Lil* Mae West wrapped that 'tough girl's style in a veil of irony. The result was genuinely enigmatic, an odd mix of roughness and artifice that baffled and tantalized a range of viewers by.(implicitly) inviting them to form their own conclusions as to what Mae West was really all about. In its ambiguity lay its strength as a means of mediating West's sexual presence: it allowed a public with diverse opinions on female sexuality to interpret Mae West in widely varying ways.

In the end West's enigmatic revamped style simply mirrored the opinions of each different observer: she could mean whatever the viewer wanted her to. To the French feminist Colette, West's manipulation of her heavy-set body (the 'powerful' breast, the 'well-fleshed thigh', 'the short neck, the round cheek of a young blonde butcher') signalled her defiant rejection of the demure and compliant Hollywood heroine. To arch-traditionalist critic George Jean Nathan, in contrast, she was the embodiment of old-fashioned womanliness, a welcome contrast to what he described as the 'endless succession of imported lesbians and flat-chested flappers' that movie audiences had been limited to before. Gilbert Seldes read West's air of good-humoured mockery as a joyous affirmation of healthy heterosexuality, a populist rejection of the 'moribund inversion' of high-culture artists like Marcel Proust. But gay novelist Parker Tyler took a different view – he saw West's irony as the essence of camp, directly inspired by the flamboyant theatricality at the heart of the gay male structure.

Mae West sustained all these interpretations and more: that was the secret of her success. By using irony to defuse 'low-class' sensationalism, she accommodated the diversity of a mass-market public. Diamond Lil, 'the finest woman who ever walked the streets', was rough enough to appeal to adventurous viewers. But as West played her she teetered on the verge of parody, thus giving viewers a chance, if they so chose, to dismiss the sex and sensationalism as a good-natured joke.

Diamond Lil was ultimately an act of self-censorship: with it, West crossed to the safe side of the line distinguishing harmless titillation from out-and-out pornography. As her story makes clear, in the post-Victorian era that line was intimately bound up with class. What was deemed porno-graphic in West's early performances was their flaunting of lower-class sexuality. To escape censure West had to ditch that identity, create an amiable, ambiguous, classless 'tough girl' who could smooth over her audience's potential unease.

Mae West's early-twentieth-century act of self-censorship raises issues that are no less potent today. As her story reminds us, definitions of pornography are never just about sex: they are enmeshed in broader social relations and function as powerful weapons of social control. In West's own time, such definitions ultimately constrained the free-dom of middle-class and working-class women alike. In an era when young middle-class women were forging a sexually expressive public identity – and looking to working-class models in the process – deeming lower-class sexuality 'filthy' and 'pornographic' helped to contain that change within acceptable bounds. Female sexuality was validated only within limits; the most subversive elements of lower-class style – its sharp social antagonism and aggressive self-pleasure – were declared deviant, ugly and crude.

With *Diamond Lil* Mae West cleansed her style of those deviant elements. It is no accident that, in so doing, she created her first mass Broadway success and the persona on which she would build her career. With the faintly tongue-in-cheek Diamond Lil, West eradicated the threat her early performances flaunted. She was provocative, yet enigmatic; sexual, but somehow not serious; or – in Lil's own words – 'a little bit spicy, but not too raw'.

Notes

Introduction *Lynne Segal*

1. For a history of 'pornography', see Walter Kendrick, *The Secret Museum: Pornography in Modern Culture* (New York: Viking, 1987).

2. Susan Brownmiller, *Against Our Will: Men, Women and Rape* (Harmondsworth: Penguin, 1976).

3. Susan Griffin, Reprint from 'Rape: The All American Crime', *Ramparts* (September 1971).

4. Some years later the US legal scholar Catharine MacKinnon would succinctly summarize this particular radical feminist appropriation of 'feminism': 'Feminism is a theory of how the erotization of dominance and submission creates gender, creates woman and man in the social form in which we know them' (*Feminism Unmodified : Discourses on Life and Law* [Cambridge, MA and London: Harvard University Press, 1987], p. 50).

5. Robin Morgan, 'Theory and Practice: Pornography and Rape', in L. Lederer, ed., *Take Back the Night* (New York: William Morrow, 1980), p. 139.

6. Beatrix Campbell, 'Sexuality and Submission', in S. Allen *et al.*, eds, *Conditions of Illusion*, (Leeds: Feminist Books, Reprinted 1974), p. 108.

7. Editorial Collective, *Scarlet Woman* **12/13** (May 1981), p. 29.

8. Anja Meulenbelt, *For Ourselves* (London: Sheba, 1981), p. 90.

9. Ann Snitow, 'Retrenchment Vs. Transformation: The Politics of the Antipornography Movement', in K. Ellis *et al.*, eds, *Caught Looking: Feminism, Pornography, and Censorship* (New York: Caught Looking, Inc., 1986).

10. Diana Russell with Laura Lederer, 'Questions We Get Asked Most Often', in Lederer, ed., *Take Back the Night*, p. 26.

11. Laura Lederer, 'Playboy Isn't Playing', in ibid., p. 122.

12. MacKinnon, *Feminism Unmodified*, p. 154.

13. See Dennis Howitt and Guy Cumberbatch, *Pornography: Impact and Influences* (London: Home Office Research & Planning Unit, 1990), pp. 7–8.

14. J. Scott and S. Guvelier, 'Sexual Violence in *Playboy* Magazine: A Longitudinal Content Analysis', *Journal of Sex Research* **23** (1987); T. Palys, 'Testing the Common Wisdom: The Social Content of Pornography', *Canadian Psychology* **27**, 1 (1986); P. Dietz and B. Evans, 'Pornography Imagery and Prevalence of Paraphilia', *American Journal of Psychiatry* **139** (1982); W. Thompson and J. Annetts, 'Soft-Core: A Content Analysis of Legally Available Pornography in Great Britain 1968–90 and the Implications of Aggression Research' (Reading University, 1990); Howitt and Cumberbatch, *Pornography*.

15. R. Baron, 'Sexual Arousal and Physical Aggression: The Inhibiting Effects of "Cheese Cake" and Nudes, *Bulletin of Psychonomic Society* 3 (1974); E. Donnerstein *et al.*, *The Question of Pornography* (New York: Free Press, 1987); K. Kelley *et al.*, 'Three Faces of Sexual Explicitness: The Good, The Bad, and the Useful', in D. Zillman and J. Bryant, eds, *Pornography Research: Advances and Policy Implications* (Hillsdale, NJ: Lawrence Erlbaum Associates, 1989); Thompson and Annetts, 'Soft-Core'; Howitt and Cumberbatch.

16. Soble, *Pornography*, p. 191; T. Smith, 'The Polls – A Review: The Use of Public Opinion Data by the Attorney General's Commission on Pornography', *Public Opinion Quarterly* 51 (1987).

17. MacKinnon, *Feminism Unmodified*, p. 15; Andrea Dworkin, *Pornography: Men Possessing Women* (London: The Women's Press, 1981), p. 69.

18. Donnerstein *et al.*, *The Question of Pornography*; Thelma McCormack, 'Making Sense of the Research on Pornography', in V. Burstyn, ed., *Women Against Censorship* (Vancouver: Douglas & McIntyre, 1985).

19. Michael Goldstein and Harold Kant, *Pornography and Sexual Deviance* (Berkeley: University of California Press, 1973); W. Marshall, 'The Use of Sexually Explicit Stimuli by Rapists, Child Molesters and Non-Offenders', *Journal of Sex Research* 25, 2 (1988).

20. P. Abramson and H. Hayashi, 'Pornography in Japan: Cross-Cultural and Theoretical Considerations', in N. Malamuth and E. Donnerstein, eds, *Pornography and Sexual Aggression* (Orlando, FL: Academic Press, 1984); Larry Baron and Murray Straus, *Four Theories of Rape in American Society* (New Haven, CT: Yale University Press, 1989).

21. Larry Baron, 'Pornography and Gender Equality: An Empirical Analysis', *Journal of Sex Research* 27, 3 (1990).

22. B. Kutchinsky, 'Pornography and Rape: Theory and Practice? Evidence from Crime Data in Four Countries where Pornography is Easily Available', *International Journal of Law and Psychiatry* 13,4 (1990).

23. Donnerstein *et al.*, *The Question of Pornography*, p. 175; see also A. Brannigan and S. Goldenberg, 'The Study of Aggressive Pornography: The Vicissitudes of Relevance', *Critical Studies in Mass Communication* 4, 3 (1987); F. Christensen, 'Effects of Pornography: The Debate Continues, *Journal of Communications*, 37, 1 (1987).

24. Neil Malamuth and James Check, 'The Effects of Aggressive Pornography on Beliefs of Rape Myths: Individual Differences', *Journal of Research in Personality* 19 (1985); P. Dietz *et al.*, 'Detective Magazines: Pornography for the Sexual Sadist?, *Journal of Forensic Sciences* 31, 1, 1986; Donnerstein *et al.*, *The Question of Pornography*.

25. Donnerstein *et al.*, *The Question of Pornography*, p. 178.

26. Lederer, in Lederer, *Take Back the Night*, p. 122.

27. Dworkin, *Pornography*, p. 128; MacKinnon, *Feminism Unmodified*, pp. 149, 59.

28. Priscilla Alexander, 'Response to Andrea Dworkin', *Gay Community News* (Winter 1986).

29. Carla Freccero, 'Notes of a Post-Sex War Theorizer', in M. Hirsch and E. Fox Keller, eds, *Conflicts in Feminism* (London: Routledge, 1991), p. 316.

30. Nina Hartley, 'Confessions of a Feminist Porno Star', in F. Delacoste and P. Alexander, eds, *Sex Work: Writings by Women in the Sex Industry* (London: Virago, 1988), p. 142.

Part 1: From Minneapolis to Westminster

Feminist fundamentalism *Elizabeth Wilson*

1. That this brief account does not mention race reflects the absence of an awareness of this issue in the feminism of the early 1970s, the period to which I am referring.

2. However, we should note that the reforms around prostitution tightened regulation and were not liberalizing. And see Jeffrey Weeks, *Sex, Politics and Society: The Regulation of Sexuality Since 1800* (London: Longman, 1981).

3. See Stuart Hall, 'Reformism and the Legislation of Consent', in National Deviancy Conference, eds, *Permissiveness and Control: The Fate of the Sixties Legislation* (London: Macmillan, 1978).

4. See Judith Walkowitz, *Prostitution and Victorian Society: Women, Class and the State* (Cambridge: Cambridge University Press, 1980).

5. Kenneth Clark in *Pornography: The Longford Report* (London: Coronet, 1972), pp. 99–100.

6 Lynda Nead, 'The Female Nude: Pornography, Art, and Sexuality'; see this volume, below, pp. 280–294.

7. This was the definition used in a resolution put to the Annual General Meeting of the National Council for Civil Liberties (Liberty) in April 1990.

8. Lynda Nead, 'The Female Nude', p. 280 *passim* below.

9. ibid., p. 280 *passim*.

10. See Carol Smart's essay in this volume, p. 184 below.

Negotiating sex and gender *Carole. S. Vance*

1. Attorney General's Commission on Pornography, Miami transcript, public hearing, 21 November 1985.

2. Attorney General's Commission on Pornography, *Final Report*, 2 vols (Washington, DC: US Government Printing Office, July 1986).

3. See *Final Report*. pp. 433–58, for a complete list of the panel's recommendations. These include mandating high fines and long jail sentences for obscenity convictions, appointing a federal task force to coordinate prosecutions nationwide, developing a computer data bank to collect information on individuals suspected of producing pornography, and using punitive RICO legislation (the Racketeer Influenced and Corrupt Organizations Act, originally developed to fight organized crime) to confiscate the personal property of anyone convicted of the 'conspiracy' of producing pornography. For sexually explicit material outside the range of legal prosecution, the commission recommended that citizen activist groups

target and remove material in their communities which they find 'dangerous or offensive or immoral'.

4. For a detailed critique of procedural irregularities, see Barry Lynn, *Polluting the Censorship Debate: A Summary and Critique of the Attorney General's Commission on Pornography* (Washington, DC: American Civil Liberties Union, 1986).

5. For changes in sexual patterns in the last century, see (for England) Jeffrey Weeks, *Sex, Politics and Society: The Regulation of Sexuality Since 1800* (New York: Longman, 1981) and (for America) John D'Emilio and Estelle B. Freedman, *Intimate Matters* (New York: Harper & Row, 1988). For a history of pornography, see Walter Kendrick, *The Secret Museum* (New York: Viking, 1987).

6. Sears went on to become the executive director of Citizens for Decency through Law, a major conservative anti-pornography group. (The group has since changed its name to the Children's Legal Foundation.)

7. Attorney Frederick Schauer argued that sexually explicit expression which was arousing was less like speech and more like 'rubber, plastic, or leather sex aids'. See 'Speech and "Speech" – Obscenity and "Obscenity": An Exercise in the Interpretation of Constitutional Language', *Georgetown Law Journal* 67 (1979), pp. 899–923, especially pp. 922–3.

8. My analysis is based on direct observation of the commission's public hearings and executive sessions, supplemented by interviews with participants. All the commission's executive sessions were open to the public, following the provision of sunshine laws governing federal advisory commissions. Commissioners were specifically prohibited from discussing commission business or engaging in any informal deliberations outside of public view.

Public hearings were organized around preselected topics in six cities: Washington, DC (general), Chicago (law enforcement), Houston (social science), Los Angeles (production and distribution), Miami (child pornography), and New York (organized crime). Each public hearing typically lasted two full days. Commission executive sessions were held in each city in conjunction with the public hearings, usually for two extra days. Additional work sessions occurred in Washington, DC and Scottsdale, Arizona.

9. Victims of pornography, as described in the *Final Report*, included 'Sharon, formerly married to a medical professional who is an avid consumer of pornography', 'Bill, convicted of the sexual molestation of two adolescent females', 'Dan, former Consumer of Pornography [sic]', 'Evelyn, Mother and homemaker, Wisconsin, formerly married to an avid consumer of pornography', and 'Mary Steinman, sexual abuse victim'.

10. Los Angeles transcript, public hearing, 17 October 1985.

11. Major works of anti-pornography feminism include Andrea Dworkin, *Pornography: Men Possessing Women* (New York: G.P. Putnam, 1979); Susan Griffin, *Pornography and Silence: Culture's Revenge Against Nature* (New York: Harper & Row, 1981); Laura Lederer, ed., *Take Back the Night* (New

York: William Morrow, 1980); Catharine A. MacKinnon, 'Pornography, Civil Rights, and Speech', *Harvard Civil Rights–Civil Liberties Law Review*, **20** (Cambridge: Harvard University Press, 1985), pp. 1–70.

Opinion within feminism about pornography was, in fact, quite diverse, and it soon became apparent that the anti-pornography view was not hegemonic. For other views, see Carole S. Vance, ed., *Pleasure and Danger: Exploring Female Sexuality* (New York: Routledge & Kegan Paul, 1984); Varda Burstyn, ed., *Women Against Censorship* (Vancouver: Douglas & McIntyre, 1985) and Kate Ellis *et al.*, eds, *Caught Looking: Feminism, Pornography, and Censorship* (New York: Caught Looking, Inc., 1986).

12. Washington, DC transcript, public hearing, 20 June 1985.

13. For the version passed in Indianapolis, see Indianapolis, Ind., code section 16–3 (q) (1984); and Andrea Dworkin, 'Against the Male Flood: Censorship, Pornography, and Equality', *Harvard Women's Law Journal* 9 (1985), pp. 1–19. For a critique, see Lisa Duggan, Nan Hunter, and Carole S. Vance, 'False Promises: Feminist Antipornography Legislation in the U.S.', in *Women Against Censorship*, pp. 130–51.

14. Women Against Pornography press conference, 9 July 1986, New York.

15. Statement of Catharine A. MacKinnon and Andrea Dworkin, 9 July 1986, New York, distributed at a press conference organized by Women Against Pornography following the release of the Meese Commission's *Final Report*.

16. David Firestone, 'Battle Joined by Reluctant Allies', *Newsday*, 10 July 1986, p. 5.

17. Statement of commissioners Judith Becker and Ellen Levine, *Final Report*, p. 199. In addition, they wrote: 'We do not even know whether or not what the Commission viewed during the course of the year reflected the nature of most of the pornographic and obscene material in the market; nor do we know if the materials shown us mirror the taste of the majority of consumers of pornography.'

18. Recent empirical evidence does not support the often-repeated assertion that violence in pornography is increasing. In their review of the literature, social scientists Edward Donnerstein, Daniel Linz, and Steven Penrod conclude: 'at least for now, we cannot legitimately conclude that pornography has become more violent since the time of the 1970 obscenity and pornography commission' (in *The Question of Pornography: Research Findings and Policy Implications* [New York: The Free Press, 1987], p. 91).

19. The only original research conducted by the Commission examined images found in the April 1986 issues of bestselling men's magazines (*Cheri, Chic, Club, Gallery, Genesis, High Society, Hustler, Oui, Penthouse, Playboy, Swank*). The study found that 'images of force, violence, or weapons' constituted less than 1 per cent of all images (0.6%), hardly substantiating the Commission's claim that violent imagery in pornography was common. Although the results of this study are reported in the draft, they were excised from the final report.

20. For recent work on s/m, see Michael A. Rosen, *Sexual Magic: The S/M Photographs* (San Francisco: Shaynew Press, 1986); Geoff Mains, *Urban*

Aboriginals (San Francisco: Gay Sunshine Press, 1984); Samois, ed., *Coming to Power*, 2nd edn (Boston, MA: Alyson Press, 1982); Gini Graham Scott, *Dominant Women, Submissive Men* (New York: Praeger, 1983); Thomas Weinberg and G.P. Levi Kamel, *S and M: Studies in Sadomasochism* (Buffalo NY: Prometheus Books, 1983); Gerald and Caroline Greene, *S-M: The Last Taboo* (New York: Grove Press, 1974).

21. The proclivity of mildly stigmatized groups to join in the scapegoating of more stigmatized groups is explained by Gayle Rubin in her discussion of sexual hierarchy (Gayle Rubin, 'Thinking Sex: Notes for a Radical Theory of the Politics of Sexuality', in Carole S. Vance, ed., *Pleasure and Danger: Exploring Female Sexuality* [Boston: Routledge & Kegan Paul, 1984], pp. 267–319.)

22. Statement of Alan Sears, executive director (Washington , DC transcript, 18 June 1985).

23. Los Angeles transcript, public hearing, 17 October 1985.

24. New York City transcript, public hearing, 22 January 1986.

From Minneapolis to Westminster *Mandy Merck*

1. Annette Kuhn, 'Public versus Private: The Case of Indecency and Obscenity', *Leisure Studies* 3 (1984), pp. 53–4.

2. Beverley Brown, 'Private Faces in Public Places', *Ideology and Consciousness* 7 (1981), pp. 3–16.

3. Mandy Merck, 'Television and Censorship: Some Notes for Feminists', in Gail Chester and Julienne Dickey, eds, *Feminism and Censorship* (Dorset: Prism Press, 1988), p. 187.

4. Donald Alexander Downs, *The New Politics of Pornography* (Chicago: University of Chicago Press, 1989).

5. Cited in ibid., p. 139.

6. Deborah Cameron, 'Discourses of Desire: Liberals, Feminists and the Politics of Pornography in the 1980s', *American Literary History* 2, 4 (1990), p. 798, fn. 1.

7. *Pornography and Sexual Violence: Evidence of the Links* (London: Everywoman Ltd, 1988), p. 8.

8. Catharine A. MacKinnon, *Sexual Harassment of Working Women* (New Haven, CT: Yale University Press, 1979).

9. Michel Foucault, *The Use of Pleasure*, trans. Robert Hurley (New York: Pantheon, 1985), Chapter 4.

10. Leo Bersani, 'Is the Rectum a Grave?', *October* 43 (1987), pp. 197–222.

11. Mandy Rose, cited by Melissa Benn in 'Adventures in the Soho Skin Trade', *New Statesman*, 11 December 1987, p. 23.

12. Catharine A. MacKinnon, *Toward a Feminist Theory of the State* (Cambridge, MA and London: Harvard University Press, 1989), p. xi.

13. Carole Pateman, *The Sexual Contract* (Cambridge: Polity Press, 1988), p. 15.

14. Catharine A. MacKinnon, *Feminism Unmodified: Discourses on Life and Law* (Cambridge, MA and London: Harvard University Press, 1987), p. 161.

15. Andrea Dworkin, *Intercourse*, (London: Secker & Warburg, 1987), p. 66.

16. Catharine A. MacKinnon, *Toward a Feminist Theory of the State*, p. 197.

17. ibid.

18. ibid., p. 198.

19. Susanne Kappeler, 'Liberals, Libertarianism and the Liberal Arts Establishment', in Dorchen Leidholdt and Janice G. Raymonds, eds, *The Sexual Liberals and the Attack on Feminism* (New York: Pergamon Press, 1990), p. 181.

20. Michel Foucault, *The History of Sexuality, Volume I: An Introduction* (London: Allen Lane, 1979) (transl. of *La Volonté de savoir* [1976]).

21. Lesley Stern,'The Body as Evidence', *Screen* **23**, 5 (1982), pp. 38–60.

22. Judith Vega, 'Coercion and Consent: Classic Liberal Concepts in Texts on Sexual Violence', *International Journal of the Sociology of Law* **16** (1988), p. 82.

23. Carole Pateman, *The Sexual Contract*, p. 224.

24. ibid., p. 207.

25. Leo Bersani, 'Is the Rectum a Grave?', p. 218.

26. Catharine A. MacKinnon, *Toward a Feminist Theory of the State*, p. 197.

27. See Elizabeth Braeman and Carol Cox, 'Dworkin on Dworkin', *Trouble and Strife* **19** (1990), p. 9.

28. Beverley Brown, 'Debating Pornography: The Symbolic Dimensions', *Law and Critique* **1**, 2 (1990), p. 151.

Part 2: Troubled pleasures

Sweet sorrows, painful pleasures *Lynne Segal*

1. Susanne Kappeler, *The Pornography of Representation*, (Cambridge: Polity Press, 1986), p. 214.

2. Michael Kimmel, ed., *Men Confront Pornography* (New York: Crown, 1989), p. xi.

3. Andrea Dworkin, 'Why So-Called Radical Men Love and Need Pornography', in L. Lederer, ed., *Take Back the Night* (New York: William Morrow, 1980), p. 153.

4. Ian McEwan, *In Between the Sheets* (London: Pan, 1978), p. 18.

5. Scott MacDonald, 'Confessions of a Feminist Porn Watcher', in Kimmel, *Men Confront Pornography*, p. 14.

6. Andrea Dworkin, speaking on 'The Late Show', BBC2, 4 October 1990.

7. Susan Sontag, 'The Pornographic Imagination', in *A Sontag Reader* (Harmondsworth: Penguin, 1982), p. 206.

8. David Holbrook, ed., *The Case Against Pornography* (London: Tom Stacey, 1972); Kimmel, *Men Confront Pornography*.

9. Steven Marcus, *The Other Victorians* (London: Corgi, 1966).

10. Stephen Heath, *The Sexual Fix* (London: Macmillan, 1982), p. 157.

11. Jean Laplanche and Jean-Bertrand Pontalis, 'Fantasy and the Origins of Sexuality', in V. Burgin *et al.*, eds, *Formations of Fantasy* (London: Methuen, 1986), p. 26.

12. Catharine A. MacKinnon, *Feminism Unmodified: Discourses on Life and Law* (Cambridge, MA and London: Harvard University Press, 1987), p. 149.

13. Sandra Bartky, *Femininity and Domination* (London: Routledge, 1990), p. 60.

14. See Judith Butler, 'The Force of Fantasy: Feminism, Mapplethorpe and Discursive Excess', *Differences* 2, 2 (1990).

15. See Joel Kovel, *White Racism: A Psychohistory* (London: Free Association Books, 1988).

16. Kimmel, *Men Confront Pornography*, pp. xiv–xv.

17. Michael Kimmel, 'After Fifteen Years: The Impact of the Sociology of Masculinity on the Masculinity of Sociology', in J. Hearn and D. Morgan, eds, *Men, Masculinities and Social Theory* (London: Unwin Hyman, 1990), p. 95.

18. Chris Nickolay, 'Men's Sex Lives', *Achilles Heel* 5 (1981), p. 33.

19. Michael Moffatt, *Coming Of Age in New Jersey* (New Brunswick: Rutgers University Press, 1989).

20. Harry Brod, 'Eros Thanatized: Pornography and Male Sexuality', in Kimmel, *Men Confront Pornography*.

21. ibid., p. 197.

22. ibid., p. 202. For an entirely different perspective, see Richard Goldstein, 'Pornography and Its Discontents', in Kimmel, *Men Confront Pornography*.

23. Alan Soble, *Pornography: Marxism, Feminism, and the Future of Sexuality* (New Haven, CT: Yale University Press, 1986), p. 73.

24. ibid., p. 52.

25. Jean Bethke Elsthain, 'Pornography Politics', in *Power Trips and Other Journeys* (Madison, Wisconsin: University of Wisconsin Press, 1990), p. 126.

26. MacKinnon, *Feminism Unmodified*, p. 59.

27. ibid., pp. 60–61.

28. Andrea Dworkin, *Intercourse* (London: Secker & Warburg, 1987), p. 67.

29. MacKinnon, *Feminism Unmodified*, p. 5.

30. Kappeler, *The Pornography of Representation*, p. 160.

31. MacKinnon, *Feminism Unmodified*, p. 99.

32. Steve Humphries, *A Secret World of Sex: The British Experience 1900–1950* (London: Sidgwick & Jackson, 1988).

33. Barbara Ehrenreich *et al.*, *Re-Making Love: The Feminization of Sex* (New York: Anchor Press, 1986); Sara Maitland, ed., *Very Heaven: Looking Back at the 1960s* (London: Virago, 1988).

34. Jane Gallop, *Thinking Through the Body* (New York: Columbia Universty Press, 1988), p. 108.

35. Shere Hite, *The Hite Report* (New York: Dell, 1976), p. 275 (emphasis added).

36. ibid., p. 271.

37. ibid., p. 194.

38. ibid., pp. 255, 612.

39. Anja Meulenbelt, *For Ourselves* (London: Sheba, 1981), p. 95.

40. Hite, *The Hite Report*; Meulenbelt, *For Ourselves*; Betty Dodson,

Liberating Masturbation, distributed by Betty Dodson; Lonnie Barbach, *For Yourself: The Fulfilment of Female Sexuality* (New York: Signet, 1975). See also Lynne Segal, 'Sensual Uncertainty or Why the Clitoris is Not Enough', in S. Cartledge and J. Ryan, eds, *Sex and Love* (London: The Women's Press, 1983).

41. Lesley Hall, *Hidden Anxieties: Male Sexuality, 1900–1950* (Cambridge: Polity Press, 1991), p. 4.

42. Freud and Stekel, quoted in ibid., pp. 117, 118.

43. Hall, *Hidden Anxieties*, p. 105.

44. ibid., p. 173.

45. Gallop, *Thinking Through the Body*, p. 131.

46. See Lynne Segal, *Slow Motion: Changing Masculinities, Changing Men* (London: Virago, 1990), ch. 6.

47. Luce Irigaray, *The Sex Which is Not One* (New York: Cornell University Press, 1985).

48. Jessica Benjamin, *The Bonds of Love* (London: Virago, 1990), p. 130.

49. ibid., p. 95.

50. Geraldine Ellis interviews Candida Royalle, *City Limits*, 7–14 February 1991, pp. 16–17.

51. Linda Williams, *Hard Core: Power, Pleasure and the 'Frenzy of the Visible'* (London: Pandora, 1990).

52. Everywoman, *Pornography and Sexual Violence: Evidence of Links* (London: Everywoman, 1988), p. 68.

53. See Ehrenreich *et al.*, *Re-Making Love*; Carole Vance, ed., *Pleasure and Danger: Exploring Female Sexuality* (London: Routledge & Kegan Paul, 1984).

54. MacKinnon, *Feminism Unmodified*, p. 15.

55. The prevalence of 'date rape' is perhaps the best indication: see, for example, Liz Kelly, *Surviving Sexual Violence* (Cambridge: Polity Press, 1988).

56. Janet Holland *et al.*, 'Pressure, Resistance and Empowerment: Young Women and the Negotiation of Safer Sex', paper delivered at the Fifth Conference on the Social Aspects of Aids, London, 1991.

57. Sharon Thompson, 'Putting a Big Thing into a Little Hole: Teenage Girls' Accounts of Sexual Initiation, *Journal of Sex Research* **27**, **3** (1990).

58. ibid., p. 253.

59. Moffatt, *Coming of Age in New Jersey*, p. 190.

60. ibid., pp. 218–19.

61. ibid., p. 201.

62. ibid., p. 212–14.

63. Shere Hite, *Women and Love* (London: Viking, 1988).

64. 'What Women Really Think', *Guardian*, 7 March 1991, p. 21; 'The Cosmo Woman's Sex Life Now', *Cosmopolitan*, January 1990, pp. 8–16.

Just looking for trouble *Kobena Mercer*

1. Audre Lorde, 'Uses of the Erotic: The Erotic as Power' (1978) and Alice Walker, 'Coming Apart' (1979), both reprinted in Laura Lederer, ed., *Take Back the Night: Women on Pornography* (New York: William Morrow, 1980).

2. Susanne Kappeler, *The Pornography of Representation* (Cambridge: Polity Press, 1986), pp. 5–10.

One important alternative to the race and gender analogy is to open the debate to include racism in both pornography and in the women's movement. This is an important point, raised in the context of a historical overview of the mutual articulation of gender and sexuality in racial oppression, discussed by Tracey Gardner, 'Racism in Pornography and the Women's Movement' (1978), in Lederer, ed., *Take Back the Night*.

3. See Kobena Mercer, 'Imaging the Black Man's Sex', in Patricia Holland, Jo Spence and Simon Watney, eds, *Photography/Politics: Two* (London: Comedia, 1986) and, for the revision of the initial analysis, 'Skin Head Sex Thing: Racial Difference and the Homoerotic Imaginary', in Bad Object Choices, ed., *How Do I Look? Lesbian and Gay Film and Video* (Seattle, DC: Bay Press, 1991). Related work on the cultural politics of black masculinity may be found in Isaac Julien and Kobena Mercer, 'Race, Sexual Politics and Black Masculinity: A Dossier', in Rowena Chapman and Jonathan Rutherford, eds, *Male Order: Unwrapping Masculinity* (London: Lawrence & Wishart, 1988).

The black male nude photographs referred to may be found in Robert Mapplethorpe, *Black Males* (Amsterdam: Gallerie Jurka, 1982); *The Black Book* (Munich: Schirme-Mosel, 1986); and Richard Marshall, ed., *Robert Mapplethorpe* (New York: Bullfinch Press, 1990).

4. Homi Bhabha, 'The Other Question: Colonial Discourse and the Stereotype', *Screen* **24**, 4 (1983), p. 18.

5. Frantz Fanon, *Black Skin/White Masks* (London: Pluto Press, 1986 [first published 1952]), p. 120.

6. Sigmund Freud, 'Fetishism' (1923), in *The Pelican Freud Library*, vol. 7, *On Sexuality* (Harmondsworth: Penguin, 1977).

7. Fanon, *Black Skin/White Masks*, p. 82.

8. The humanist critique of objectification is taken up by Essex Hemphill, 'Introduction', in Essex Hemphill, ed., *Brother to Brother: New Writings by Black Gay Men* (Boston, MA: Alyson Press, 1991).

Gonad the Barbarian and the Venus Flytrap *Anne McClintock*

1. Michael S. Kimmel, ed., *Men Confront Pornography* (New York; Crown, 1989).

2. ibid., p. 167.

3. Fred Small, 'Pornography and Censorship', in ibid., p. 63.

4. A brilliant exception is Linda Williams, *Hard Core: Power, Pleasure and the 'Frenzy of the Visible'* (Berkeley: University of California Press, 1989).

5. Thomas Laqueur, *Making Sex: Body and Gender from the Greeks to Freud* (Cambridge, MA: Harvard University Press, 1990).

6. Avicenna, *Canon*, 3. 20. 1. 44. Quoted in ibid., p. 51.

7. Quoted Laqueur, p. 49.

8. Patrick Geddes and J. Arthur Thompson, *The Evolution Of Sex* (London: Home Universal Library, 1899), p. 266. Quoted in Laqueur, *Making Sex*, p. 6.

9. See Sheila Jeffreys, '"Free From All Uninvited Touch Of Man"; Women's Campaigns Around Sexuality, 1880–1914', *Women's Studies International Forum* **5**, 6, pp. 629–45.

10. I am indebted to Margaret Jackson, '"Facts Of Life" or the Eroticization of Women's Oppression? Sexology and the Social Construction of Heterosexuality', in Pat Caplan, ed., *The Cultural Construction of Sexuality* (London: Tavistock, 1987), pp. 52–81.

11. ibid., p. 63.

12. ibid., p. 71.

13. Paul Robinson, *The Modernization Of Sex* (London: Paul Elek, 1976), pp. 105, 133, 142, 154.

14. See Williams, *Hard Core*, for a valuable account of the history of the porn genres preceding these classics: chs 1–3.

15. *Feminine Sexuality: Jacques Lacan and the Ecole Freudienne*, ed. Juliet Mitchell and Jacqueline Rose, transl. Jacqueline Rose (London: Macmillan, 1982), p. 89.

16. Cindy Patton, 'Hegemony and Orgasm', *Screen* **30**, 1 (London: 1989) p. 105.

17. See the excellent Chapter 4 of Williams, *Hard Core*.

18. ibid., p. 107.

19. Catharine MacKinnon, *Feminism Unmodified* (Cambridge, MA: Harvard University Press, 1987), p. 10.

20. Linda Lovelace and Michael McGrady, *Ordeal* (New York: Berkley Books, 1980), p. 114.

Pornography and fantasy *Elizabeth Cowie*

1. There is also a conflation of the distinct forms, orders and genres of sexual imagery as well as its different modes of consumption and production. These include the sexual joke, the sexual story and the pin-up in the workplace, as well as the stag film.

2. In contrast, a writer such as Catharine MacKinnon sees desire and sexuality as socially determined and constructed by the hierarchical social relations in society: 'Sexuality to feminism is, like work to marxism, socially constructed and at the same time constructing' (p. 49) while later she defines sexuality 'as whatever a given society eroticizes' (p. 53): Catharine MacKinnon, *Feminism Unmodified: Discourses on Life and Law* (Cambridge, MA and London: Harvard University Press, 1987). *However, sexuality here rapidly becomes equivalent to male power, since 'sexuality arises in relations under male dominance', which tends to imply an essential male sexuality which is identical to aggression.*

3. *Final Report*, 2 vols, p. 383, vol. 1 (Washington, DC: US Government Printing Office, July 1986), quoted in Kendrick, *The Secret Museum* (New York: Viking), p. 235.

4. Jean Laplanche, *Life and Death in Psychoanalysis*, transl. G. Mehlman (Baltimore, MD and London: Johns Hopkins University Press, 1976) (Paris: Flammarion, 1970), p. 86.

5. Moustafa Safouan, 'Men and Women: A Psychoanalytic Point of View', *m/f* **9** (1984), p. 65, reprinted in P. Adams and E. Cowie, eds, *The Woman in Question* (Cambridge, MA: MIT/October Books and London: Verso, 1991).

6. Richard Dyer, 'Male Gay Porn: Coming to Terms', *Jump Cut: A Review of Contemporary Media* **30** (1985), pp. 27–9.

7. But not an 'empty' sign, as many writers assume. A sign always has meaning, or rather is always part of a production of meaning. Moreover, as semiotics has shown, signs do not name concepts, or objects, but produce meaning through a structure and play of differences within the sign system. As a result, 'woman' could never be a simple or pure sign of 'herself', since the sign's meaning is not inherent in the 'woman' but in the structure of signification produced: for example, in the differences between mother, sister, daughter, or woman, man, animal, or husband, wife, child.

8. Freud's major discussion of this is in his case study of the 'Wolf Man' in 'From the History of an Infantile Neurosis' (1918 [1914], vol. XVII, *The Standard Edition of the Complete Works of Sigmund Freud* (London: The Hogarth Press, 1961). The concept of the primal scene and its fantasies is reconsidered by Jean Laplanche and Jean-Bertrand Pontalis in 'Fantasy and the Origins of Sexuality', *International Journal of Psycho-Analysis*, **49** (1968), Part 1, reprinted in Victor Burgin, James Donald and Cora Kaplin, eds, *Formations of Fantasy* (London: Methuen, 1986).

9. This passivity is now seen by some analysts, including notably Jean Laplanche, as being primary and prior to any active wish. This is discussed in his book *New Foundations for Psychoanalysis*, transl. David Macey (Oxford: Basil Blackwell, 1989) (Presses Universitaires de France, 1987).

10. Published in Lady Winston, ed, *The Leading Edge: An Anthology of Lesbian Sexual Fiction* (Denver, CO: Lace, 1987), and quoted in Sara Dunn's perceptive discussion 'Voyages of the Valkyries: Recent Lesbian Pornographic Writing', *Feminist Review* **34** (1990).

11. As Sara Dunn observes: 'The otherness of sex (i.e. heterosexual and gay male) generates the erotic charge, coupled, of course with the butch's realisation of the perversity of her own desires.' Difference remains a means of erotic coding for the lesbian (or gay man) just as much as for the heterosexual, for whom sexual difference alone is never enough; instead he or she must pile on class, race, etc as structuring differences. ('Voyages of the Valkyries'). She illustrates this point by quoting another lesbian story involving an Irish woman and a woman barrister.

12. Jean Laplanche has traced this primary passivity in his discussion in *Life and Death in Psychoanalysis*, transl. and introduced by Jeffrey Mehlman (Baltimore, MD and London: Johns Hopkins University Press, 1976) (Paris: Flammarion, 1970), ch. 5.

13. '"A Child is Being Beaten": A Contribution to the Study of the Origin of Sexual Perversions' (1919), *SE* vol. XVII.

14. ibid., p. 189.

15. ibid., p. 191.

16. While for both boy and girl the fantasy is passive, Freud sees it as a heterosexual fantasy in the girl, for whom the figure who beats is her

father, whereas for the boy it is the mother. This is discussed by Parveen Adams in 'Per Os(scillation)', in James Donald, ed., *Psychoanalysis and Cultural Theory: Thresholds* (London: Macmillan, 1991).

17. Gilles Deleuze presents a forceful challenge to Freud's claim that sadism and masochism are a pair of opposites in his discussion of Sacher-Masoch's writing. Deleuze sees these as two different forms which do not interrelate and are manifested in the work of de Sade and Sacher-Masoch by radically different aesthetic strategies: *Masochism – Coldness and Cruelty* (New York: Zone Books, 1989). However, Laplanche's discussion of sadomasochism in *Life and Death in Psychoanalysis* offers a rereading of Freud's arguments to show that sadism and masochism are related to a primary passivity. The two forms do have an interrelationship; moreover, the features of suspense and delay Deleuze assigns to Sacher-Masoch's work can also be found in de Sade, while the repetition characteristic of de Sade is equally present in Sacher-Masoch, in his endlessly repeated scene of unconsummated masochism.

18. Lynne Segal, drawing on the work of Nancy Friday, Wendy Hollway and the findings of sex workers, has pointed out that fantasies of 'overpowering women against their will seem to be the exception, rather than the rule, of men's fantasy', and that 'Men are almost as likely as women to select a masochistic role in fantasy, seeing pain as the symbolic price for pleasure, feeling guilty about wanting something they see as "dirty"': *Slow Motion: Changing Masculinities, Changing Men* (London: Virago, 1990), p. 213; Wendy Hollway, 'Women's Power in Heterosexual Sex', *Women's Studies International Forum* 7, 1 (1984). Nancy Friday's survey shows that, by a ratio of four to one, men's fantasies were masochistic: *Men in Love: Men's Sexual Fantasies* (New York: Arrow Books, 1980).

19. As Linda Williams points out, this investigation in much film pornography is organized to produce the desired answer – she wants the man's penis. *Hard Core: Power, Pleasure and the 'Frenzy of the Visible'* (Berkeley: University of California Press, 1989).

20. Sigmund Freud, 'The Loss of Reality in Neurosis and Psychosis' (1924), *SE* vol. XIX, p. 187.

21. ibid., p. 185.

22. John Forrester's discussion in 'Rape, Seduction and Psychoanalysis' offers a valuable review of the psychoanalytic position and argues that it is clear that Freud did not see unconscious wishes for sexual relations as 'relevant to the question of whether the assault was against the woman's will or not', S. Tomaselli and R. Porter, eds, *Rape* (Oxford: Basil Blackwell, 1986), p. 62.

23. The corroboration warning and its role is discussed in Jennifer Temkin's *Rape and the Legal Process* (London: Sweet & Maxwell, 1987), pp. 132–50.

24. Jennifer Temkin gives a series of examples: ibid., pp. 135–6.

25. In Britain the Heilbron Committee (1975) proposed that the use of sexual history evidence should be firmly regulated; however, although the Sexual Offences (Amendment) Act 1976 places a general embargo on the use of

sexual history evidence, the defence may apply to the judge in the absence of the jury for leave to include it, and this has been successfully applied for in a number of trials, as Jennifer Temkin notes: ibid., p. 121.

26. Pat Califia, 'Feminism and Sado-Masochism', *Heresies* **3**, 4 (1981), p. 31.

27. ibid., p. 30.

28. Joyce McDougall has suggested that there is a distinction between compulsive fantasy, in which the same scenario is repeated, with a rigid set of elements played out in a fixed order of variation, and neurotic fantasy, in which creative variation, together with complex structures of substitution and displacement, present a changeable and playful scenario: 'Primal Scene and Sexual Perversion', *International Journal of Psycho-Analysis* **53** (1972), p. 371.

29. 'The Splitting of the Ego in the Process of Defence' (1940 [1938]), *SE* vol. XXIII, p. 276.

30. 'The Loss of Reality in Neurosis and Psychosis', p. 187.

Part 3: The personal as political

Liberalism and the contradiction of sexual politics *Mary McIntosh*

1. Beverley Brown, 'Debating Pornography: The Symbolic Dimensions', *Law and Critique* **1**, 2 (1990), pp. 131–54.

2. See, for instance, Diana E.H. Russell, 'Pornography and Rape: A Causal Model', *Political Psychology* **2**, 1 (1988), pp. 41–73.

3. Dorchen Leidholdt and Janice G. Raymond, eds, *The Sexual Liberals and the Attack on Feminism* (Oxford: Pergamon Press, 1990).

4. In ibid., p. 4.

5. 'Pornography and Rape', p. 49.

6. ibid., p. 50.

7. These are terms that have acquired a certain glamour in cultural analysis, but it is important to recognize that even something as unequivocally reprehensible as rape may have some ambivalent and challenging aspects. It may, in other words, be subversive of an imaginary sexual order, and be perceived as such by some rapists, without this justifying it in any way.

8. Andrea Dworkin, *Pornography: Men Possessing Women* (London: The Women's Press, 1981), p. 203.

9. ibid., p. 202.

10. ibid., p. 200.

11. ibid., p. 224.

12. 'The Homosexual Role', *Social Problems* **16** (1968), pp. 182–92.

13. Peggy Reeves Sanday, 'The Social Construction of Rape', *New Society* 16, 1037 (1982).

14. For a fascinating interpretation of this history, see Walter Kendrick, *The Secret Museum: Pornography in Modern Culture* (New York: Viking, 1987).

15. *Oxford English Dictionary*.

16. Outside the realm of pornography, too, bourgeois men could enjoy images of nude women displayed for their delectation in the highly respectable genre of oil painting – see John Berger, *Ways of Seeing* (London: Pelican, 1972), ch. 3.

Delightful visions *Robin Gorna*

1. 'Aids' is used broadly to refer to the complete concept, which includes the virus and the syndrome as well as people living with them, and the diverse reactions to the epidemic and those affected. Where the purely medical phenomena are intended, the acronyms HIV and AIDS are used.

2. ACT UP – the Aids Coalition To Unleash Power is a diverse non-partisan group of individuals united to end the Aids crisis. The group started in New York City in early 1987 and now has chapters throughout the world.

3. ACT UP/NY Women and AIDS Book Group: Marion Banzhaf *et al.*, *Women, AIDS, and Activism* (1990), p. 24.

4. 'Positive Feedback: Needs Unmet', *The Pink Paper* (6 March 1991), p. 166.

5. Lee Chiaramonte, 'Lesbian Safety and AIDS: The Very Last Fairytale', *Visibilities* (January/February 1988).

6. Svein-Erik Ekeid, Co-ordinator, Global Programme on Aids, Regional Office for Europe, from paper given at 'Promoting Sexual Health', Cambridge, 24–27 March 1991.

7. ibid.

8. Robin Gorna, Frankie Lynch, Sue O'Sullivan; Simon Hall, Edward King, Simon Watney.

9. Tamsin Wilton, paper given at 'Social Aspects of AIDS' Conference, March 1991.

10. 'AIDS Charity "Should Lose Public Grants"', *Daily Telegraph*, 7 May 1991.

11. Simon Watney, 'The Simon Watney Column,' *Gay Times*, April 1991.

12. 'AIDS Charity "Should Lose Public Grants".

13. Quoted in Bruce Kemble, 'Safe Sex Shock for Unshockable Oxford', *Evening Standard*, 5 October 1990.

14. Roger Mortlock, 'Student Safer Sex Leaflet Had "Marked Impact"', *HIV Exchange*, March/April 1991.

Further reading

Denis Altman, *AIDS and the New Puritanism* (London: Pluto Press, 1986).

Tessa Boffin and Sunil Gupta, *Ecstatic Antibodies: Resisting the AIDS Mythology* (London: Rivers Oram Press, 1990).

Erica Carter and Simon Watney, eds, *Taking Liberties: AIDS and Cultural Politics* (London: Serpent's Tail, 1989).

Cindy Patton, *Sex and Germs: The Politics of AIDS* (Boston, MA: South End Press, 1985).

Simon Watney, *Policing Desire: AIDS, Pornography and the Media* (Minneapolis: University of Minnesota Press, 1987; 2nd edn 1989).

Unquestionably a moral issue *Carol Smart*

1. Catharine A. MacKinnon, 'Not a Moral Issue', in *Feminism Unmodified: Discourses on Life and Law* (Cambridge, MA and London: Harvard University Press, 1987).
2. Catharine A. MacKinnon, 'On Collaboration', in *Feminism Unmodified*.
3. MacKinnon, 'Not a Moral Issue', p. 147.
4. Mariana Valverde, *Sex, Power and Pleasure* (Toronto: The Women's Press, 1985).
5. MacKinnon, 'On Collaboration', p. 200.
6. Mary Whitehouse, *Whatever Happened to Sex?* (London: Hodder & Stoughton, 1977), p. 214.
7. Phyllis Schlafly, *Pornography's Victims* (Westchester, Ill.: Crossway Books, 1987), p. 89.
8. Everywoman, *Pornography and Sexual Violence: Evidence of the Links* (London: Everywoman Ltd, 1988), pp. 64–5.
9. ibid., p. 85.
10. Michel Foucault, *The History of Sexuality, Volume I: An Introduction* (Harmondsworth: Pelican Books, 1981) (transl. of *La Volonté de savoir* [1976]).
11. Edward Bristow, *Vice and Vigilance: Social Purity Movements in Britain Since 1970* (Dublin: Gill & Macmillan, 1977).
12. Select Committee of the House of Lords on the Law Relating to the Protection of Young Girls, British Sessional Papers, 1881, vol. 18, p. 464.
13. Everywoman, *Pornography and Sexual Violence*, pp. 24–5.
14. The question of truth and falsehood has, of course, preoccupied many in the field. The Select Committee in 1881 pointed out how many of the women who give evidence of coercion to Mr Dyer and his associates said the exact opposite to other investigators. Moreover, some of the women complained that Dyer had tried to remove them forcibly from the 'houses' where they worked. Similarly, Linda Marchiano has given very different accounts of her period as Linda Lovelace. The problem with these competing accounts is that the teller can be disqualified as a known liar. But her account will live on to be harnessed to different political goals, while she becomes little more than a pawn in the game of political rhetorics.
15. MacKinnon, 'On Collaboration'.
16. Sandra Harding, *The Science Question in Feminism* (Milton Keynes: Open University Press, 1986); Dorothy E. Smith, *The Everyday World as Problematic: A Feminist Sociology* (Milton Keynes: Open University Press, 1988).
17. Carol Smart, *Feminism and the Power of Law* (London: Routledge, 1989).

Classroom conundrums *Jane Mills*

1. Ruth Hall, ed., *Dear Dr Stopes: Sex in the 1920s* (London: Deutsch, 1978).
2. ibid.
3. Survey of 4,000 young people aged 15–24 living in the southwest of England, Institute of Population Studies, University of Exeter, 1991.
4. Quoted in an article entitled 'You Can't Get Pregnant the First Time, You Know', by Dina Rabinovitch, *The Times*, 20 May 1991.

5. David Shears and Stephen Cliff, *A Survey of AIDS Studies in Secondary Schools* (London: Avert, 1991).

6. Circular No. 11/87: *Sex Education at School* (London: Department of Education and Science, 1987).

7. David Shears and Stephen Cliff, *A Survey of AIDS Studies*.

8. Thomas Szasz, 'The Case Against Sex Education', *British Journal of Medicine* 8 (1981).

9. David Shears and Stephen Cliff, *A Survey of AIDS Studies*.

10. Nancy Garden, *Annie on My Mind* (London: Virago Upstarts, 1988). Judy Blume's teenage fiction is published by Piccolo (Pan) Books.

11. *Sex Education*, videos and booklet (London: BBC Education, Autumn 1988).

12. Education (No. 2) Act 1986, Chapter 61 (London: HMSO).

13. Quoted in an article entitled 'Learning the Hard Way' by Judy Sadgrove, *Guardian*, June 1991.

14. Eileen Phillips, ed., *The Left and the Erotic* (London: Lawrence & Wishart, 1983).

Further reading

Association of London Authorities, *ALA Briefing: Section 28's Effects* (London 1989).

Jane Cousins Mills, 'Putting Ideas into Their Heads: Advising the Young' in *Family Secrets/Child Sexual Abuse, Feminist Review* 28 (1988).

Suzie Hayman, *Say Yes, Say No, Say Maybe* (London: Brook Advisory Centre, 1991).

Janet Holland *et al.*, *Don't Die of Ignorance. I Nearly Died of Embarrassment: Condoms in Context* (London: WRAP, The Tufnell Press, 1990).

M. McNair, 'Homosexuality in Schools', *Education and the Law* 1, (1989).

Philip Meredith, *Sex Education: Political Issues in Britain and Europe* (London: Routledge & Kegan Paul, 1989).

Alan Rusbridger, *A Concise History of the Sex Manual 1886–1986* (London: Faber & Faber, 1986).

Stonewall, *Clause 25 of the Criminal Justice Bill* (London, 1991).

Rachel Thomson and Sue Scott, *Learning about Sex: Young Women and the Social Construction of Sexual Identity* (London: WRAP, The Tufnell Press, 1991).

So long as it's not sex and violence *Harriett Gilbert*

1. Donatien Alphonse François, Marquis de Sade, *Justine* (New York: Lancer Books, 1964), (France, 1791).

2. Andrea Dworkin, *Mercy* (London: Secker & Warburg, 1990).

3. Susan Brownmiller: *Against Our Will: Men, Women and Rape* (New York: Simon & Schuster, 1975).

4. Gloria Steinem, 'Erotica and Pornography: A Clear and Present Difference', in Laura J. Lederer, ed., *Take Back the Night* (New York: William Morrow, 1980).

5. Annette Kuhn, *Women's Pictures: Feminism and Cinema* (London: Routledge & Kegan Paul, 1982).

6. Paula Webster, 'Pornography and Pleasure', *Heresies* **12** (1981).

7. Angela Carter, *The Sadeian Woman* (London: Virago, 1979).

8. ibid., p. 1.

9. Georges Bataille, *Story of the Eye* (New York: Urizen Books, 1977) (Paris, 1928).

10. *Mercy*, p. 269.

11. *Mercy*, p. 161.

12. *Mercy*, p. 328.

13. Pauline Réage, *Story of O* (London: Corgi, 1972) (France, 1954).

14. Lisa Duggan, Nan Hunter and Carole S. Vance, 'False Promises: Feminist Anti-Pornography Legislation in the US', in Gail Chester and Julienne Dickey, eds, *Feminism and Censorship* (Bridport: Prism, 1988).

15. Carter, *The Sadeian Woman*, p. 3, quoted from Michel Foucault, *Madness and Civilization* (London: Tavistock, 1967).

Part 4:   To each their own

Pornographies on/scene *Linda Williams*

1. In his book *The Secret Museum: Pornography in Modern Culture* (New York: Viking, 1987), Walter Kendrick traces the history of nineteenth-century pornography through attempts to censor it. Defining pornography as whatever representations – and knowledge – a dominant class or group determines it does not want in the hands of another, less dominant class or group, Kendrick locates the origins of the idea of pornography in the erection of the 'secret museum' at Pompeii to house 'obscene' art that had once been available for all to see.

2. Alexander Downs's book *The New Politics of Pornography* (Chicago: University of Chicago Press, 1989) offers a useful summary of the legal battles that have been fought over this term.

3. Andrea Dworkin, in *Pornography: Men Possessing Women* (Chicago: University of Chicago Press, 1979), has suggested that one possible root meaning of the word obscene is the ancient Greek for 'offstage'. Thus obscenity could mean literally that which should be kept off (*ob*) stage (*scaena*). However, since the word *caenum* means filth, it is also possible that the etymology derives more simply from filth and that the 'offstage' meaning is a false etymology. It is perhaps only in the modern age, which has found so many classical references to sexual functions obscene, that this 'offscene' etymology would gain credence. Nevertheless, the etymology is worth rethinking now that sexual functions are so forcefully placed back *on* the scene. Dworkin's book is an excellent example. The very crux of her argument against pornography cannot be made without graphic descriptions of several pornographic works. The entire feminist anti-pornography strategy, of which this was the first volley, depended, in fact, upon the strategic placing of obscenity onscene.

4. Sprinkle's career is especially interesting. It has moved from male-orientated burlesque and live sex shows, to film and video porn – most

recently that of Femme Productions to the Franklin Furnace, Performing Garage and other avant-garde performance spaces where she has performed various parodic show-and-tells describing her role in the sex industry, including the famous 'Deep Inside Porn Stars' (see Linda Williams, *Hard Core: Power, Pleasure and the 'Frenzy of the Visible'* [Berkeley: University of California Press, 1989], pp. 246–8). In the Cleveland performance deploying the speculum Sprinkle was observed by the vice squad and forced to omit the speculum in her next show. Ironically, when Sprinkle used to do live sex shows in her porn-star days in Cleveland she was never even visited by the vice squad (see Cindy Carr, 'War on Art: The Sexual Politics of Censorship', *Village Voice*, 5 June 1990, p. 28).

5. See Laura Mulvey, 'Visual Pleasure and Narrative Cinema', *Screen* **16**, 3 (1976), pp. 6–18.

6. Gayle Rubin, 'Thinking Sex: Notes for a Radical Theory of the Politics of Sexuality' in Carole S. Vance, ed., *Pleasure and Danger: Exploring Female Sexuality* (Boston: Routledge & Kegan Paul, 1984) p. 308.

7. Teresa de Lauretis 'Freud, Sexuality and Perversion', forthcoming in *Politics, Theory and Contemporary Culture* (New York: Columbia University Press, 1992).

8. Parveen Adams, 'Of Female Bondage' in Teresa Brennan, ed., *Between Feminism and Psychoanalysis* (London: Routledge, 1989), p. 251.

9. Sigmund Freud, *Three Essays on the Theory of Sexuality*, transl. James Strachey (London: Hogarth, 1953–66 [1905]), pp. 147–8.

10. Michel Foucault, *The History of Sexuality, Volume I: An Introduction*, transl. Robert Hurley (New York: Pantheon, 1978) (transl. of *La Volonté de savoir* [1976]).

11. Jonathan Dollimore, 'The Cultural Politics of Perversion: Augustine, Shakespeare, Freud, Foucault', *Genders* **8** (1990), pp. 1–16 (p. 1).

12. Linda Williams, *Hard Core: Power, Pleasure and the 'Frenzy of the Visible'* (Berkeley: University of California Press, 1989).

13. Foucault, *The History of Sexuality, Volume I: An Introduction*, pp. 51–73.

14. Stephen Ziplow, *The Filmmaker's Guide to Pornography* (New York: Drake, 1977), pp. 31–2.

15. Dollimore ('The Cultural Politics of Perversion') has shown how perversion is regulated by the binary opposition between the natural and the unnatural. Yet this binary opposition is, like all binaries, actually a hierarchy. It attempts to impose metaphysical fixity – of origin, nature, identity and aim – on processes that are by nature unfixed.

16. Richard Dyer, 'Gay Male Porn: Coming to Terms', *Jump Cut: A Review of Contemporary Media* **30** (1985), pp. 27–9.

17. See David Pendleton, unpublished manuscript (1991).

18. For a fuller discussion of the complex and controversial theories of sadomasochism and sadomasochistic fantasy, see Williams, *Hard Core*; Kaja Silverman, 'Masochism and Male Subjectivity', *Camera Obscura: A Journal of Feminism and Film Theory* **17** (1988), pp. 31–66; Parveen Adams, 'Per Os(cillation), *Camera Obscura* **17** (1988), pp. 7–29; Gaylyn Studlar, *In the Realm of Pleasure: Von Sternberg, Dietrich, and the Masochistic Aesthetic*

(Urbana: University of Illinois Press, 1988). In this brief discussion I am not so much interested in explicating the nature and aetiology of sadomasochistic fantasy as I am in the relation of s/m, as one kind of pornographic fantasy, to other 'perverse' fantasies.

19. Gilles Deleuze, *Masochism: Coldness and Cruelty* (New Yard: Zone Books, 1989), pp. 56–68.

20. See B. Ruby Rich, 'Review Essay: Feminism and Sexuality in the 1980s', *Feminist Studies* **12**, 3 (Fall, 1986), p. 536.

21. Jean Laplanche and Jean-Bertrand Pontalis, 'Fantasy and the Origins of Sexuality', *International Journal of Psycho-Analysis* 49 (1968).

22. See Parveen Adams, 1989.

23. In one classic s/m narrative, *The Story of Joanna* (Damiano, 1975) this indifference to sex is dramatically demonstrated. In the context of a narrative that assumes heterosexual desire and is focused on the shift from a male dominator, Jason, who passes on his role to a female dominatrix, Joanna, who fulfils his or her desire by becoming his murderer, there is a remarkably transgressive scene in which Jason is massaged by his butler. The massage turns into the butler fellating Jason. This scene, absolutely anomalous in heterosexual porn, suggests the extent to which fixed sexual identities can be upset by the play of sadomasochistic pleasures which challenge the forms of heterosexual identity organized around phallic control.

24. An excellent example is almost any 'lesbian' number performed by Georgina Spelvin in heterosexual pornography throughout her career. See especially the two numbers in *3 A.M.* (MacCallum, 1984). Susie Bright includes the shower scene from this film in her current 'All Girl Action' show on lesbian representation in film and video.

25. Williams, *Hard Core*, pp. 229–64.

26. See, for example, the cosmetics sale vignette from Candida Royalle's *Femme* (Neimi, 1984).

27. See, for example, some of the early filmic celebration of lesbian sexuality, such as Barbara Hammer's *Dyketactics*, which tend to emphasize androgyny and happy-go-lucky frolicking in nature, and to eschew differentiation.

28. Major exceptions are the work of de Lauretis (1992) and Adams ('Per Os(cillation)'; within the Lacanian tradition, and Jessica Benjamin *The Bonds of Love* (New York: Pantheon, 1988; London: Virago, 1990) within the object-relations tradition.

29. Adams, 1991, pp. 248–9.

30. Kate Davy, 'Fe/Male Impersonation: The Discourse of Camp', in Joseph Roach and Janelle Reinelt, eds, *Critical Theory and Performance* (Ann Arbor: University of Michigan Press), p. 23.

31. Cindy Patton, for example, has written that at a recent Lesbian and Gay Health Conference workshop on sex, lesbians who liked 'raunchy' lesbian porn also liked raunchy gay male porn. In both cases what appealed to them in low production values was the connotation 'illicit'. Similarly, a number of gay males who did not like gay porn said they enjoyed the lyrical and less raunchy lesbian porn film *Erotic in Nature*. Patton argues that 'the ability of lesbians and gay men to identify with characters across sex lines – though

perhaps not across gender roles – suggests that porn may work in a more complicated way than the porn-causes . . . violence-against-women argument indicates' ('The Cum Shot: Three Takes on Lesbian and Gay Sexuality', *Out/look* (Fall 1988) pp. 72–7 [p. 76]). I would go further – the cross-sex identifications would seem to work in a variety of ways, for 'straight' viewers as well.

32. Foucault, *The History of Sexuality, Volume I*, p. 157.

33. Williams, *Hard Core*, pp. 248–64.

34. ibid., pp. 164–6.

Bad girls *Loretta Loach*

1. J. Kristeva, *In the Beginning Was Love: Psychoanalysis and Faith* (New York: Columbia University Press, 1987).

2. D. Hebditch and N. Anning, *Porn Gold* (London: Faber, 1988).

3. A variety of surveys are cited in D. Hebditch and N. Anning, *Porn Gold*. Also Linda Williams, *Hard Core: Power, Pleasure and the 'Frenzy of the Visible'* (Berkeley: University of California Press, 1989; London: Pandora, 1990); *Guardian*, 19 April 1991; and D. Howitt and G. Cumberbatch, *Pornography: Impacts and Influences* (London: The Home Office, 1990).

4. Williams, *Hard Core*.

5. Kate Soper, 'Postmodernism, Subjectivity and the Question of Value', *New Left Review* **186** (1991).

The female nude *Lynda Nead*

This article first appeared in *Signs: Journal of Women in Culture and Society* **15**, 2 (1990).

1. Quoted in Lord Longford, *Pornography: The Longford Report* (London: Coronet, 1972), pp. 99–100.

2. The published material on pornography is extensive, so it is difficult to extract a handful of texts that accurately represent the debate. A very useful selection of British feminist writings is reprinted in Rosemary Betterton, ed., *Looking On: Images of Femininity in the Visual Arts and Media* (London and New York: Pandora, 1987), pp. 143–202.

3. John Ellis, 'Photography/Pornography/Art/Pornography', *Screen* **21**, 1 (1980), pp. 81–108, quote on p. 83.

4. It is Kant's theory of the self-contained aesthetic experience that is at the bottom of all this, but in Clark's usage it becomes simplified and popularized, an accessible formula for cultural definition (see Immanuel Kant, *Critique of Aesthetic Judgement*, transl. J.C. Meredith [Oxford: Clarendon, 1911]).

5. Stuart Hall, 'Reformism and the Legislation of Consent', in National Deviancy Conference, ed., *Permissiveness and Control: The Fate of the Sixties Legislation* (London: Macmillan, 1980), pp. 1–43, quote on p. 18.

6. See Jeffrey Weeks, *Sex, Politics and Society: The Regulation of Sexuality since 1800* (London and New York: Longman, 1981), pp. 273–88, on which this discussion of seventies moralism is based.

7. ibid., p. 280.

8. See Longford, pt 1, ch. 7. Longford discusses the American congressional 'Report of the Commission on Obscenity and Pornography, September 1970' (Washington, DC: Government Printing Office, 30 September 1970), which rejected any clear correlation between pornography and acts of sexual violence and advocated a liberalizing of sex education in order to foster 'healthy' sexual development. The report resulted in a split between members of the commission and was rejected by the Senate and president.

9. Kenneth Clark, *The Nude* (Harmondsworth: Penguin, 1976); Arthur Goldsmith, *The Nude in Photography* (London: Octopus, 1976); Michael Busselle, *Nude and Glamour Photography* (London: Macdonald, 1981).

10. Victor Burgin, *The End of Art Theory: Criticism and Postmodernity* (London: Macmillan, 1986), p. 42.

11. Quoted in Longford, *Pornography*, p. 100.

12. John Berger, *Ways of Seeing* (London: BBC & Penguin, 1972), p. 54.

13. ibid., p. 57.

14. Linda Nochlin, 'Eroticism and Female Imagery in Nineteenth-Century Art', in Thomas B. Hess and Linda Nochlin, eds, *Woman as Sex Object: Studies in Erotic Art, 1730–1970* (London and New York: Allen Lane, 1972), pp. 8–15. For a detailed discussion of this collection of essays, see Lise Vogel, 'Fine Arts and Feminism: The Awakening Conscience', *Feminist Studies* 2, 1 (1974), pp. 3–37.

15. Peter Webb, *The Erotic Arts* (London: Secker & Warburg, 1975), p. 2.

16. Interestingly, both Webb and Berger argue that oriental art offers honest and frank representations of sex as opposed to the repressed and unhealthy sexuality of Western bourgeois art. In this way, they support the racist mythology of the unrestrained sexuality of non-European races and perpetuate the particular art-historical version of the ideology of primitivism.

17. For an important discussion of the metaphor of penis-as-paintbrush, see Carol Duncan, 'The Esthetics of Power in Modern Erotic Art', *Heresies* 1 (1977), pp. 46–50.

18. Lawrence Gowing, *Matisse* (London: Thames & Hudson, 1979), p. 63.

19. Michael Jacobs, *Nude Painting* (Oxford: Phaidon, 1979), p. 24.

20. Malcolm Cormack, *The Nude in Western Art* (Oxford: Phaidon, 1976), p. 25.

21. On the mythology of male artistic genius, see G. Pollock, 'Artists, Media, Mythologies: Genius, Madness and Art History,' *Screen* 21, 3 (1980) pp. 57–96.

22. William Feaver, *The Observer*, 25 March 1986, p. 25.

23. In the social sciences there have been many publications on the relationship between exposure to images and resulting action. The publication in Britain of the Minneapolis public hearings on pornography (1983) endorsed the link between the use of pornographic material and acts of sexual violence; see *Pornography and Sexual Violence: Evidence of the Links: The Complete Transcript of Public Hearings on Ordinances to Add Pornography as Discrimination against Women: Minneapolis City Council, Government Operations Committee, December 12 and 13, 1983* (London: Everywoman, 1988).

Notes on contributors

ELIZABETH COWIE teaches film studies and psychoanalysis at the University of Kent. She co-founded and co-edited the feminist journal *m/f*, and is the author of a forthcoming book on the representation of women, film theory and psychoanalysis.

HARRIETT GILBERT is a writer who lives in London. Her most recent novel was *The Riding Mistress* and her most recent non-fiction work a 'feminist companion to sex and sexuality' whose title, as we go to press, has not yet been decided.

ROBIN GORNA has worked with the Terrence Higgins Trust as a volunteer and was on the Board of Directors (1988–90). She is author of *Action on Aids*. She has been an Aids Liaison Officer in Oxford and is currently a consultant to the EC Commission on Aids and Drugs.

MARYBETH HAMILTON is a writer and lecturer who teaches American popular culture at West London Institute. She is completing a book about Mae West.

LORETTA LOACH is a journalist who has worked on a range of television documentaries and has also written for the *Guardian*, *Observer*, and *New Statesman & Society*. She is an editor of *Feminist Review*.

ANNE MCCLINTOCK teaches cultural and feminist studies at Columbia University. She is currently writing a book on women and the sex industry, entitled *Power To Come*.

MARY MCINTOSH teaches sociology at the University of Essex and is a member of the editorial collective of *Feminist Review*. She has written on the family, social policy and sexuality. She is active in Feminists Against Censorship.

KOBENA MERCER was active in the Gay Black Group in London in the early 1980s; he has lectured and published widely on the cultural politics of race and sexuality in representation and currently teaches art history at the University of California, Santa Cruz.

MANDY MERCK has edited *Screen*, and the Channel 4 lesbian and gay series *Out on Tuesday*. A collection of her essays entitled *Perversions* is forthcoming from Virago.

JANE MILLS is a writer and documentary film-maker. Her films include *Rape: That's Entertainment?* Her books include *Make It Happy, Make It Safe* (Penguin) and *Womanwords* (Virago). She has just completed a dictionary of sexual terminology for teenagers, and is editing *The Bloomsbury Guide to Erotic Literature*.

LYNDA NEAD lectures in the history of art at Birkbeck College, University of London. She is author of *Myths of Sexuality* (Oxford: Basil Blackwell, 1988) and has a book forthcoming on the female nude (London: Routledge).

GILLIAN RODGERSON is a journalist at *Gay Times* magazine and a regular contributor to *Capital Gay*. She is a member of Feminists Against Censorship and the co-editor, with Elizabeth Wilson, of *Pornography and Feminism* (London: Lawrence & Wishart, 1991).

LYNNE SEGAL teaches psychology at Middlesex Polytechnic and is a member of the *Feminist Review* collective. Her previous works include *Is the Future Female?* (Virago, 1987) and *Slow Motion: Changing Masculinities, Changing Men* (Virago, 1990). She is a member of Feminists Against Censorship.

CAROL SMART teaches sociology at Leeds University and formerly taught sociology and women's studies at Warwick University. She is author and editor of several feminist books, including *Feminism and the Power of Law* (Routledge, 1989) and *Regulating Womanhood* (Routledge, 1992).

CAROLE S. VANCE is an anthropologist who writes about gender, sexuality, and public policy. She is editor of *Pleasure and Danger: Exploring Female Sexuality* (1984) and a contributor to K. Ellis *et al.* (eds), *Caught Looking: Feminism, Pornography and Censorship*, 1986. She has been active in many feminist groups and teaches at the School of Public Health at Columbia University.

LINDA WILLIAMS teaches film studies and women's studies at the University of California at Irvine. She is author of *Hard Core: Power, Pleasure, and 'the Frenzy of the Visible'* (Pandora, 1990).

ELIZABETH WILSON played an active role in the Women's Movement campaigns of the 1970s, such as Women's Aid, and was on the editorial collectives of *Red Rag* and *Feminist Review*. She is the author of a number of books including *Adorned in Dreams: Fashion and Modernity* and *The Sphinx in the City*, both published by Virago.

Index

SEXUAL ANARCHY
Gender and Culture at the *Fin de Siècle*

Elaine Showalter

'A triumph . . . gleams with wit and wry insight'
– *New Statesman & Society*

'Sexual anarchy' – dire predictions, disasters, apocalypse –
became the hallmark of the closing decades of the nineteenth
century. The New Woman and the Odd Woman threatened
male identity and self-esteem; the emergence of feminism and
homosexuality meant the redefining of masculinity and
femininity. This is the terrain which Elaine Showalter
explores with such consummate originality and wit.

Looking at parallels between the ends of the nineteenth and
twentieth centuries and their representations in literature, art
and film, she ranges over the trial of Oscar Wilde, public
furore over prostitution and syphilis, and in our own time,
moral outrage over the breakdown of the family, abortion
rights, AIDS. High and low culture – from male quest
romances to contemporary male bonding movies (*Heart of
Darkness* reworked into *Apocalypse Now*), Freud to *Fatal
Attraction* – all are part of this scholarly and entertaining study
of the *fin de siècle*.